WHY DO I DO WHAT I DO?

How To Understand Yourself and Others

Virginia Dunstone, M.S.

Published simultaneously in the United States and Canada by Gate Publishing.

For information:
Gate Publishing
P.O. Box 4261
Scottsdale, AZ 85261
(602) 991-2660 Fax: (602) 661-4091

Cover and text design by Ashley Key, Inc.
Consultants - Wright & Co. Publishers, Inc.

Library of Congress Cataloging-in Publication Data

Dunstone, Virginia R., 1946 -
Why Do I Do What I Do?
How To Understand Yourself and Others / Virginia Dunstone. - 1st ed.
p. cm.
ISBN 0-9638282-0-7 : $15.95
CIP 95-80810
1. Psychology 2. Self Help I. Title

First Edition
2 3 4 5 6 7 8 9 10

To My Mother And Father Whom I Now View
As The Most Valued Of Teachers.

To Darcy, Deanna, Donald, Derek And Duane
For The Honor of Being Your Mother
And Your Teacher.

Acknowledgements

Thank you to all the special people who contributed to the completion of this book. These people include those who were involved in the hands-on effort required to publish this book, as well as those who have crossed my counseling path. It was through these clients that I acquired the deep understanding that lives can become empowered when the concepts within these pages are a part of daily living.

A Special Thank You:

To Carr and Shelley Wells whose initial financial investment enabled me to take time from my private practice and concentrate on writing.

To Ed Gagle, president of American Family Resources, Scottsdale, Arizona, whose charitable organization sponsored the project for the women in prison. Ed also was a constant source of support and encouragement as he assisted in edit after edit. For his help I will be forever grateful.

To my editor, Adelle Budnick whose time, effort, and expertise will forever be appreciated.

To my sister Ardyth Bakken and my friend Pam Spector for their valuable comments regarding copy and concepts.

To Jennifer Snyder whose words of enthusiasm regarding LifeScripting became the title for this book.

To Kelly Fitzpatrick whose understanding of human photography allowed for a picture on the back cover.

To Steve, Cathy and Alicia Perry for being the instruments that created the artwork of Alicia and my hands in Section III.

To Bonnie Johnson, D. L. Bud Wright and Ashley Key for their artistic talents in creating the cover and design of the book.

CONTENTS

Introduction

The journey of my life as a person and as a therapist has brought me to a place of deeply believing that each life has individual meaning. I have also come to believe that all life events have positive significance which, when properly understood, can become the basis for unlimited personal growth and self knowing. With this self knowing, individuals can experience a life filled with purpose, joy and fulfillment.

The book you are about to read is for anyone who wants to obtain greater personal understanding and experience the life changing rewards of "free choice" rather than the slavery of deeply ingrained "conditioned responses." This book is equally valuable for individuals who believe their lives have been a struggle, as well as for those who feel their lives have been relatively easy. For each reader, the psychological processes presented within these pages will provide tools to convert all past experiences, as well as future events, into a meaningful and rewarding life.

How I came to believe in the workable concepts of this book involves my personal history. For years I had a deep sense of something not being totally complete within myself even though my exterior life had all of the dynamics that should have created personal happiness. To the world I was the mother of five, chief volunteer at the church, member of the P.T.A., supporter at the kids' games, and the mother who welcomed all children into the family home. Yet inside of myself I continued to have a sense of incompleteness and the feeling of never having quite arrived at a place of personal meaning. As a result of these feelings, I embarked upon a journey to discover what was wrong. I began to look for who had done what to me, why it had happened, and what I was going to do about what "they" had done. I joined groups, I labeled myself, I went to therapy, I even became a therapist; yet the desire for internal completeness still continued to persist.

That longing has now become an awesome journey of joy and satisfaction, not only for myself, but also for the thousands who have shared in the processes that are contained within this book. Because of my personal experiences and the positive experiences of my clients, I am convinced this therapy can, and does, open individuals to a deep self-awareness of the love that already exists within. I call this therapy *LifeScripting*℠.

Through *LifeScripting*, I have come to know that we need not beat ourselves up for one second of our lives, nor do we have to blame and then forgive others to become fully who we are. I have also come to realize that a loving acceptance of our lives as meaningful and purposeful (no matter what the experience) can create a power of love within a person that connects them to themselves as well as to others. The process to accomplish this is simple and very specific. It requires only information and the use of methods that are easily applied, once understood. This book contains the information, the method, and the *LifeScripting* process.

We have often heard that the answers to life are within. However, very rarely, if ever, are we told how to discover them. Simply stated, *LifeScripting* is a precise and usable method to find the answers that have eluded so many for so long. In this book you will learn how to look inside yourself, when to look inside, and what to do with what you find. Through *LifeScripting*, you will grasp the significance of each of your life's experiences and understand how they guide you to your highest purpose. As a result of this knowledge, no experience will ever again be viewed as negative. Every experience can become positive, loving, and one of perfect timing and order for your life.

My Story

As a child, I had a burning desire for people to live their lives loving each other. That desire came from the fact that my parents were not always happy with the life they had chosen to live together. As a result, much of the time I perceived life as difficult and stressful. I frequently thought, "If only people could see the good in each other and concentrate on that, things would be so very different." This youthful desire has been the driving force behind the therapeutic and personally empowering work that I do for both individuals and organizations.

My life began in North Dakota where I was born the youngest of three girls. After experiencing what I perceived to be a difficult childhood, I graduated from high school and moved to Seattle where I married the man I felt would be with me forever. We had five children in six years and shared what most would consider a fantasy relationship. In the thirteenth year of our marriage our relationship greatly deteriorated, and as a result I enrolled in college with the intention of establishing a career. Because of circumstances, it was necessary for me to work full-time while being a full-time student and mom. In four years I earned, with honors, my B.A. degree in psychology and got divorced that same year. I was now a single mom with five children and had a need and desire to earn my masters degree. Without missing a heartbeat, I continued my education on a full-time basis while working countless hours. Since we were living in Las Vegas, Nevada, I knew that working as a valet parking attendant was the best way to support a family. By working as a substitute parking attendant at two of the major hotels I was able to work all night. This enabled me to go to school and be a mom by day. During the day I also worked as a part-time therapist. In two years I completed my masters degree in counseling, again with honors, and moved to Arizona to begin my career.

During the years I was living the life I just described, many internal discoveries were occurring. One of these discoveries occurred during my masters program, when Dr. Marchant presented an overview of Adlerian Theory which involved the concept that our childhood beliefs have significant meaning in our adult lives. Because my childhood had been so very challenging, I had decided long ago that to review it again and again was too painful. I had concluded it would be better to just let the past be the past. However, what kept haunting me was the deep knowing that our belief systems were formed by age six and that we all live these beliefs over and over again. Consequently, I became obsessed with the idea that if we could learn to unlock our belief systems, why couldn't this knowing empower us as adults, rather than cause us pain or unwanted behavior repetition. Because of these thoughts, I became more and more troubled with the therapeutic processes that looked for what was wrong, then spent countless hours hoping to find a way of "fixing it." This internal discomfort has guided me away from traditional therapy and into the development of *LifeScripting*. *LifeScripting* enables each person to look at his or her life as a powerful classroom for personal knowing and understanding. *LifeScripting* also assists individuals in looking within their experiences for positive empowerment and, as a result, finding their purpose, direction, and uniqueness.

The development of *LifeScripting* has been a part of my work since 1983. The information has come from many sources, including concepts of my own which I designed based upon my positive experiences with clients. As a result of combining my experiences and the positive experiences of others, I have created tangible processes that, if applied, can truly empower your life.

So for the little girl I was who desired that people love each other, I have found a way to fulfill her dream. Her dream has not only become my reality, it has become a reality for many others. By using this book as your tool, it can also become part of your experience. It is, therefore, with deep honor that I offer you a road map for life and welcome you to the possibility of recognizing the limitless love you have within yourself.

With a deep sense of oneness,

Virginia

SECTION I

LifeScripting Principles

The information in this section is designed to provide you with a basic understanding of the key psychological principles of *LifeScripting*.

For the most complete experience please read and understand this section before attempting to answer the 96 Questions in Section II.

LifeScripting

Have you ever wondered why you do what you do? Have you ever found yourself repeating behavior patterns after saying, "I'll never do that again!"? Do you often conclude your repetitious behavior with confusion about yourself because, after all, you were so sure you would never do "it" again?

What if you could know and understand every action and thought you have? What if you could recognize what is causing what in your life and, as a result of that recognition, could consciously choose your behavior? What would it also be like for you to discover your personal meaning and the ultimate purpose for your life?

The book you are about to read takes you on a journey that provides all of this information and more. The question, "Why do I do what I do?" will be answered. As a result, any confusion you have had about yourself and your behavior will end. Within these pages you will be shown how to find answers for all of your past, present, and future behavior. You will be given information about where to look for the answers, how to look, when to look, and what to do with what you find. When you apply this information to your life you will be impacted in a profound and positive way.

This book is divided into three sections. Each section presents an entire process and requires the other sections to be complete. This is much like the concept of a jig-saw puzzle; it is one picture with many pieces, all of which are vital to the completion of the puzzle. Like the pieces of the puzzle, each idea, when understood and properly placed, will ultimately create a total understanding of the picture called ***you***.

Section I contains information that will assist you in understanding how your childhood belief systems determine your adult behavior. You will discover that behavior is programmed, much like a computer, and that it is necessary to understand your programming in order to discover what is causing what in your life. With this knowledge, you will be able to consciously choose future behavior. You will also learn how your thinking creates your reality and how your early childhood thoughts created the beliefs which are now governing your adult behavior. You will be taught how to access this valuable past information. With this knowledge, you will come to understand that all past events can become your personal power, and, as a result, you will never again regret any experience or view any part of your life as negative.

In Section II, you will be given 96 questions that, when answered, will identify the beliefs that are running your adult life. Based upon your answers, you will understand why you react and respond the way you do to the events and people in your world. With this newly acquired information, you will be able to determine all future behavior. Among the 96 beliefs you are to identify will be your individual beliefs for: What is a man? What is a woman? Who am I? What is the world like for me? How do I best interact in the world? How do I handle stress? How do I problem solve? What are my beliefs about relationships? What is my life's purpose?

In Section III you will learn several methods for personal empowerment. You will be introduced to a dimension of thinking that will enable you to experience yourself internally in such a way that you will be able to understand the completeness of all that you are.

I have chosen the word *LifeScripting* to identify the process detailed in this book. This word best describes the concept that we all have a valued script in the play of life. In a play there are many parts. One part is of no greater value than another since all parts fit together to produce the complete play. Each individual who is properly cast and plays his/her* part to the fullest adds to the success of the entire play. We all must discover the part we are to play in life so we can become all we were designed to become. If we successfully play our part, we add to the lives of others because the entire play is effected by our performance. When this occurs, personal fulfillment is heightened and life takes on a new and positive dimension.

LifeScripting will assist you, as it has my clients, in experiencing the genuine inner peace and joy that comes from knowing yourself and understanding the part you play in life.

* For easier reading, throughout the remainder of the book I will interchange the words he, she, him, and her, when he/she, him/her is appropriate.

Beliefs = Your Reality

Your personal beliefs run your life by controlling your behavior. All behavioral choices are a direct result of beliefs and perceptions. If you believe something, then that is exactly what you are experiencing in your life.

Experts in psychology state that your current beliefs were formed by the time you were six years old. Your life is therefore being directed by the child you were. If the child believed something, the adult has a silent, loving contract to fulfill what the child believed. To understand the beliefs of the child you were is to understand the adult you have become. Once you recognize and comprehend the beliefs of the child, you will understand what has been guiding your life and why you do what you do! This awareness will also provide you with a basis to understand all future behavior choices.

The process of discovery will be both gentle and enlightening. It involves knowing the child you were, understanding the experiences and perceptions of that child, then looking at those experiences in a whole new and loving way. In my opinion, it is not necessary to analyze childhood experiences in an intense or negative manner. It is only necessary to review childhood experiences for the information they provide in assisting us with our adult decisions. In Section II you will be given the guidelines for reviewing your childhood experiences.

Psychology States Beliefs Are Formed By Age Six

Psychological research has validated that our beliefs are ingrained by the time we are six years of age. Recent evidence suggests that beliefs are formed as early as three years of age. At three you can barely put the correct words together to get your basic needs met, yet your beliefs are totally established for who you are in the world and what the people in your world are like for you. It is a mind-boggling concept to realize that what you actually believed by age three is what continues to occur for you throughout your entire life. To verify this truth, simply look to your life experiences. How many times have you said you would never repeat a behavior and then found yourself doing the same behavior over and over? How many people in your present world remind you of people in your past? Do the relationships you now have contain familiar dynamics that match those you have had before? Does it often seem the life you are living is the life you have already lived? This happens because belief systems run your life, and they are what you use as the basis for all of your choices. We would all like to believe we are free thinkers who are totally in charge of our ability to make good choices for ourselves. What actually occurs, at deeper levels, is that our unremembered belief systems sub-consciously rule us as we make our adult decisions. As a result, we often feel powerless because we repeat our behavior no matter what we have seemingly convinced ourselves to do in our own minds.

Once you realize your childhood beliefs rule your adult choices, you can learn methods to work with those beliefs. As a result, you will never again feel powerless. You will know that, if you identify the beliefs of the child, you can manage those beliefs rather than allow them to subconsciously run your life. With the recognition of childhood as the place of your personal power, you can go to the appropriate childhood experiences to know yourself like you've never dreamed possible.

Mind As Computer

As a computer stores data on a disc, so the human stores beliefs in the brain. Both the computer and the brain are limited in their ability to access only information contained within. Your brain has stored the belief systems you formed in childhood, and these beliefs appear again and again on the screen of your mind. The impact of these beliefs is of such magnitude that they are perceived as "the truth" regarding your experience of the world in which you now live. To truly be in charge of your life and your choices is to learn how to access the stored data and to selectively bring it up on the screen of your mind. Once the information is on the screen and you recognize that this is the data influencing your choices, you can then decide how best to integrate the information into your life. Without first bringing the data onto the screen, you, like the computer, will be run by hidden programming deep within.

Belief Storage

Let's look at the basic dynamics of the computer to understand how your beliefs were formed and stored. At a very elementary level the computer is a machine that stores information. Information is placed on a floppy or a hard disc which makes it available for later reference. This stored information can be accessed only if the right buttons are pushed by the person operating the keyboard. By pushing these buttons, the desired information appears on the computer's screen.

We humans are very similar to computers, particularly when it comes to the process of gathering and storing information. Most of our data about life is gathered by the age of six, and it is stored on the floppy disc of our heart and brain. Both the heart and brain are involved in the storage of data. This occurs because as children we assimilate the world through our perception of love and belonging, rather than through our ability to think logically and use deductive reasoning.

There are only two ways to bring stored data from the brain onto the screen of our memory. One way is to voluntarily access the data with questions about the past. The second is to access data through emotional responses triggered by present events. Triggers by-pass the normal process of bringing information onto the screen in an orderly manner. When triggered information is brought onto the screen, it is the result of an emotional situation occurring in the "now" which parallels data stored in the past. We will discuss triggers thoroughly in Chapter 14.

You cannot work with stored information until you bring that information onto the screen of your memory. You can talk about change, wish things were different, and mentally dissect life. However, until you know how to access your belief systems and work directly with them, change or empowerment cannot occur. With information from your memory, accessed past data will become both visible and understandable. You can then decide if you want to change it, use it as it is, add to it, or just return it to storage. Chapters 14, 15 and 16 will give you information about when to look, how to look, and what to do with what you find.

Like computers, people may appear to be similar, but no two people or computers contain the same stored information. We all see the world through individual eyes. Therefore, our personal computers (brains) store our uniqueness. When we learn to access our individual experiences and perceptions we will become connected to ourselves at the deepest of levels.

To further understand the process of data storage and belief system formation, let's discuss the words "I love you." There are five and one-half billion people on the planet. Yet, many times we have a false concept that there is only one "I love you." Of course we believe it is our "I love you," which is based solely upon our personal belief about love. Once we have formed our beliefs regarding love we usually try to get everyone, or at least the people we care about, to see love though our eyes. However, what is actually occurring is that we each have a deep belief about love based upon our personal experiences prior to age six. These beliefs create our choices and behavior about love. Two examples will help illustrate this concept:

Example #1 - A little girl named Valerie is born into a family that loves her very much. Valerie is often told she is loved. She is put to bed at night with Mom and Dad reading to her, tucking her in, kissing her good-night and saying, "I love you." Valerie stores in her mind's computer the message that love is soft, warm, wonderful, and that she is safe because of it. She grows up and meets Tom who, one moon-lit night, says the words "I love you." Valerie's emotional buttons are pushed. This brings onto her mind's screen the information from her childhood floppy concerning the words "I love you." As a result, she immediately feels warm, soft, wonderful and safe, since that is the information entered on her disc before she was six years old. When Valerie internalizes Tom's words she is not consciously remembering the little girl she was, rather, she believes she is an adult responding to the words "I love you." In reality, it is the belief system of a child dictating Valerie's response to Tom.

At the same time, Tom's childhood beliefs about "I love you" are dominating his response to the "now." Both adults are unaware of the circumstances of their individual pasts. To understand what is happening at the deepest levels, they eventually must ask each other the following questions: How did you learn about love when you were a child? How did your dad show you that he loved you? How did your mom show you that she loved you? These questions, as well as many others, will be reviewed in Section II. They are important questions to answer because the beliefs formed from early childhood experiences will eventually control how love evolves in the life of this couple.

Example #2 - A child named Rocky is born in the ghetto. Rocky is raised by his mother, since his father left the family when Rocky was six months old. His mother does what she can to keep the family of four together. Because of work and survival needs, she has no time for her children. She becomes so discouraged about love that she never utters the word because of her pain. As a result, Rocky never hears "I love you" and rarely, if ever, feels secure. Because of circumstances and peer pressure, Rocky becomes part of a gang early in life. This reinforces his view that love is painful and not something to believe in or trust. He becomes filled with anger because his basic need to love and be loved has not been met. As an adult, a woman named Tonya enters his life. She sees his pain and wants to make a difference to him. Tonya falls in love with Rocky and one night looks into his eyes and says, "I love you." Rocky's emotional buttons are pushed and the information from his childhood floppy reminds him that love is not safe. Rocky's resulting adult behavior is one of both anger and distrust. Tonya is hurt because he pulls away saying he does not believe in love. She blames herself for his reaction and wonders what she has done to create his response. At the same time, Rocky feels both confused and suspicious. He wonders why he had the unexplainable need to pull away. What has happened? The beliefs from their separate childhood experiences are in charge of their present behavior. The adults do not understand that their individual childhood beliefs about love override all other desires and data.

Your childhood floppy stores your individual self. When you realize this you will no longer wonder what is happening to you or why you respond the way that you do. To function best in the world you will simply need to learn how to consciously access your floppy disc. *LifeScripting* will teach you a method for accomplishing this. When you use this method of accessing, everything you need to know or want to know, in the area of who you are and what you believe, will be available to you.

Belief System Formation

Before beliefs are stored in the brain of a child they are first filtered through the child's need to love and to belong. As children we do not have the capability to analyze love, we simply perceive love through our feelings. With these perceptions we form a belief about the world and all that is in it. Because our beliefs are being filtered through love it is important to first look at the dynamics of love before we attempt to understand our individual beliefs about life.

To verify the need for love, think of any time you have loved. What happened to you? Think now of any time you have chosen to withhold love. What happened to you? Think of the deepest need you have within yourself. Isn't it to be happy by experiencing love and a sense of belonging? If your inner knowing is that you desire happiness through love and belonging, then isn't the key to a full and joyous life contained in the ability to love and to belong?

My experience as a therapist daily validates the importance of love and belonging being present in an individual's life. I have observed time and again that miracles occur when clients turn their thoughts from stress and pain to thoughts of love. Therapy need not be centered on fixing a broken life, or on healing the pain of the past by reliving it, or on constantly working on what has happened to you; therapy is simply about thinking differently and opening your heart to love. To grasp this truth ask yourself, "Has hate ever created happiness or healed a life?" No! Hate separates and destroys and can only be present when love is absent. Therefore, approaching life with a loving human heart is truly the key to a balanced, healthy, happy life.

Science's Recognition Of The Need To Love

Our basic human knowing about the need to love is now being validated by science. With this new information there is a solid basis to speak about the true empowerment of individuals through the dynamics of love.

Before detailing the steps of "how" to discover the love you have for yourself, it is important to understand what research has verified about love. From the volumes of data, I will present an abbreviated version of the findings.

Psychology states that the primary need of the human being is to love and to belong. When these needs are met the individual feels secure and desires to expand. When these needs are not met the person feels incomplete and rarely, if ever, reaches his full potential. Psychological studies have also validated that love affects the physical growth patterns as well as the general health and well being of both animals and individuals. Studies conducted with rabbits validated these findings. In these studies rabbits were injected with cancer cells and divided into two groups. One group was simply fed and left alone. The other group was fed and nurtured. The rabbits in the group that were left alone quickly died. However, the rabbits in the group that were nurtured lived much longer. The study of babies and their growth patterns also verifies the need for love and belonging. Simply stated, babies who received loving touch grew at a faster pace than babies who did not receive loving touch.

The medical profession is also beginning to acknowledge the powerful dynamics of love as it affects the human body. Dr. Joseph Chilton Pearce, the author of several books including ***Magical Child***, presented a summary of these findings during a workshop in Phoenix, AZ. This workshop was mind enhancing to say the least.

Dr. Pearce contends that to understand the reality of love we must first understand the connection of the heart to the brain - not - the brain to the heart. It is now evident that the heart is connected to the human system in several vital ways. One of the vital connections of the heart to the brain is the discovery that the heart is truly the organ that empowers love and ignites human expansion. It has been proven that the heart speaks to the head (brain), not the head to the heart. When the heart feels love, neuro-transmitters fire to the brain and these firings cause the human mind to expand to abstract thinking and limitless possibilities. When the heart feels love it also sends neuro-transmitter firings to the immune system which greatly assists in the physical health and personal well-being of an individual.

According to Dr. Pearce, there are also specific stages of early human development that must first occur before an individual is capable of expanding to love. If these stages aren't correctly sequenced, the person cannot reach her full potential. Individuals who fail to progress properly through all the developmental stages will tend to focus primarily on the physical world as their source of personal fulfillment. Individuals who properly progress will tend to experience life from a perspective of love for self and love for others, and thereby fulfill their basic need for love and belonging.

According to Dr. Pearce, 95% of individuals in our society were not properly assisted through the sequential stages of growth and development. As a result, it is difficult for these individuals to arrive at the place of expansion and love. This has occurred for many reasons. Two of the primary reasons are: 1) The bonding process at birth has, in many instances, been taken away from mothers because of hospital settings. 2) The need for heros in the teen years has not been met by our society. Chapter 5 will assist you to more fully understand the dynamics of these stages and what needs to happen for an individual to be able to arrive at a place of expansion and love.

For now, it will be helpful to grasp a very simplified version of the layers of the brain and their function. The brain has three layers, each developing at a specific age. The first layer of the brain is concerned with basic survival needs, physical boundaries and territorial defense. This is the layer of animal instinct and animal behavior. It is the most basic layer in the development of the human brain. The second layer of the brain is the portion that governs pleasure, pain and understanding of the physical world. This area is the second layer to develop and the portion in which many spend their life, according to Dr. Pearce. The third layer is unique to humans. It is the area of the brain where abstract thinking occurs, the place of limitless possibility and expanded thinking. This layer provides us with the ability to be empathic, cooperative and conscious of more than ourselves. It contains the capacity and ability to respond to life for the mutual well-being and fulfillment of ourselves and others.

For individuals to expand to the place of loving connection, they must be able to experience areas within the third layer of their brain. Since this layer has so much to offer, how do we get to it? And better yet, how do we stay in it? The answer is the heart! The heart is the key to unlocking this area since it has a direct connection to the third layer of the brain. This connection can be accomplished by opening your heart to love, which ignites the firing of your neuro-transmitters. This firing elevates you to the third layer of your brain where limitless thinking and feeling are possible. If your heart is not opened, you will spend much of your energy in the lower two layers of your brain. If you are in the second layer of the brain, in your search for personal satisfaction, you will find yourself looking to possessions for your fulfillment. If possessions do not satisfy you, you will tend to revert to the first layer of your brain where basic animal instincts rule.

If love is the solution for the human being, then it is also the solution for the larger societal issues that have caused 95% of our people being driven by the lower layers of the brain. The awareness and use of love will enable individuals to expand their hearts, thereby activating the third layer of the brain where no one is a "victim," and where anger turns to understanding because love exists. Opening to love is totally possible and can be accomplished by fully understanding and deeply loving yourself. The information in this book will provide the method.

The next chapter presents the perfect scenario that would theoretically accomplish all stages of development for an individual and, as a result, create a fully developed and loving human being.

The Perfect Person

To further explain the evolution of the three layers of the brain, I have created an imaginary child who progresses perfectly through all of the childhood stages. His name is Eddie. Be aware before experiencing Eddie, that the perfect life does not exist and that all people, at some time, experience the absence of love in their life. Nevertheless, through the dynamics of *LifeScripting* it is possible to convert the areas in your life where you have sensed a lack of love, into the very places where deep personal empowerment will occur.

Now meet Eddie. Imagine that little Eddie is conceived in love and that he is in the environment of Mom's womb where he is receiving never ending sensations about his world. He is deeply wanted by Mom and Dad, and they express this love by calmly and lovingly talking to him in the womb. They even read to him and play beautiful music as they wait for his birth. Eddie is born in a birthing center where his entire birth process is centered around connection with his mother and father. He is born naturally, Mom receives no drugs, and there are no complications. After Eddie takes his first breath he is immediately placed on his mother's stomach. When the umbilical cord stops pulsating the cord is cut, and he is taken by his mother and lovingly placed on her left side where her familiar heartbeat reminds him of his connection to life. Mom gazes into his eyes as she nurses him with a total feeling of love. He looks back into her eyes and feels her love, and as a result experiences complete human bonding. He is now taking in his world through the five senses of taste, smell, touch, sight and sound. He is content next to his mother as he experiences the most crucial moments of human development. Dad is there with support and love for both his newborn son and for Mom. As Eddie keeps looking at his mother he feels a powerful shift in her energy. What has happened to her, as a result of properly bonding with her beautiful child, is a chemical shift within her brain. Because of this shift she moves to a place where values, ideals, intuition, understanding, self-assurance and all possibilities exist. She now has a feeling of total power and capacity to sustain her own life and the life of her child. Child and mother have just shared an incredible internal process that is life enhancing for both. For the next two months (an important time frame) and beyond, Eddie is held and nestled in the arms of those who love him. Much of the time he is held heart to heart because his parents are aware that hearts must connect to create total bonding. Mom and Dad talk to Eddie and interact with him because they are keenly aware that the quality of life for a child is basically determined by his relationship with his parents. This bonding has created for Eddie a deep sense of love and belonging, and has allowed him the possibility of utilizing all three layers of his brain.

By the time Eddie is twelve months old he has developed his essential sensory-motor system. This has occurred because Mom and Dad have kept him out of walkers and rarely put him in a swing or playpen. Eddie has spent time on the floor and has been allowed to crawl. As a result, his brain and coordination skills have developed, and Eddie is open to later learning skills. He is now ready to branch out and move away from Mom and Dad to explore everything in his world by feeling it, tasting it, smelling it, playing with it and talking to it. Mom keeps Eddie safe from harm as he builds his knowledge base about the physical world and his emotional relationships with others.

By the age of eighteen months, Eddie's brain has developed all the pathways for learning that will ever be available to him. He now has the capacity to learn from any and all experiences.

By age four, he has learned 80% of everything he will ever know about the physical world. His language system is 80% complete and all emotional connections and perceptions are fully ingrained.

Until age six or seven, it is vital for Eddie's mental development that he use his imagination which will result in his later ability to grasp symbolic concepts such as math, language, poetry and metaphors. Therefore, Eddie is given toys which stimulate his imagination and allow for his creativity, not toys that are already assembled by the manufacturer. He loves his blocks, pots, pans, play dough, tinker toys, crayons, etc., because he can make them become anything he wants. A match box becomes a car, and a stick becomes a magic wand. Mom and Dad also read Eddie stories and provide him with cassette tapes to further develop his imagination. They read or have him listen to each story at least six times so Eddie can develop and experience the characters in his mind. Eddie's favorite stories are about animals since they appeal to his animal brain (the first layer of the brain), and they allow his imagination to flourish. Eddie is seldom exposed to television because the radiant light inhibits constructive learning needed for his developing brain. Television also hinders Eddie's later ability to use abstract thinking.

By age six, Eddie is ready to move out into society and will demonstrate only what has been modeled for him up until that time. Approximately 95% of his learning has come from watching the behavior of the individuals with whom he has been in contact. Eddie will therefore respond and act out the subtle, as well as the obvious characteristics of his parents and his significant others. Eddie's brain is as large as it will ever be, and he is enormously susceptible to the slightest suggestions from society as to his possibilities. This is a critical learning phase because all possibilities appear equal. Play, story telling, and the use of imagination are vital experiences at this time.

From ages seven to eleven, all learning experiences are simply a continuing reinforcement of Eddie's earlier learning, with the added dimension that he is able to consider additional possibilities.

At age eleven, something happens to Eddie internally. A chemical is released in his brain which dissolves any pathways that haven't been developed through repetition. Because of this process Eddie will no longer consider all possibilities. He will only expand in the areas, and consider the possibilities, that have already been established by his earlier learning.

By age fifteen, Eddie is noticing a profound urgency inside of himself. (This urgency is not sexual by nature.) He now has the feeling that something tremendous is going to happen to him and he becomes extremely idealistic. He looks for a role model that matches his ideals. Fortunately, Eddie finds powerful heros in both his dad and his favorite uncle. The connection to his heros causes his heart to open which enables the neuro-transmitters to fire from his open heart to his brain. The heart is actually speaking to the head and this miraculous event enables him to move to the third level of the brain, the place of limitless possibilities. Eddie has now become one of the rare 5% that has accomplished the transition which enables him to lovingly create and become all that he desires. Eddie's life will, of course, have it's normal issues but these issues will be mainly external. They will not be internal because Eddie knows who he is, and he has love as the basis for his happiness and future.

Now that Eddie's life is in order, let's look at what would have happened if he had not found a hero at age fifteen. If Eddie had not found a hero he would have continued to feel the internal awareness that something profound was going to happen to him until about the age of twenty. Then, as with most, he would have become discouraged. As a result, his heart would have shut down and he would have become one of the 95% who live life in the arena of the two lower brains where self and possessions rule.

Through Eddie we have seen that reaching full human potential is dependent upon specific needs being met in several vital stages of growth and development. The need to be bonded at birth is the first crucial event that creates a connection to self and to others. For generations, because of hospital procedures, many babies were not bonded at birth. The result is obvious in our society. We are a society that screams, "What about me?" and at the same time wonders, "Who am I?" We could accomplish much for our world and for future generations if our babies were immediately given back to their mothers at birth.

The second vital stage that provides us with an opportunity to become all we can become occurs at about age fifteen, when we open to more than ourselves by finding a hero or a role model. The need for our young people to find a true hero is a vital stage in helping them open to their abstract brain (the place of limitless possibility). Yet, as a society, we are sadly lacking true heros. As a result, our teenagers worship sports and entertainment celebrities who seldom qualify as genuine heros. By not producing valid heros, we have hindered our teens in the simple process of opening their hearts. With this missing heart connection, the human experience is dominated by the two lower parts of the brain - the parts that function totally with the emphasis on the physical world.

Without heros, individuals automatically revert to the mid-brain in an attempt to satisfy their needs. Here they will be motivated and obsessed by the pleasures of possessions. If these pleasures do not satisfy them, they will then turn to the first layer of the brain where animal instincts dominate. In this part of the brain they will attempt to find meaning through base desires. This is the place where drugs and self indulgence become the substitute for a true connection to the heart. This endless process of searching for the self in the two lower layers of the brain leads most individuals further and further away from experiencing their basic need to love and to belong. The missing stage of heros is one reason why today's youth are experiencing escalated gang activity, drug addiction, teenage suicide and an all-time high level of discouragement and despair.

It is never too late for the heart to open. To open the heart later in life, a person must be willing to experience love. This love can occur as a result of finding a hero, having a spiritual awakening, or finding a cause or purpose beyond the self. Assistance in opening the heart can also be brought about by art, visualization, meditation, playing, fantasizing, storytelling, singing, dancing, or by going lovingly back to the child.

The need of all people is to love. If we are not assisted in expanding to the place of love we automatically contract into being less than we were intended to become. If the key is opening the heart, thereby creating a connection to the brain, then the heart, not the head, is the key factor in the equation. We cannot think our way into empowerment, we must love our way into consciousness. When this occurs we will automatically want to lovingly share ourselves with others.

Thoughts Create Reality

After studying Eddie's life, it becomes obvious that most of us have not experienced the perfect life. With so much missing what chance do we actually have to be fulfilled in our adult lives? Fortunately, we have every chance if we can arrive at a place of empowered thinking. Notice the key words "empowered thinking." This does not mean you can randomly think differently and your life will automatically become empowered. We have all tried to just "think differently" to change our lives, and we usually become frustrated with the sameness of the results. When self effort fails, most then go to the next step for change and experience seminars and/or books where they become exposed to new information and thinking. Many times the effects of these new found processes last for only a brief moment in time. The person then begins to notice that his old patterns of thought and behavior are again dominating his life. The reason for this return to the old patterns is that the foundation for integrating the new information has not been properly laid. Without the proper foundation, change becomes difficult if not impossible. *LifeScripting* will provide you with the ability to establish a proper foundation for lasting change.

If your thinking is the place of personal empowerment then you need to understand the process of thinking, and how your thinking determines both your internal and external life. Once you understand the components of your thinking, any new information presented to you can be filtered into your consciousness in a whole new way.

It is first necessary to understand that your thoughts create your personal reality. The events of life happen, and even though these events cannot be changed, your thoughts about past events do influence your present reality. There are several concepts that will assist you to internalize this life-altering truth. As these concepts are presented in this chapter you will begin to realize the power of your thoughts.

First Thought, Second Thought

Your thinking creates your entire reality, and yet how often do you stop to think about what you are thinking? Most people go through the day reacting to their thoughts but seldom do they pause to ask themselves, "What am I actually thinking?" For most people, thoughts are either random, or they are the thoughts they have been told to have. Rarely do people pause and realize that what they are thinking is creating their reality. There is great hope in knowing that if you choose a different thought, you could create a different reality.

Take a moment and ask yourself, "What am I thinking?" Now close your eyes and lock in that thought. Next ask yourself, "What else could I be thinking?" Now close your eyes and hold that thought for a moment.

When you pondered the first question, "What am I thinking?" a very interesting process began. It may have been difficult to decide what it was you were actually thinking. In all likelihood once you decided to lock the thought in, it then became difficult to hold the thought. When you asked the second question, "What else could I be thinking?" things got even more interesting. You discovered at that point the countless possibilities that existed for you. You could have thought about anything, the options were limitless. The choices about what you can think are totally yours. Your thinking is your place of personal power! Yet, on a daily basis we give up this power to our conditioned responses rather than becoming aware of the limitless choices in our own minds.

The first thought about an event may be a random thought, or a trained response. However, the second thought about the event is totally a choice. Realizing this, you may want to occasionally monitor your thinking by asking yourself, "What am I thinking?" If the thought is not one you feel serves your life, ask the next question, "What else could I be thinking?" Remember, the power of choice is all yours.

Neutral Events

All events are neutral. Seeing or hearing this statement usually causes a quick review of the events in your life that you certainly did not believe were neutral.

The concept that events are neutral does not suggest that the events of your life were not important to you. However, it does suggest that events have no meaning until you decide what you think about the event. The specific impact each event has in your life is directly related to the meaning you place upon it. There is no right or wrong placement of meaning, the choice is yours. You will, however, emotionally respond to an event based solely on the thoughts you have about it. When you realize you can choose what you are thinking, and that you have the ability to replace unwanted thoughts with wanted thoughts, then the response to each life event is in your hands.

To illustrate the concept that all events are neutral, imagine a group of people sitting in a room into which a rattlesnake crawls. How will the people choose to respond? Three people run from the room screaming, because the meaning they place on the snake is fear. One man freezes because he remembers the time he was bitten by a snake and almost died. Several others climb upon their chairs and observe from a safe place. One lady approaches the snake and picks it up. She is a snake charmer and feels this snake is a gift from someone special. With all of these responses to the same snake, the snake still remains neutral. The snake is just being a snake crawling on the floor. The responses to this neutral event are a result of what takes place in each individual's mind. No one's reaction to the snake was right or wrong. The internal thoughts of each person simply controlled their emotional and physical response to the event.

All events are neutral until we place meaning on them. What meaning are you placing on the events in your life? What other meaning could you place on these events that might positively alter your life?

Viewpoint

Viewpoint is not an opinion, it is the point from which you view. There are more than five billion people on the planet all with a different point from which they are viewing the world. No two people can observe the same event from the very same vantage point, if for no other reason than the different placement of their bodies and the position of their eyes. For example, when a family is sitting around the dinner table they do not see the objects on the table in the same way. Each person's perception is based on her position at the table. Imagine a large milk pitcher in the middle of the table. If Dad, who is at the head of the table, described the pitcher from his position he would describe the handle since that is what he sees. Mom is seeing the side of the pitcher with writing on it and one of the children sees the other side which is clear and round. Each person is looking at the same object, each is correct in what she is seeing, yet each would describe the pitcher differently. Why? Because each is seeing through her eyes only. Even if we were to put all of their descriptions together we would have a difficult time reproducing the milk pitcher.

If we add the concept of personal histories to the dynamics of viewpoint, we will gain an even deeper understanding. If one of the children had spilled milk from the pitcher, he might look at it and be afraid to touch it. Mom could be remembering the day her mother gave her the pitcher and she could be feeling love. Dad could be looking at the pitcher and thinking of the cost of milk today in comparison to when he was a child. The object is neutral, the personal thoughts about it are not.

When each person describes the pitcher, her vantage point, as well as personal history, must be considered in that description. If the members of the family were to listen to each other's point of view, they would all have a more in-depth understanding of not only the object on the table, but of each other as individuals.

Viewpoints, when understood as the point from which we view rather than opinions, can help create a broadened picture of the events we experience. Ideally, viewpoints can become a means of connecting people rather than a means of creating turmoil and separation. There are no right or wrong viewpoints, there are simply different points from which we view.

You Create Your Reality With Your Thoughts

You create your reality about any situation based upon your viewpoint and your personal experience. The story of two brothers from Oregon vividly illustrates this truth. The brothers went to therapy and were asked in separate sessions to recall an early childhood memory. Their stories went as follows:

Brother #1: "I remember a wonderful childhood experience. My brother and I were invited to a friend's birthday party. We asked Mom if we could walk to the party even though it was raining. She said yes. My brother and I had a great time on the way, splashing each other in the puddles and getting our friend's present wet. We arrived at the door laughing as we handed our friend his wet present. During the party the cake was accidentally knocked on the floor and we asked the mother of our friend if we could just eat it off of the floor since it was already a mess. She said we could, and we had the best time playing with the cake and getting ourselves covered with the frosting. It was a great party and a wonderful day."

Brother #2: "I want to tell you about the most humiliating day. My brother and I were invited to a friend's birthday party. It was a rainy, dismal day. We asked our mom to drive us to the party and she refused, so we had to walk. I was so upset. On the way to the party my bully brother kept splashing in the puddles and got me soaking wet. The present also got wet. I was totally embarrassed when we handed our friend the present, but my brother just laughed. During the party some kid knocked the cake on the floor and the mother of our friend was so mad she made us eat the cake off of the floor. I wanted to disappear. It was a horrible day."

What is the difference in the perceptions of the brothers? The event was the same, yet the way they viewed the event was what created their reality. One brother viewed the party as a fun event, and all of his perceptions reinforced that view. The other brother viewed the party as a horrible event, and as a result he remembered only negatives. It is not events that create our reality but rather our perception and thoughts about events.

You Choose Your Thoughts

No one has the power to put thoughts into your head. No one can make you think anything you do not want to think. Every thought is totally yours by choice.

Even though no one can choose your thoughts, you are constantly being programmed by others as to what to think and how best to define what is actually happening to you. Most people have become accustomed to hearing words like, "You make me happy! You make me sad! I need you!" Messages like these make it difficult to arrive at the belief that we alone choose what we think. Yet when you live life realizing you can choose the thoughts that ultimately create your reality, your world can become a positive place regardless of the events.

Studies of prisoners of war validate the truth that your personal power to choose your thoughts is the determining factor for a positive or negative life experience. These studies involved two types of prisoners. The first group were men who seemed to have a fairly smooth transition back into life after their experience with war. The second group had an obvious struggle with the transition. What was the difference, since each apparently had the same experience? It was discovered that the difference involved their thinking while they were in the war camps. The men who did well realized the one thing they had complete control over was what they were thinking. They realized the guards had charge over their bodies and daily agenda, but they had no control over their thoughts. These successful prisoners chose thoughts of their families, they imagined their children growing, they planned things they would do when they returned home, and they kept their life's purpose foremost in their minds. The other group allowed thoughts of fear and pain to take over their internal world. The result was a pattern of fear that lasted even when they were safely back at home.

What you think truly creates your reality, and you are the only person who chooses your thoughts. Once you are aware of this, your future thinking will become your personal responsibility. Your freedom to empower your life will then become your ability to freely choose your thoughts.

Mind Time

How do you spend your mind time? The actual time we spend with people and things is easily measured. However, what is seldom measured is the time we spend pondering people and things in our mind. And yet mind time is what is truly creating our internal reality. For example: 1) Carla and Mark end their romantic relationship. Mark goes on with his life and seldom thinks of Carla. Carla, however, thinks of Mark daily. Even though the relationship is over, how much time is Carla actually spending with Mark? As much time as she allows in her mind. 2) Georgia has a three-minute meeting with her boss. In the meeting he indicates that her performance has been sub-par. During the next several days, Georgia spends countless hours reflecting on the three-minute discussion.

A beneficial exercise is to make a list of what occupies your mind on a daily basis, then write how much actual time you spend with each item and how much mind time you spend. Once finished, look again at the list and write if your thoughts about the entries are positive or negative. You will soon develop a clear understanding of how your thoughts are affecting your reality.

For most, the past is usually a place of much mind time, both conscious and subconscious. I have helped my clients develop greater personal power by reviewing their pasts in a whole new way. The process is dependent upon your ability to choose the thoughts that allow you to see all past events as positive. This new point of view requires skills that will enable you to actually "change your thoughts" about your past. The *LifeScripting* concepts presented in Sections I and II will enable you to further develop this life-altering process.

Reframed Thinking

Reframing is the process of consciously choosing the thoughts you have about your memories and experiences. You cannot make past events go away. The past did happen and it is a part of you. However, the power to control your future and the ability to experience happiness is directly connected to how you view your life experiences. Since thinking creates your present reality, you have the option of putting a new frame of thought around any and all past events. This new frame will enable you to create a positive present experience regardless of the events. To illustrate this concept, imagine an old picture with a worn out frame. You do not want to replace the actual picture because it has sentimental value, but you do want to change the frame so it will blend better with your new decor. The act of reframing the picture creates the look you want without altering or forfeiting the original picture.

If the pictures from your past bring you pleasure, there is certainly no need to change your mental frame of reference about them. However, if a picture (memory) is causing you stress or pain, then changing the frame of reference can help create a new and beautiful dimension to your present life.

Reframing is dependent upon your ability to emphasize what is right in a situation rather than what is wrong. This can sometimes be difficult since we are often trained to look for what is wrong. Something as simple as red check marks on school papers reinforced that what was wrong was more important than our correct answers. These and many similar past messages have skewed our thinking and, as a result, we primarily tend to look for the problem. When this occurs, we fail to see the valuable gift within each and every situation. When looking for what is wrong, we inevitably perceive a negative picture we are forever attempting to fix. When looking for what is right, however, we see potential and develop an understanding of the gifts that life is providing us.

Reframing your thinking can become a simple process of answering several life-altering questions about your experiences. They are:

- Can I change what happened?
- What is right about this picture?
- What does this situation teach me?
- Who would I be without this experience?
- Who are the teachers in this memory?
- What did they teach me?
- How can I serve others with what I have experienced?

When you understand and work with the process of reframing, you will discover positive perspectives to empower your past experiences. As a result, your memories both of joy and pain will become powerful pieces of personal knowledge. You will come to recognize your uniqueness and realize that your past experiences were designed to empower your adult life.

It is important that you reframe your life from a perspective of love. Love is your birthright, and when you begin to look at your life with love, you can and will embrace everything that has happened as a gift of learning, knowing, and serving. What you previously rummaged through as your past garbage will become your buried treasures. When reframing becomes a natural process in your life, you will never again say to others, "What did you do to me?" Instead you will say, "Thank you for the experience because it has helped me to become all that I am."

In Section II you will further learn how to reframe each memory for its content and belief system formation.

Thoughts Are Things

Your thoughts not only affect your personal life by what they create for you, but they also influence others. Thoughts are things and can be measured. It has been determined by scientific instruments that thoughts travel at 186,000 miles per second (the speed of light). Your thoughts go out like radio waves and are felt by those around you.

The affect of thoughts on others can easily be demonstrated by a muscle strength test called applied kinesiology. In seminars, I use applied kinesiology to have the audience experience a visual demonstration that thoughts are truly things and that they affect both sender and receiver. I do this by having a volunteer leave the room. I instruct the audience to send positive thoughts to the person when I hold one finger above the individuals head, and to send negative thoughts when I hold up two fingers. When the volunteer re-enters the room I explain that I am going to test his muscle strength by having him extend one arm and push it upward as I put pressure on his wrist to create resistance. I then stand behind the volunteer and signal the audience with one finger. After waiting a few seconds to allow the audience to send positive thoughts I apply resistance to his extended arm. The arm of the volunteer remains solid and able to resist me. I ask the volunteer to relax as I signal the audience to send negative thoughts. After a short pause, I test the arm resistance of the volunteer. Each and every time his arm loses strength and falls to his side. The subject usually looks at me in amazement and asks, "What did you do?" I then re-signal the audience to send positive thoughts and his arm strength returns. This measurable demonstration vividly suggests that thoughts are truly things. What we think not only affects ourselves, it greatly affects others.

To comprehend this phenomena is literally life changing. What actually happens when we think negative thoughts? Not only do we pay the price of our internal unhappiness, we also add to the negativity in the world. If we want our world to be a better place, then the best place to begin this change is with the self. This can be accomplished by thinking positive thoughts.

If you are having a difficult relationship with another and want the person to respond favorably, then positive thoughts are the path. Negative thoughts greatly reduce the inner strength of the other person and add to the conflict. The most powerful tool we have to affect our lives and the lives of others is to think positively and send out thoughts of love. This process also applies globally. We may not be able to go with Mother Theresa to feed the hungry, but we can send her positive thoughts of love and support at 186,000 miles per second, thereby assisting her in her work. The power we have within our minds is limitless.

In realizing our thoughts affect others, it is also important to understand that the thoughts of others also influence us. What will happen to you if someone is thinking negatively about you? We have proven that negative thoughts alter the strength of an individual in a measurable way; you are no exception. If someone is thinking negatively about you it can weaken you. However, there is something that can be done to counteract the negative thoughts of others. Imagine again the volunteer and the arm strength test. After the earlier demonstration I then ask the person to close his eyes and remember a time when he felt love. I signal the audience to send negative thoughts. When I apply pressure to his arm it remains solid and strong. What happens to the volunteer is the feeling of love sends neuro-transmitters to his brain which puts him into abstract limitless possibility where negatives cannot enter. Through this demonstration, it becomes visibly evident that if we stay positive and loving, the negatives of the world cannot create weakness in our lives. I encourage you to try these demonstrations with your friends.

Another visual demonstration involving the arm strength of a person happens when the volunteer hears positive or negative statements. When I make a positive statement about the person such as, "You are a powerful person," his arm remains strong when tested. However, when I make a negative statement such as, "You will never be able to succeed," his arm loses strength. If I again ask him to think about love then speak a negative, his arm remains strong. If the individual makes the positive or negative statements about himself, the same strength and weakness happens to his arm.

Thoughts and words are a source of strength or weakness in our lives and the lives of others. Consciously choosing positive thoughts and words should be one of life's most serious considerations.

Transformational Thoughts

For *LifeScripting* to have its greatest impact, it will be helpful for you to consider the following three transformational thoughts. These perspectives, when perceived as truths, will greatly assist you in discovering that the complexity of life can be viewed in very simple terms. So for a moment please set aside your existing perceptions and open yourself to these possibilities becoming your truth.

Thought #1 - You Are Not An Accident

Have you taken the time to notice the order in the universe? The seasons come and go, the planets orbit, the sun rises and sets, and every atom has an incredible, intricate design. From a distance, as well as up close, the purpose and order of all things can be seen. We observe this and we stand in awe, yet when we look at our own lives we often think we are the "big accident." We seldom have this thought when life is wonderful, but we often find ourselves with this thought when life seems overwhelming.

To believe your life or its circumstances are an accident creates, at the deepest subconscious level, a belief that you are not an important and loved part of this universe. If you believe in the concept of a higher power, or a being called God, or an energy called Universe, then the belief that you are an accident suggests you are not loved by this higher power. As a result, you will feel your life does not have deep purpose or meaning because, after all, God doesn't even have a plan for you.

Some existing therapies are inadvertently reinforcing this very message. Many well-intentioned therapists have given clients the feeling that they are truly an accident in the universe, and only through sheer effort on their part will they fix what has been broken in their lives. One way this has occurred is by having a client go back to the memories of her past, and through these memories find out who did what to her. Clients are then asked to re-live these experiences to somehow fix them. This process creates blame, not only for the people involved, but blame for the universe having given the person the "wrong experience" and, therefore, the "wrong life." This process is unnecessary and not compatible with personal growth. In fact, it inhibits true empowerment since expansion can only come from love. When someone believes she is an accident, or blames others for any event that has occurred, her heart immediately contracts and negative thinking dominates her life. On the other hand, to perceive life as meaningful assists each of us in arriving at the desired goal of love and belonging.

Note: Even if you do not believe in a higher power and have concluded that life is truly an accident, or at best a random event, *LifeScripting* will still provide you with tools to help you live at the highest possible level. As I have often said to my clients, "The life you are living is the life that you have. You and only you will live it, so why not make it the best experience possible?"

Thought #2 - Life Has A Cycle

Expand now to the idea that by viewing the sequential events of your life you can create a new perspective that will enable you to determine the cycle or pattern you are living. Once this pattern is identified, the events of the past will take on a whole new meaning for your future.

An analogy of the yearly cycle of a tree best illustrates this truth. Imagine a beautiful, large tree. In the fall the leaves of the tree turn brown and fall to the ground. If you pick up the fallen leaves and look only at the leaves you can logically say, "Look at the dead leaves; certainly the tree must be dead." By looking only at the dead leaves you become convinced that the tree has indeed died. Yet if you observe the entire life cycle of the tree, a very different picture can be seen. In the fall, the leaves of the tree turn brown and fall to the ground. They then decompose and fertilize the soil which provides nutrition that enters the root system. This food actually assists the tree in becoming taller, fuller, stronger, and more beautiful in the spring. It is in the context of the complete cycle of the tree that the dead leaves become vital to the overall life and beauty of the tree.

The isolated events of our lives are similar to the fallen leaves of the tree. When focused on as dead, bad, or destructive, we fail to recognize their potential for good. Yet many are viewing their past as the place of broken pieces which must be mended before they can move forward in "the now." With this perspective, individuals will "work" on a piece of their life and seem to get better for awhile. However, in a relatively short period of time they usually find themselves slipping back into old negative feelings and patterns. The person will then either "work" again on the same perceived broken piece of life, or he may find another piece of his life that he thinks could be the problem and try to fix it. As long as the person is viewing things as wrong or broken, or in need of being fixed, the events of his life will remain negative and disconnected. However, when the events of the past are viewed as a part of an evolving picture, a deeper, richer, and more rewarding perspective of life is realized.

All past events have occurred; they cannot be changed. Yet each memory, like the dead leaves, can have value in the total picture of our lives. Memories provide us with valuable information about ourselves and therefore become the building blocks for personal growth. Once we begin to look at each and every memory for its positive information, we will come to understand ourselves in the most expansive way possible.

Thought #3 - Our Lives Are Like A Tapestry

A tapestry is a series of intricate threads that when properly woven together comprise a complete picture. Each thread has incredible purpose and must be woven exactly as intended or a flaw will appear in the picture. When looked upon separately, each thread does not appear to have great significance; however, the entire picture is affected if only one thread is not placed in its proper position.

Our lives are like a thread in the tapestry called humankind. We each have been given a specific thread to weave that no one else can weave. Our purpose and power comes from knowing what our thread is and saying yes to weaving it. It is in the process of weaving our thread that we find our joy and purpose, while at the same time assisting in the completion of the entire picture called humankind. Unfortunately, finding the right thread oftentimes becomes our greatest challenge because we are bombarded with countless messages that seem to invite us to weave threads that do not belong to us. When we follow these erroneous messages, we lose contact with ourselves and do not reach our full potential. Some of the most common messages that sabotage us are:

Society Says, "Be Someone Else"

Today there is great pressure within our society to become someone other than who we really are. We long to find ourselves in the truest sense of the word and become all we can become. Yet on a daily basis, society bombards us with messages that distract us from this noble goal. The marketeers of life tell us what to look like, what to wear, what to eat, what kind of car to drive, and how to succeed. The suggestions for our lives are limitless. Seldom are we told how to find our unique life thread, and rarely are we given the instructions to weave it well. As a result, the temptation to become someone else dominates our thinking as we desperately try to weave the threads suggested by parents, teachers, friends, television, etc. This perversion has resulted in deep internal stress for individuals, and has fostered a society in rapid decline.

The 96 questions in Section II will assist you in finding your personal tapestry thread. With the tools of *LifeScripting*™ as your guide, you will be assisted through the steps that will enable you to weave your thread well.

Some Therapies

Early in my career as a therapist, I practiced the type of therapy I am about to comment upon. I did it out of love for others, as I'm sure most other therapists are doing. I believed books had to be correct as they outlined the various methods of applying therapy. Yet when I implemented some of the techniques, I sensed something was wrong. Because of this awareness, and with my knowing that love is the key, I have come to believe that therapy which does not empower the person by creating love for self and others should not be used.

Today, much of what is happening in therapy is actually preventing people from weaving their personal tapestry thread. This occurs because many clients are being engulfed in the relentless process of figuring out what is wrong with their lives. They are then encouraged to discover who did what to them. The final step is to discover what to do about what was done. As a result, countless hours of therapy are spent reviewing and fixing lives as if they are broken. This approach keeps people preoccupied with their apparent problems but does not assist them in getting to the process of developing a life designed to utilize their full potential. If people are busy in total self analysis, how can they give and receive the love they are so desperately seeking? How can they weave their threads when all they are doing is staring at them?

Labels

Another therapeutic method of personal sabotage is to label yourself, and then to become that label. People do this when they identify their issues and call themselves by those issues. When this occurs, they then walk the path of trying to fix the habit, fear, or phobia.

Psychological research positively confirms that "self talk" creates our deepest belief about ourselves. We also know that those who speak or think negatively about themselves, or label themselves, create a feeling of not being whole. Labeling usually leads those who have become its victims into placing their personal tapestry threads into the hands of others, who then attempt to help them fix the "problem." A modern phenomenon seems to be that the methods people are choosing as a means for helping themselves are becoming the place where they become dependent. Many join groups which are lovingly designed to provide growth and support. However, far too often the overall message of "I am broken" so prevails that life becomes something to be forever "worked upon." This attitude can destroy the hope of ever overcoming the problem and can create dependency in and of itself. When our labels win we become trapped with the feeling of being "less than," and that idea permeates our daily life and keeps us in bondage.

Please understand that self-help support groups have greatly assisted, even virtually saved, millions of lives by providing people with support systems of encouragement and love. However, the process of wearing a label and living with the feeling of being forever broken is, in my opinion, what has created a negative within this positive framework. I strongly suggest that when you awaken every morning you do not reconfirm your feeling of brokenness by saying, "I am a/an_____" because this statement creates a negative about the self. However, a statement such as, "I choose not to______ today" generates positive reinforcement because it creates in the mind a sense of personal success.

If one of your past behavioral patterns included the excessive use of substances, I suggest you do not forever beat yourself up for acts committed while under the influence. Although you are responsible for your choice to use, and therefore responsible for the consequences of that choice, it was the drug which many times dictated your behavior. I recommend you always look to your past for the places of learning and reframing, rather than for your character defects. If you use this positive process daily, all past experiences can and will become places for your personal growth.

Relationships

We are led to believe by advertising, television, books, and music that we should experience a certain kind of relationship. If we do not, something is wrong with our life. As a result of this message, far too many people are spending countless amounts of time searching for their perfect "other" and ignoring the weaving of their personal tapestry thread.

I am not suggesting that relationships are unimportant, but to spend a lifetime searching for another is certainly a way to avoid finding oneself. It is important to realize that all people are not destined to be in a relationship. Who would tell Mother Theresa to stop doing what she is doing and find a relationship in order to reach her full potential? She is so obviously weaving her personal thread for the entire well being of humanity that to ask her to weave the thread of a romantic relationship seems absurd.

If a relationship is one of your goals and you feel it is an integral part of your life purpose, then within the pages of this book you will discover the type of relationship to best assist you as you weave your personal tapestry thread.

Properly weaving the human tapestry is the ultimate responsibility of each individual. This responsibility is best assumed by those who believe they are not an accident, that everything has a cycle, and that their essence is a valuable part of a tapestry called life. Detailed in the next chapters are principles that will assist you in finding your thread and methods of how to weave it well.

The Classroom Of Life

An additional principle necessary to understand before discovering your individual beliefs, is the concept that your life has been a classroom for learning. With the knowledge that your belief systems were formed by the time you were six and that those belief systems are running your adult life, it becomes important to consider the learning process of the child. By doing this, you will not only understand the adult you have become, but you will view childhood as the foundational classroom for all learning.

To further grasp the dynamics of what happened to you as a child, let's closely analyze the components of a classroom as they relate to your childhood learning.

The Purpose Of A Classroom

A classroom is a place designed for learning. Its purpose is to create an environment where students gain knowledge. The information provided in a classroom is intended for the future empowerment of the student.

A student does not use all the information gained from a class each and every day, but rather she uses portions of the information as it is needed along the path of life. When information is needed, the student does not go back into the classroom to sit at the desk and retake the class. The student simply taps her memory to access the stored data that applies to the present.

Childhood is your first classroom, therefore childhood is where your foundational learning has taken place. To tap into that learning, it is not necessary to go back and re-live your childhood experiences. You can simply access your memory for what you have learned. What you have learned in childhood then becomes valuable information on file and can be used for daily choices in your adult life.

The Language Of Childhood

During childhood you learned two languages. The first was the language you speak, the second was the language of your behavior. You do not usually judge your verbal language by telling yourself to stop speaking English (or whatever language you have learned), but many times you do judge your behavioral language and tell yourself to stop doing certain behaviors or repeating certain patterns. You mistakenly do this because you do not understand that your behavioral language is as deeply ingrained as your verbal language.

Both languages are a part of your stored data and came from the core of what you learned in the first few years of your life. To judge your language or behavior does not assist your life, it only creates negative thoughts and feelings that can lead to a process of self-destruction. Your verbal language, as well as your behavioral language, can only be changed by conscious choice. Conscious choice can only occur after the information is brought onto your computer screen (the mind) for viewing. Once available for viewing you can become aware of your options and make decisions about your future behavior. The processes of *LifeScripting* will assist you in discovering how to retrieve information from your past and also teach you how to reframe that information for future empowerment.

Teacher/Student

In a classroom there are assigned teachers. The teachers are in charge of the class and the learning process. Some teachers are more challenging than others. The degree of difficulty can be an indicator to the student that much can be learned from the teacher if reframing is applied to the experience. For example: in the classroom of childhood, James had a teacher called Mom who belittled him for his every move. James, as an adult, knows the depth of this feeling and now works with children who feel criticized and unable to align with their parents. Who taught James this skill? His mother, the teacher. Valuable information becomes a part of a student's knowledge base when the student chooses to learn rather than chooses to reject the teacher because of the perceived degree of difficulty.

The curriculum of a classroom is designed to provide the specific information needed by each student. The degree of difficulty is based on the learning capability of the student. Some classrooms are for first graders, some for second, third, college level students, post graduates, etc. No classroom is a wrong classroom, nor is one classroom any better or worse than another. Each and every classroom is designed to provide the student with the information he requires. The classroom of your childhood was the perfect classroom for you. It provided the precise information and experiences you needed to become the person you were intended to become.

In a classroom, the teacher is not always just the teacher. Many times the teacher becomes the student by learning from those officially called the students. When this happens, the student indirectly becomes the teacher. This dynamic can occur for a brief moment or extend over long periods of time. Both roles enhance learning and are gifts to all involved. In your childhood classroom, your teachers were your parents, your caretakers, your siblings, your peers, and anyone else that significantly crossed your life path. Conversely, you were also their teacher.

It is also important to understand that as a child you learned and assimilated information that formed your beliefs in two distinct ways - through what you heard and through what you observed. Verbal information accounted for 5% of your learning. The remaining 95% of your learning came from perceptions of your environment, and from your observations of the behavior of others.

Building Blocks For Learning

In a classroom, you learn basic information about specific subjects so you can use that information as a foundation upon which to build your future learning. For example, in math you learned that 1+1=2. You learned this by having this concept demonstrated over and over. As a result, when you see the math equation 1+1=? you automatically write the answer 2. If you could (and you can) find a method of discovering what is causing what in your adult world (the 1+1s that =2), then you could be totally in charge of your life's answers. You could even choose the equation that would guarantee your desired results. You could also know the ingredients that would lead you to undesirable results. With this knowledge, you would be able to avoid destructive relationships and behavior.

Until you know what causes what, you will repeat the same behavior and continually wonder why you get the same results. For example: Imagine you are in a chemistry lab and you have little knowledge of chemistry. As you begin to combine chemicals, you are unaware that two specific chemicals, when brought together, will create an explosion. You randomly mix these two chemicals and an explosion occurs. After you clean up the mess you wonder what happened, but you do not investigate what caused what and soon you accidentally combine the same two chemicals. Once again an explosion occurs. You still don't realize what is causing the explosions so you continue to mix the chemicals and the result is always an explosion. Finally, you back up and ask yourself, "What is causing what?" You discover that when you put the two chemicals together you get an explosion. At this point you have new options because you now have knowledge and understanding about what is causing what. With this new data you realize you cannot change the chemicals but you can predetermine whether you desire an explosion. If you want combustion because you want a rocket to fly, then you will put these chemicals together and expect an explosion. If you would rather not have the explosion, then you will keep the chemicals apart. The same is true in your life. You can discover what is causing what in your life by reviewing the stored information from childhood. With this awareness you will have the ability to choose the specific life results you desire.

By way of illustration, assume a woman believes men will hurt her. She assumes this because that is what was stored on her childhood floppy disc. As a result she is experiencing hurt from men in her adult relationships. If she could discover what is causing what by recognizing the type of men that create hurt for her, she could then choose whether she wants the resulting hurt, or wants to avoid the hurt. She could accomplish this by her choosing to engage, or not engage, in relationships with the type of men that the child knows will hurt her.

Since your beliefs from childhood create your beliefs for what causes what in your adult world, it becomes extremely important to know what caused what in your childhood. With this knowledge, you will be able to consciously choose the results you want by properly choosing your behavior.

To illustrate this in a deeper way, let's look at a real life situation. A business woman named Tracy is noticing that every time she invests money with women she ends up both frustrated and with no money. Tracy tries again and again to invest with women but the result is always the same. To find out what is occurring she needs to ask herself, "What happened to me in the classroom called childhood with regard to money and women?" The answer for Tracy is in the interactions she had with her mother in relation to money. When Tracy was a child most of her interactions with her mother involving money resulted in Tracy having nothing. Tracy would do household chores and neighborhood jobs to earn money. Her mother would then borrow the money and not repay Tracy. In high school, Tracy worked part time and loaned the money she earned to her mother. They agreed the money would be repaid when Tracy entered college. When the time for college arrived, Tracy's mother didn't have the money to pay her debt to Tracy. Consequently, Tracy was never paid back. The belief that women and money cause loss dominates Tracy's viewpoint. As a result, all of her adult financial investments with women have concluded in a monetary loss for Tracy.

What is causing what for Tracy becomes obvious when we look at the history and belief of the child. In childhood, whenever money was involved with Mom (a woman), the child lost. As a result, the adult also lost when she invested money with women. The belief of the child became the reality of the adult. Women + money = loss.

To reframe this experience for its power is to first remember that there are no accidents. Everything that happened to Tracy in the classroom of childhood is for her information and can serve her once she becomes aware. Secondly, all people who cross Tracy's path can be and are her teachers. With this in mind, the empowering reframe of this experience is as follows: Tracy, realizing the gift of learning from the child, knows that investing with women minimizes her financial success as an adult. Consequently, she chooses not to invest her money with women because she already knows the inevitable result. Tracy also realizes that the child she was never stopped working and giving to her mother, regardless of the financial loss. As a result, Tracy knows that a part of her life purpose is working with women, however, she is to never assume the end result of this will be financial gain. This interaction in her childhood has become one of the many unique threads in Tracy's personal tapestry. This thread, when placed as a part of the entire picture of Tracy's life, helps guide her in her life's work.

Many have come to believe that it is necessary to "overcome" the experiences of childhood. Conversely, *LifeScripting* suggests looking to your childhood for information about what causes what in your adult life. With this awareness, you can predict, in advance, what results you will encounter because it has already happened! With this foresight, you can then choose to engage or not engage in behavior because you will already know the predictable result. With these new insights, it now becomes possible to understand why the same actions recreate the same results. This knowing becomes your compass because you can recognize the 1+1s that cause the 2s. With this power, you will be able to decide to embrace or avoid the 2! When you know what caused you joy as a child, you can create that experience knowing that joy will be your result as an adult. When you know that certain experiences caused you pain, you will stop doing them over and over again. The gift of *LifeScripting* is in discovering what is causing what and using it as a guidance mechanism to empower your daily life. When this occurs, life then becomes excitement over asking, "What do I know?" rather than experiencing sorrow and confusion created by asking "Why did these things have to happen to me?" Life will no longer be seen as being done to you, but rather it will be seen as being done for your knowledge, power and direction. The child then graduates from being the pupil to becoming your teacher, guidance counselor, and hero.

Once you truly grasp the 1+1s that = 2 in your life, the information becomes like an automatic pilot system that guides you daily. Through reframing, you will see the gift of each childhood experience in terms of information that serves you, the adult. As a result, you will never again look at your past experiences as something you wished had not occurred, but rather you will be honored to be the vehicle that carries the child's experiences forward. It is the child that can adequately guide the adult when the adult knows how to look to the child for information.

Each of us had different experiences in childhood because we needed different pieces of information to guide us in weaving our individual threads in the tapestry of life. The answers for what threads you are personally weaving and how best to weave them are truly within yourself. In later chapters you will discover when to look, how to look, and what to do with the information you find.

Classrooms Provide Multi-leveled Information

There seems to be a two part learning process in each childhood experience. Each experience provides information for both your public life and your private life. The same experience can produce an opposite result depending upon which part of your life you choose to apply the learning.

A client's experience will help you understand this somewhat complicated process. Robert came to my office with the complaint that his private world was in confusion. His primary issues at home were about communication. Robert could not get his wife to listen to him, and he always seemed to be the man mediating between his step-children and their mother. In the world of business, things were great. Robert earned six figures annually by dealing with the very thing he could not deal with at home. His job involved traveling nationally to help people in corporations to hear and understand each other. He helped management listen to employees and taught employees how to be heard by management. Yet in his own home Robert was not heard, and he was totally frustrated at always being the voice for the children. To understand what was happening was to discover the experience of the child he was and therefore isolate Robert's beliefs about being heard.

Robert was the first-born baby of deaf parents. He was born at a time when there wasn't any equipment to alert his parents when he cried. Imagine how many times and how long he must have cried before someone came to his rescue. When Robert was three, his sister was born. Every time she cried, Robert would wake up Mom and Dad so they could take care of her. He became the voice that got all of her needs met. When his brother was born he became his voice also. As a child, Robert learned how to get people to hear each other. He also learned how to get the basic needs of others met. Because of this childhood learning, Robert, as an adult, is a natural mediator who helps management understand employee needs. He also has an intuitive ability to assist the employees in voicing their specific needs. He did not learn these skills in a college class, he learned them from a child who provided a voice for the members of his family. With that voice, he helped them meet their needs.

In the business environment, these skills are his gifts; but at home in his private world, Robert re-experiences the frustration of the child he once was. Each time the members of his family do not personally hear him, he reacts as if he is again the lone child who is not being heard by his deaf parents. So the very thing the child learned for his career causes him pain and frustration in his private world. Prior to our session, Robert had not realized that the childhood lessons were to be taken to the world for adult power. Without this awareness, his adult home reminded him of the childhood classroom called family, and therefore his belief that he wasn't going to be heard at home emerged as truth. Once these insights were explained, he had the choice to thank the child for the learning that serves him in his business world, and to also understand the child's message for his private world. Robert's childhood learning confirms that he will not be heard at home. Thus, he needs to stop making it a requirement and go with the flow. He now knows that family members tend not to listen to him about his personal needs, and he understands that his job is to help them recognize each others needs. He is also grateful to the child he was for teaching him the skills necessary to assist others in hearing both sides in the world of business.

Robert's life has drastically changed since he honors the child he was. He uses the knowledge about his childhood experience to become an empowered adult in both of his worlds. His entire life was served once the significance of the past was brought to a conscious level.

An example from the classroom of my personal life will also help illustrate this dynamic. My mother had a view from her past that one of her roles as a parent was to break the spirit of her children. Someone had told her that this was the spiritual thing to do since God required humility in His people. I was born a spirited child, so oftentimes my interactions with my mother became a clash of wills. I never gave in no matter what the cost to my body. As I grew older, I realized that freedom for my spirit was outside of the house. Consequently, I took advantage of every opportunity possible, and enthusiastically participated in many events outside of my home. When I got married I carried the belief of the child to my marriage and many times perceived that the intent of my spouse was to cap my spirit. Consequently, like the child, I found every excuse to be outside of the house. I would do this by being with the children or volunteering in ways that provided my spirit with the ability to soar. Often I would return home to experience the frustration on my spouse's part as he complained about my free spirit. I was seeing and feeling the very same pressures I experienced as a child, and I responded the very same way the child did so many years earlier.

By reframing the experience, this scene from childhood has given me a source of great awareness about my life. What I see now is beautiful. If Mom is my honored teacher and not my abuser, then what did she teach me through this interaction? She taught me that in the world outside of my home I was to be free spirited and become involved with many people and many projects, my job description so to speak. She also taught me that when I returned home there would be a need to rest and re-group for the next event in the world. As a result of this knowledge, I now have a home I thoroughly enjoy. It is a space of peace and softness where I rest and nurture my being. This space provides me with the balance necessary to be fully involved with the events of the world which require a spirit that is fully charged and enthusiastic.

The child also learned from these interactions with Mom that spirits cannot be capped or killed. As a result, I teach people how to empower their spirit and how to find the freedom in their life that comes from living their hearts' desire. I also teach them how to relax and still the spirit which helps them find their internal self. For this reason, and many more, I now see my mother as a valued teacher.

Classrooms Are To Teach The Teachers

Once the student grasps the curriculum of the classroom, then, when appropriate, the student can become the teacher of others. The key question is always, "What did the child learn for me?" It is never, "How was I hurt?" Confusion will go on forever when responding to the second question. Learning will go on endlessly when the emphasis is on the first question. It is up to each of us to determine if we want to spend negative-thought-time tearing down our personal life and trying to rebuild what we think is broken, or if we want to learn from and reframe our past experiences. Through *LifeScripting,* you will realize that childhood is a personalized classroom of learning. The purpose of that learning is to take the knowledge from the classroom and use it in the world. You cannot change what has already occurred, but you can empower your life when you are aware that you are not an accident and that all of your experiences can provide positive information for your choices. Childhood then becomes a classroom for your learning, not a place to hurt or be hurt.

How To Recognize Your Teachers

The following simple exercises will enable you to determine your past and present teachers. Remember, what you believed as a child is what you are living in your now world. The characters of your past, in some form or fashion, express themselves in your daily life. There are two ways to recognize the teachers who are serving you:

1) List or draw a picture of the people involved in your childhood. How close or distant were these characters to you? Next to each name write who in your present experience is most like each of these people. You will soon determine that your past is your present.

2) List or draw a picture of the characters on your present stage of life. Next to each of these names note who in your childhood most resembles the people who are now in your life. With this exercise you will discover that your present is your past.

To help you further empower your life, ask yourself the question, "What did each of these individuals teach me, and how can I reframe my experience with them so I can use the information to enhance my life and better serve others?"

The idea that life is a valued classroom is a key *LifeScripting* concept that will help you find your purpose, your power, and your joy.

What Happens To All Children

Before discovering the specific events that formed your personal belief systems, it is first necessary to take a more in-depth look at the actual process of belief system formation. Remember, like the computer, information about life is stored in the files of the brain. This data becomes your belief, your truth, and therefore your behavior. The precise dynamics of this process will be presented to you in this chapter. If you follow the unfolding diagrams and explanations, this complex process will be easily understood. It is important to pause and review each number on the diagrams in order to understand the dynamics that took place for you in determining who you have become. With this new understanding will come new possibilities for your future choices.

The Human Process

Recall from Chapter 4 that the need of all children (and adults) is to love and to belong. If love and belonging are present, an individual grows both psychologically and physically. If, however, a perception exists that love and belonging are absent, then an individual contracts emotionally and physically. It is both purposeful and wonderful that this need is primary in our life because it connects adults to children and children to adults.

It is important to realize that in your early years, when you were totally dependent upon others for your survival, you were given the basics by someone or you would not be alive today. This truth alone should give you a new perspective and sufficient reason to say "thank you" to others for your life.

With this thought in mind, let's look at what happens to all children and begin diagraming (below) the events of childhood. With love and belonging as the primary need (#1) a baby is born (#2). This newborn baby ("me" in the small circle) symbolizes every birth that has ever occurred. At birth each child is born into a situation/classroom that is already in process, which is represented by the larger circle (#3). This "situation" is always bigger than the child and represents the initial challenge of every newborn.

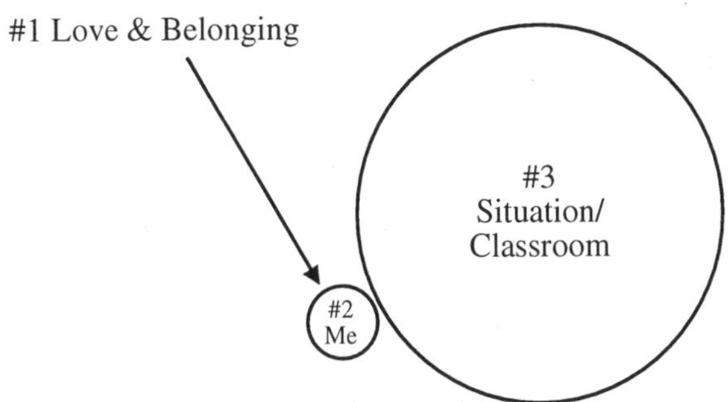

The uniqueness of each situation is as individual as the number of children who have been born. This occurs because each child views life through her own eyes and perspective. Therefore, there cannot be two identical situations, even if all perceived circumstances seem exactly the same to an outside observer.

Regardless of the circumstances into which a child is born, the fact remains that the child is involved in a scenario already in progress. The child can only experience the situation through her eyes and from her perception. From her vantage point, the child forms a series of beliefs about life. This process is much like going into a movie theater with the movie well in progress and having the task of figuring out not only the plot, but who each individual character is and what role each of them is playing. Some children are born into healthy movies, some into fairy-tales, some are a part of a drama, some are born into love stories, some into boredom, some are in a mystery, others are a part of a horror movie, etc. No matter what the movie, the child will view the situation through her eyes only. It is this childhood perception that forms lifelong belief systems. As I help people review the movie of their life, it always becomes apparent that it is the child, age six or younger, who decides the core belief for: Who am I? What is a man? What is a woman? Who are the people I will associate with in life? How will I relate with them? How will I handle stress? How will I problem solve? What is my purpose? and How will I love? Your personal beliefs in these areas and others will be discovered as you answer the 96 questions in Section II.

Right Family - Right Child

Since there are no accidents, each child is born into the right situation with the right parents. Each child will experience in his childhood exactly what is needed for the potential possibility of becoming all that that child can become. In simple terms, all children are in the right classrooms experiencing the right situations to learn what they personally need to know so they can competently weave their life threads.

How Beliefs Form

Looking at a specific family event will assist you in understanding belief system formation. The situation I will use will be imaginary even though it may apply to many readers. Please be aware that I will use a negative scenario in order to graphically illustrate the possible behaviors that can result for a person experiencing an event. After viewing the event as negative I will show you how to reframe the situation to turn it into positive power.

Imagine a little girl named Sarah is the first born child (#2 - in the following diagram) of a family unit that consists of a mother and father. Sarah, like all children, views her entire world from her need to love and belong. Life should be beautiful, however Mom and Dad are experiencing major stress in their lives and as a result are in constant turmoil with each other (#4 - in the diagram). When Sarah is about five, Dad, because of his feelings of powerlessness, begins to incest her. (As the layers of *LifeScripting* and belief system formation unfold, you will discover that what created Dad's behavior was a direct result of what happened to him as a child. When Dad was a child he was in a situation where someone harmed him, and he is now carrying his learning forward.) Sarah is told by Dad not to talk about the incest and she becomes very confused. Since she is unable to understand the dynamics happening for Dad (he doesn't even understand), she can only conclude that the situation is about her. Sarah, like all children, believes that everything happening is about her because she cannot reason that something is occurring for the people interacting with her. Because of this, all situations and events become beliefs about self. These beliefs then become the entire reality of the individual (#5 in the diagram).

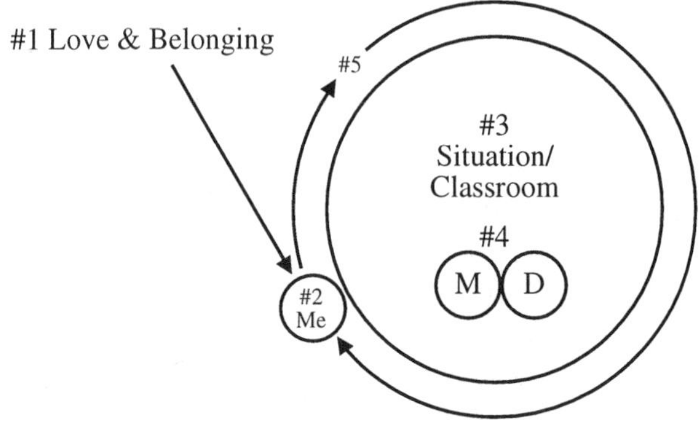

In belief system formation, Dad represents (for all children) the beliefs for: What is a man? Who is a man to me? and also Who is God? (These specific beliefs will be personally addressed for you in Section II.) Because of this process, Sarah's interactions with Dad form an entire belief about men and their future relationship to her.

As Sarah grows into an adult she will respond one of several ways to men in her life. Her responses are based solely on her original perception of the events with her Dad.

Her possible choices are:

Option #1 - Pushing Men Away

Let's say the internal message and perception of Sarah is, "Men hurt me and confuse me." With this message as a belief, Sarah establishes a deep emotional contract with the child that no man will ever hurt her or confuse her. Sarah then grows up around the child and this contract becomes the core of her interaction with men. As the years pass, she builds thick walls of defense. These walls are built totally out of love for the child since they serve in protecting her from being hurt by men. Sarah is experiencing, at the deepest levels, the love of self. At a conscious level Sarah may have forgotten the child and the experiences with Dad, however, regardless of her ability to remember, she will inevitably honor her loving contract to protect the child.

The adult Sarah becomes will push men away in defense of the child. People will respond to her behavior by staying away, and they will wonder why she is so intense and defensive. Most people interacting with her will believe her behavior is about the woman they see in the present moment. But in actuality, a deep and beautiful love for a child is the driving force behind Sarah's observed adult behavior.

Until Sarah fully understands this loving contract and realizes her options for reframing, she will continue to believe that deep committed love will never be available to her. She will experience, time and again, her belief that love is painful, resulting in an unsettled feeling of being less than she knows she was meant to be.

Option #2 - Bringing Men Into Her Life Who Hurt Her

This option is a little more complex in its dynamics and is based on an internal message which says, "Men hurt me and it can't be my fault." Because of this belief, Sarah will grow up around the child and have an incredible desire to bring into her experience men who hurt her. This seems illogical until you look at the deeper dynamics of the contract Sarah now has with the child she was. Since the message of "it can't be my fault" prevails, Sarah becomes driven to find only men like Dad who hurt her. She does this because she is trying to make a positive difference in the life of men who act like Dad. Sarah wants to be powerful enough (for the sake of the child) to change just one man into a person who loves and cherishes her. If she can accomplish this, she can then prove she is better than Dad, and that the sexual behavior had to be Dad's fault and not her's. After all, she believes someone like Dad truly loves her and therefore she must be lovable. Unfortunately, what will happen to Sarah when she chooses men like Dad is that she will again experience the same dynamics she experienced as a child with her dad (1+1=2).

With this behavior, Sarah will forever feel powerless in her life as she continues to attract only men who match her picture of Dad. These men will hurt her as she interacts with one after another - all for the love of a child! Sarah's behavior will persist for as long as she subconsciously holds the contract with the child, which internally states she must make a positive difference to a man. Sarah's intentions are so loving, yet the results are so heartbreaking. Sarah's life could change if she understood the positive options that would result from reframing this childhood experience.

Option #3 - Reframing For Power

Most adult behavior will fall into the two categories of behavior just described: 1) Pushing the situation away from the adult self to protect the child. 2) Bringing the same situation into everyday life in an attempt to change the end result.

A third choice is also possible but it is seldom discovered in the natural course of events. This option is the choice to consciously reframe events. The process involves thinking in a new and positive way about the already existing situations in your life. It includes the realization that the situations in your life have already occurred and can never be changed. You can, however, change your thoughts about any situation and, in so doing, alter your reality. With changed thoughts, you will create new behavior resulting in an empowered life.

To change your thoughts is not to just say, "Oh, I'll just change my thinking!" It also involves a realization of what you are thinking and the willingness to choose different thoughts about situations that are creating negatives in your life. This new thinking is based on a belief that the "new thoughts" are the ones you really want to have, because these thoughts will create a more positive and productive life for you.

To develop a positive frame of reference about life is to remember that there are no accidents in your life and that all events are necessary for your personal growth. Add to this the awareness that you are in a classroom of learning, and you will recognize that your experiences can serve in determining who you are. With these beliefs as the basis of your thinking, it is possible to look to all of your childhood experiences as being the right events for the child, and, therefore, the right events for you. Each experience can then provide clear knowledge of your uniqueness and what you have to offer the world in which you live. The end result will be deep joy because your heart will open in meaningful ways to both yourself and others. To accept this view is to acknowledge that the events of your childhood provide the purpose, the direction, and the guiding information for you the adult.

The ability to reframe your life experiences is your ultimate freedom. Your reframing is based entirely upon your personal thinking and frame of reference. No one can tell another what an experience should mean to him. The experience is what it is to only you, and you alone are the deciding factor in the interpretation of its meaning.

If we were to help Sarah reframe her experience with incest, we would first look at the situation as being over. We would not have her go back to re-experience the event. We would simply have Sarah access her memory for information about the event by watching it like a movie. When watching it like a movie, she is not re-living the experience, she is simply looking for the information necessary to reframe her thinking in a positive manner. A positive way to look at the event of incest is to believe that at the highest of levels Sarah is loved, and that there is something about the experience that will enhance her knowledge so she can better serve herself and others. Perhaps Sarah's resulting job will include helping incest victims because she now has a deep understanding of the dynamics of incest. Or she may choose to help perpetrators to develop an understanding of their actions. As a result of her incest, she could also become a more aware parent and greatly impact her children's lives. She could also realize that she must choose someone unlike Dad to ensure a healthy relationship.

However, if Sarah does not become aware that her behavior is the result of a deep love for the child that she was, she will continue to blindly create self-destructive relationships. If she chooses the self destructive approach, she will feel a closing of her heart and miss the opportunity to experience love in her life. It is only through the act of reframing that she has an opportunity to open her heart and live a powerful and purposeful life.

A memory like Sarah's incest can create an empowered adult when the adult realizes that the child was a part of an experience that can, with different thoughts, serve both herself and others. Sarah's adult thinking process would include thoughts such as, "If I am loved, how does this experience serve my life? How can I love myself and others with my knowledge from this experience? How can I understand and love the people (teachers) who were a part of my experience?" Sarah will be able to answer these questions with love because of her understanding that all people involved in her life were once beautiful children who had something happen to them. Foremost in her mind will be the knowledge that they too grew up around the child and formed a contract of love to protect the child. This contract causes them, as well as her, to repeat or repel their original experience.

It is important to remember that if Sarah's dad is hurting a child, he was a hurt child. If her dad came to you as a little boy and said he was being hurt, you would not push him away, you would love and hold him, and you would help him through the situation. If you can begin to see the child that he was as valuable, then you will feel a oneness with him that will open your heart. This is a much better option than choosing thoughts of anger about another which closes your heart and causes negatives to rule your life.

This is not to say that we are condoning the behavior of Sarah's father. Consequences for his behavior are required until he understands his experience, chooses to reframe his life, and changes his behavior. Until he reaches that point, consequences are the only method to keep him from possible behavior repetition. Ideally, if Sarah's father were helped to understand what actually happened to him as a child, he could then begin the process of opening to the awareness of the love he has for the child he was. He could then use his experience to change his life and serve the life of others. However, it is important to remember that even if he does not come to an awareness of how to reframe his life, we still need to approach him with love and understanding.

Discernment Not Judgement

If someone does not choose to change his behavior, it does not mean, even with awareness, that it will be comfortable to be around him. If this is the case, then it becomes necessary to practice discernment rather than judgement. Discernment says, "I see your behavior and this is not a place I would choose to put a child. Therefore, I am not going to stay." It also says, "I realize that others may never change so I choose where I place myself based on their choices." Conversely, judgement says, "You are bad and things should be different because I want them different." In the process of judging another, the heart shuts down, love is absent, and the result is negative for all concerned.

To approach all of life with only positive thoughts will not change your past experiences, but it will change your attitude and behavior in the now moment. If you see your experiences as gifts, you will come to value everything that has ever occurred in your life.

The Gift The Adult Has To Offer The Child

In this chapter you have seen the incredible influence of the child in your adult life. Without the child's experiences of both joy and pain, who and what would you be? To review childhood with new eyes of understanding is to recognize only love for the child's experiences. The next logical question then becomes, "What do we as adults have to offer this child for all that the child has taught us?"

The answer becomes obvious when we contemplate what the significant difference is between an adult and a child. That significant something is life experiences coupled with the ability to reason and understand. When the child's experiences are combined with our adult knowledge, reframing can occur. When we utilize this powerful step, all childhood experiences will be seen in terms of how they have served us as individuals.

When I first began to realize the child/adult connection, I experienced much confusion about the order in life. This confusion came when I contemplated, "If only we had our adult understanding in our childhood bodies, most of our negative life issues could have been avoided. Why do we have to wait until adulthood to have the experience and understanding that the child so desperately needed?" After much thought, I realized there truly is perfect order in the process of life. Much of this awareness came from reviewing my own life. If I had been my adult self when Mom was beating me and sitting me on the cold, hard radiator for punishment, I would never have allowed the experience to occur because I would have removed myself. If the child had been removed I would have missed the learning experience that eventually created the woman I have become. I learned much by enduring Mom's punishment, including how to stand tall in my truth. Not once during the entire process with Mom did the child ever falter or back down. Those experiences taught me how to handle immense amounts of pressure. They also taught me how to persevere.

An additional reframed gift from my radiator experience involves my mother telling me to think about how my "bad deed" had created Christ's death. I sat there wondering how something so significant as Christ's death could possibly be the result of a little girl not following her mother's orders. As I sat there for what seemed like hours, I remembered how the priests had said Christ died to show us love and the beauty of a life beyond our bodies. What I concluded during those long moments on the radiator has now become the core learning for my adult work with clients. People come to me feeling crucified and dead, and I spend the necessary time helping them realize they are alive. I do this by helping them understand the connection to their spirit, where they have true life and personal freedom. Who taught me this lesson and gave me such a beautiful gift to share with others? The little girl who sat on a radiator!

I shudder when I think that I used to reject my childhood experiences as if they had no value in my adult life. I now see the child I was as my honored friend and teacher. I no longer go back and wish my childhood were different. I am forever grateful to the child I was for my life experiences, and I am glad that I cannot change those experiences. Today, my mom has become a valuable teacher, and the child I was has become the loving student who is now my teacher. With this perspective, I have become the honored vehicle to carry the child's lessons forward by loving myself and serving others. To accomplish this deep reality within myself, I simply reframed my thinking.

Changed Thinking Requires Changed Behavior

The idea of perfect order and reframed thinking does not mean non-action. It means total involvement in your life because you realize there is purpose in every situation. For example, imagine a car accident has just occurred and you need to decide your role in the incident. The last thing you want to say is, "Oh, it's in perfect order so I am not to get involved." Instead you would realize that perfect order is based on the fact that you are a part of this scene for a reason. You would then decide what part you are to play.

If your role is to call for help, then that is what you must do. If you determine that calling for help is not your role but rather your skill with CPR is what is needed, then you must quickly use your ability in CPR to do your part.

Once you begin to view life with the question "How can I participate because I am part of the complete picture?" your life becomes one of total involvement and service to others. Your job then becomes one of recognizing your part and enthusiastically playing it well.

Summary

It is the child who internalizes all experiences as beliefs, and it is the adult who acts on these beliefs as truth. With this knowledge, we now realize the importance of consciously connecting the adult with the child. This connection enables the adult and child to become a unit of loving power that will serve the self as well as others.

We are told to search for the love of self, yet for most, finding this love has been illusive. The truth is, we are already loving ourselves at the deepest of levels because we are honoring, with our adult behavior, the belief systems and contracts we have made with the beautiful children we were. We only need to look at our behavior and our lives to recognize that in both our loving and in our withdrawing we are speaking and acting for the child within.

Forgiveness And Understanding = Thank You

The next step to an empowered life is to love others with the same understanding you now have for yourself. This can be accomplished in two ways. The first is to approach forgiveness in a whole new way, and the second is to see life through the eyes of another.

A New Approach To Forgiveness

Forgiveness has become a word with many meanings and much emotional attachment. We are told we must forgive in order to become whole, and yet the standard approach to human forgiveness creates a feeling of something being very off-balance. This occurs because most forgiveness first includes judging someone. After we judge a person we then say, "I forgive you." The person being forgiven many times feels the sting of judgement and inevitably feels inferior to the one who is doing the forgiving.

Please understand that the intent of most people when forgiving another is pure, and is generally based on the idea of compassion and connection. However, to comprehend why forgiveness does not always cause us to feel better is to look at the deeper dynamics of forgiveness.

The event of my mother's death will best illustrate for you (as it did for me) the deeper truths about forgiveness. I share this emotional experience with you only because the story says it all, and hopefully it will assist you in developing a more in-depth understanding of forgiveness.

I was raised Catholic so the concept of forgiveness I came to know was based on the idea that if someone said or did something to you, you would lovingly say, "I forgive you." This process never felt right to me for several reasons. If I were the one forgiving, I first had to judge someone and then say that her behavior was really okay. As a result, to be a good and forgiving person I had to be better than others, so to speak. On the other hand, if I were the one being forgiven, I would only feel better for a brief moment before an unsettled feeling would "creep in" about being judged by the person forgiving me.

When my mother was dying and I was called by my sisters to be with her, I came face-to-face with my preconceived ideas about forgiveness. I began to ponder how I was going to forgive and say goodbye to the person who had caused me so much pain. At that point in time, I had not reframed my mother as the single most impactful teacher in my life. I only saw her as my abuser, and so it seemed to me that the honorable thing to do was to forgive her for what she had done to me.

As I was flying to Seattle, I planned the entire scene of forgiveness. I made a mental list of all that I had perceived she had done to me. The list included: she had not wanted me, she had not accepted me, she had beaten me, she had deprived me of joy, she had taken the money I had earned, she had rented half of my bed to others for extra money, she had always told me how to act, and most of all, I believed she did not love me. With my list in mind, I arrived at the convalescent center and waited for the ideal time to look into her eyes, tell her all of my grievances, and inform her that I would forgive her.

At the appropriate time, I looked into my mothers eyes and, with deep emotion, attempted to recite my list of her wrong doings. But the words would not come out. In that profound moment, I realized a truth about forgiveness that will go with me to my grave. I realized that the things for which I was attempting to forgive my mother were the very things I had never given to her. I was going to forgive her for not accepting me - I had not accepted her. She did not want me - I had not wanted her. I felt she did not love me - yet I had withheld my love from her. Suddenly, I became aware that forgiveness is not a process of judging another, it is rather a process of giving to another. I realized that it is the very thing we want from another that we must be totally willing to give. Otherwise, we are guilty of the same behavior we are forgiving.

With this overwhelming awareness, I fell into my mother's arms and sobbed, "Will you ever forgive me for having judged you?" The moment for me was deeply moving and lovingly connected. However, my mother the profound teacher still had one more lesson to teach. She whispered in my ear as I was crying in her arms, "I always said you should be an actress." Since I did not comprehend, at that moment, that my mother was taking me to the next step in my learning about forgiveness, I was horrified by her words. I ran into the hall and said to my sisters, "How could she be so cruel when I was sharing my very essence with her?" Now I see the beauty and the gift in her words. What my mother taught me in that painful moment was the complete process of forgiveness. She taught me that forgiveness includes giving what you desire without holding back, including the component of not expecting what you give to come back from the person to whom you gave it. Forgiveness is totally an unconditional event. The word forgive, when dissected, contains the answer to true forgiveness. "For" "give" = Forever give.

Forgiveness, as I now experience it, is a beautiful process since it opens the heart to both the self and to others. Prior to the event with my mother, I had only seen my side of the story and had never wanted to hear or see her side. By withholding my love from her, I had created an impossible situation for both of us. I never allowed an opportunity for her to enter my world, consequently, there was no room for me to enter hers. The walls of resentment I'd built by my sense of what should have been, could not be penetrated in all of our years together; yet in just one moment my heart opened and my mother became part of my loving.

My mother died several days later. My experiences with her have since become the core of the work I do in helping others to find the key that opens their hearts to a full and empowered life.

Through The Eyes Of Another

The expression "walk a mile in my shoes" has great significance in the process of understanding and accepting people for who they are, rather than for whom we want them to be. With understanding and awareness of others, we can make loving choices about our behavior as it pertains to each and every individual.

To understand another involves a deep realization that we were all once children forming belief systems about life, and that as adults our behavior is nothing more than acting on those belief systems. To truly know another and understand the behavior of another is to become aware of the experiences he had as a child. Furthermore, it is important to understand that these childhood experiences of others are "locked in" as their beliefs. If we could see these individuals as children, instead of the adults they have become, we would then be able to approach each person in a whole new and loving way. With this awareness, we would also know when it is best to avoid individuals who might cause us discord and stress. To help you understand how this view can create empowerment is to share with you a part of Kate's story.

Kate's life story has many pieces, but for the purpose of this illustration we will only review a few of those pieces. When Kate came to my office to do a *LifeScript,* she had seven spots of possible cancer on her liver. She had already had several cancer surgeries and she was very concerned about her health and well-being.

Kate was filled with anger. She was angry about her cancer, and she was angry about the negative interactions with her family. One of the specific issues about which she was particularly angry was her brother's attitude toward her. She felt he constantly told her she was always taking from him. Kate kept saying, "What have I ever taken from him? He is so angry and I don't understand what it is he thinks I have taken from him."

To understand her brother's anger is to look at the lives of the children Kate and he once were. When Kate was born, her mother already had an 18 month old son by the name of Ken (the now angry brother). Because of circumstances, their mother was unable to care for the children and placed them in an orphanage. They were both in the orphanage for 18 months when a family adopted them. The family who adopted them really wanted only a girl, but discovered that Kate had a brother. Since the adopting parents had just miscarried twins, they decided to accept both children. The couple already had two older boys named Ken and Robert. Because they had a child named Ken, they decided to change their adopted son's name from Ken to Paul. Kate's name was changed to Prudy.

There was much drama between the already existing children and the new children. Ken, now Paul, became resentful and constantly blamed Kate for "taking from him." For years his anger and resentment built and their relationship grew further and further apart.

Kate, now the adult who was facing possible death, had a desire to reconcile the situation with Paul but did not know how. In the process of her *LifeScript,* we looked at Paul's anger by investigating the child he was. What was it that he, the child, felt Kate had taken from him? The answer to this question clarified Paul's adult cry of, "You take from me!" Paul had been involved in a relationship with his mother for the first 18 months of his life. Kate was born and because of her birth they were both placed in an orphanage. As a result, he lost his mother. What did the child believe Kate had taken from him? His mother! If an 18 month old little boy were crying for his mother and wondering why he had a sister and not his mother, we would approach him with a deep sense of love and understanding. This is what Kate now does every time she faces her brother's anger. She sees a beautiful little boy crying for his mother and she approaches him as that little boy. To further add to Ken's losses because of Kate, remember that the adopting family wanted Kate and only took Ken as a tag-along. Because they already had a son named Ken, they changed little Ken's name to Paul.

Because of Kate, he believed he lost his mother, then his name, and ultimately his identity.

Paul has not changed because of Kate's insights, but Kate has. She now sees her brother through the eyes of the children they once were. She now approaches him with deep love. Her anger has subsided and she no longer has spots on her liver. Her cancer tests are coming back clear. Her loving approach to life has changed her attitude, and her body has co-operated with this positive change.

To understand "the child" helps all of us to interact in a more connected way with the adults in our world. To know the adult, you must first ask about and know the child. If this is not possible, then realize that the behavior of the adult indicates what might have happened to the child. If for some reason, even with this understanding, the adult's behavior is such that you cannot be a part of it, use discernment rather than judgement and adjust your interactions accordingly. Always remember, as you make the necessary adjustments, that we were all once children and we all have equal value in the universe. Also remember the experiences of a child last a lifetime. If you can learn to love the child in others, you will add an empathetic dimension to your interactions that will be felt by others. This will automatically occur because you will approach everyone with unconditional love.

With this new frame of reference, it is possible for you to love others in a whole new way, though this is not to say you must spend time with others if they do not exhibit acceptable behavior.

An excellent way to decide where best to place yourself with people or situations is to ask this question, "Is the child I was safe in this situation?" If the answer is yes, then stay. If the answer is no, removing yourself then becomes the behavior of choice.

With the awareness that forgiveness is giving what you desire from another, and that understanding another is walking mentally in their shoes, the next chapter contains specific examples of reframing which will help you further grasp these concepts for use in your own life.

Examples Of LifeScripting Applied

Before demonstrating how and when to look at your past, I first want to share with you several examples of the life changing dynamics of reframing. I believe these examples will help you better understand how to use your life experiences for power rather than for pain. The stories are taken from the files of lives I have *LifeScripted*.

Richard

Richard's story is very intense in terms of the experiences he had as a child. (With the dynamics of reframing he now views his childhood as a powerful place for information not only for himself but for others.) To help you understand Richard's power to reframe, I will emphasize only one part of his life. But first a brief overview of Richard's life story is necessary.

Richard was born to parents who were in great confusion and drama about life and about each other. Richard's dad was Irish and his mom was Native American. Richard's dad was an active alcoholic. At some point, his dad decided that his love for his wife had died and he replaced it with hate. Unlike his father, Richard had a deep attachment to his mother and she became the center of his life. Consequently, he became the favorite of her five children. When Richard was eight, he and his mother were taking their usual Sunday walk, when suddenly she slumped down and could not breath. He ran for help but when he returned she was dead. She died because his dad had poisoned her with rat poisoning. Richard's dad led him to believe his mom had committed suicide. For years, he felt she had left him when she had promised she would always be there for him. Richard's deep sense of loss was complicated by trauma within the family, which resulted in Richard being placed in an orphanage. Numerous negative situations occurred in the orphanage, all of which had a lasting effect upon Richard.

Richard's life story is a book unto itself, but for the purpose of understanding reframing I will isolate Richard's story to his experience with policemen. As Richard grew into manhood he became an active alcoholic. When Richard got drunk he would often perpetrate crime. He would wait for the police to arrive at the scene of the crime, and he would then become violent with them. The end usually resulted in Richard's arrest and some type of sentence being served. No one ever got to the core of what was happening within Richard; they simply responded to his behavior and arrested him. Time after time he was released from jail and told that if he returned, the next punishment would be more severe. These threats did not stop Richard because driving him was the love he had for the child he once was.

When Richard came to me for *LifeScripting*, I asked him a question that enabled both of us to begin understanding his behavior. The question was, "What was your experience with policemen when you were a child?" Why this question? Because I know that behavior is not random, and that the Richards of the world do not just get up one day and act out. Therefore, it becomes necessary to find the source of the belief of the child. When you find this, you find the script for adult behavior.

Richard told the story of the night he and his mother were walking through the park and his mother became alarmed by something. She told Richard to hide behind the bushes and wait until she came to get him. As Richard waited and watched, a policeman entered the park and raped his mother. The reason for Richard's adult behavior is now obvious. Richard would drink, he would miss his mother who had died, he would remember their loving connection and he would set up a scene to appease her rape.

Another part of Richard's story needs to be reviewed to fully understand how he reframed this event to empower his life, and now the lives of others.

When Richard was very small, he would go with his mother to bars where she performed as a steel guitar player. Sometimes, to earn extra money, his mother would go to hotel rooms with men she had met at the bar. She would take Richard with her, telling him everything was okay and that he should just play in the corner. At these times with his mother, he felt no fear or abuse. For this small boy it was just the way life was; after all, Mom said it was "okay." He learned from these hotel room experiences that "permission" is a necessary ingredient for a man to be with a woman. This experience further reinforced the ugliness of the rape of his mother where permission was not granted and fear was present.

Richard's reframe has many parts. First he realized that all experiences contain positive power once he stopped trying to change them or push them away. He then asked himself what insight or information he possessed as a result of the child's experience. Richard began to see how he could use this information in a positive way in his adult life. He accomplished this by understanding that to love his life was to love the child and honor the child's experiences. (He was certainly aware that his past method of behavior and thinking had caused severe problems in his life and the lives of others.) Through *LifeScripting*, he discovered ways to reframe those experiences in such a manner as to love himself and serve others.

Richard is now an active member of AA and he also works in prisons. He assists both men and women in the area of respect for women, speaking for women in such a way that his message is more acceptable than women speaking for themselves. One of the many messages he delivers to men is to respect women by always getting permission before engaging in any sexual behavior (who knows better than the child who witnessed permission verses rape). He works well with rapists as well as with those who have been raped. He talks to people about understanding the child/adult connection and how it determines and empowers behavior.

Richard has become a powerful example of a reframed life. He believes everything that has happened to him has been a source of information that enhances his adult life and enables him to touch and affect the lives of others. Today Richard lives an addiction-free life of peace, joy, and purpose.

Sue

Sue's childhood, like Richard's, contains many intense life situations. For the example of reframing, we will look only at the beatings she received from her father. Sue's father used to stand before her and look at his watch as he said, "You have one minute to answer the question!" The question could be about anything. If Sue did not give him the response he wanted in the allotted minute, she would be severely beaten. These beatings led to court hearings and foster placement.

Reframed: As an adult, Sue is a person who handles confusion and intense demands very well. She is able to very quickly make the complicated seem very clear. She never submits a project at school or work unless it is concise, clear, and to the point. One of her many jobs involves training the staff of an agency. Sue is clear and precise in her presentations, and creates materials that are easily understood. Because of the child's experience, Sue is a valued member of any team.

Jim

Jim's story, like Sue's, also involves beatings, but Jim's beatings created a very different end result for his adult life. In Jim's early childhood, his father asked him to tell the truth about an event in which Jim was involved. Jim told his father the truth, but his father believed he was lying and beat him saying, "Tell me the truth." Jim again told the truth and his father again beat him. The beatings continued for five hours. Jim knew if he lied, his father would stop beating him but he never veered from the truth.

Reframed: Jim is a man filled with integrity. He can, and does, take immense pressure from the world of business where he is constantly being asked to veer from his values. He believes if the child could endure beatings for five hours to teach him not to lie, then he will be the man who honors the child's learning.

Jackie

Jackie is a powerful example of how early our programming is set in place for our adult behavior. When Jackie was *LifeScripted* I asked the usual question, "What do you know about your birth?" She said she knew nothing except what her mother had told her when she was thirteen. According to her mother, her dad did not want another child and decided a home abortion was the best solution to the unwanted pregnancy. Jackie's father convinced her mother to get into a bathtub filled with hot water so he could use a hanger to abort the baby. When Jackie's mother got into the tub, her father started to use the hanger, but her mom screamed, "I won't let you kill the baby!" She got out of the tub and refused to complete the process.

Knowing that the adult will either pull the childhood experience toward her or push the experience away, I asked, "Do you take excessive numbers of baths or do you avoid the bath tub?" She said, "I would rather die than take a bath. In fact, I have always thought I was crazy because I go insane around the idea of a bath." She continued by telling the story of the time her husband rented an apartment unequipped with a shower. Jackie was furious that he didn't consider her desire to never take a bath. She said they stood at the edge of the apartment tub and her husband demanded she get into the water. With total terror and a feeling of death, Jackie screamed, "I'll divorce you before I get into the tub!"

The connection of this apartment bathtub scene and the bathtub scene between her mother and father is phenomenal. Jackie was again faced with a man (just like her dad) who was demanding that she get into a bathtub - the exact scene she lived while in her mother's womb. Her response was to save the unborn child she was.

It is mind expanding to realize that Jackie was in the womb less than three months when she formed her perception of danger about bathtubs. It has become evident to me, as I work with clients and groups, that the age of an individual at the time of an emotional event is not relevant to the storage of that event. Intense events store as beliefs and those beliefs dictate adult behavior.

Reframed: Is Jackie going to be a bathtub sales person? No. The reframe for Jackie is more in the area of awareness. She now knows how connected every experience (even in the womb) is to adult behavior. Today, Jackie is a therapist who uses the story of her "in-womb" experience, and resulting experiences, to assist others in going as deeply as necessary to find the origin of their programming. As a result, this little embryo's experience has assisted many in understanding the depth and the complexity of the human process.

Virginia

I would like to share a loving reframe from my life experience. When I was a little girl, my father was away much of the time. I loved my dad and looked forward to the times when he was home. On occasion, my father would bring his friends home late at night, and as the proud father, he would awaken us girls to "show us off." During these late night events, he asked us to talk about anything we wanted to talk about. My two sisters would get quickly bored and go back to bed, but I would stay up as long as possible talking to Dad's friends as if I were an adult and they were my peers.

The reframe for this event is so very obvious to me when I look at my adult life. I am a public speaker. I have no fear of speaking before large crowds of total strangers about any subject. I can accomplish this because the child taught me that Dad's friends were my friends and I could talk to them about anything. To prepare for a speaking engagement, I review what I am going to say late the night before I am scheduled to speak. This behavior correlates to being awakened by my dad late at night. I can also be called to speak on a moment's notice because as a child I never knew when I would be invited to talk with my dad and his friends. It is clear that the dynamics of my public speaking ability are all contained in my childhood interactions with my father and his friends.

Bev

When Bev was a little girl, one of her favorite experiences was to get dressed up and go with her prominent psychiatrist uncle when he made rounds at the mental hospital. While he was with his patients, Bev would play and visit with the other mental patients. She felt totally comfortable in this environment and looked forward to her visits.

Reframed: As an adult, Bev's job is supervisor and therapist at a mental health facility. Like the little girl of the past, she dresses in the most expensive clothes while she works with, and places, patients in the ward. Bev loves her job. Who trained Bev for this job?

Debbie

Debbie was born with a serious heart condition. At the time of her birth, the condition was more severe than medical doctors had the capacity to correct. But they knew if Debbie could be kept alive for several years, technology would catch up to her needs. Debbie was kept still and protected, and at age seven her surgery was scheduled. The night before surgery, the minister of her church came and talked to her about the possibility of dying. He said the surgery was very serious and only if it was "God's will" would she survive. They prayed together and Debbie released herself into God's hands. On the day of surgery, Debbie was totally prepared for whatever God had planned for her. After a successful surgery, Debbie faced days of being in an oxygen tent. When her family visited, they were instructed not to touch Debbie because they would disturb the oxygen tent that supported her life. Debbie laid in her tent of isolation and longed to be held and kissed.

Reframed: Debbie is now a healthy woman on a mission to help cardiac patients. She works for a team of cardiac specialists and does an excellent job with their patients. Why? Because she has a deep understanding of what others are truly experiencing when they face heart challenges. She is especially gifted at interfacing with the families of cardiac patients when surgery turns to stress. She sits with the families, as the minister sat with her, and says, "This is in God's hands. Let's pray together." Debbie reports that many times she has seen impossible situations turn around as a result of prayer. Debbie has also designed seminars to assist patients and their families in understanding the importance of touch and connection in the emotional and physical recovery of a patient. She is driven to speak in this area because after her surgery no one was allowed to touch her. For the little girl she was, Debbie now reaches out to others, assisting them in giving the touch she did not receive.

Examples of reframing are limitless; as limitless as all of the possible life experiences multiplied by the number of people who have ever lived. Your personal power comes from your ability to reframe your own experiences. Section II will provide you with 96 foundational questions to assist you in this process.

When To Look At Your Past

With the knowledge that your past is the key to your adult behavior, it becomes crucial to know how and when to access your past experiences. There is a time to look at your past, and a time to leave your past alone.

When Not To Look

A simple way to know when not to look to your past is if your now moment is working. The positive flow of life is a clear message that you are in the right place, doing the right thing, with no need to adjust. You are designed to be happy, and when happiness is present you need to recognize it, be grateful, and enjoy the process. At these times, leave the past alone and enjoy your life.

To help you further understand the importance of when not to look at the past, I will share the story of my friend Diane. Diane was one of the most internally joyful people I have ever met. We spent hours together planning ways to be of service to mankind, constantly laughing and enjoying the process of life. One weekend Diane decided to attend a seminar specifically designed to help individuals empower their lives by looking at past events. She returned from this seminar a totally different person. She began looking at every event for the emotion it created for her, and how the event applied to who had done what to her in her past.

At the weekend seminar, Diane was taught a technique which enabled her to vent and release her feelings. With this technique she spent countless hours releasing, screaming, and crying. I watched my friend develop a heavy heart and age ten years before my eyes. Diane was no longer easy to be with because she made everything a suspicious event that was tied to her past. As a result, we drifted apart, though I often remember the joy that was once a major part of my friend's life.

Diane taught me several valuable lessons I now share with others. The most intense lesson is to not tie every now moment to a past event. To do this causes a loss of joy in the present. Diane also taught me, in a very visual way, that a painful review of the past blocks life rather than enhances it.

Unfortunately, some of the modern therapeutic approaches incorporate making every now moment a suspicious past event. With these approaches, we are invited to look at the past for who did what to us, and once we have determined this, we are to decide what we must do about what they have done. Furthermore, we are often asked to relive past experiences, to feel the feelings, so we can theoretically release the problem. We now know that looking at the past for its negative consequences closes the heart and creates unwanted stressors in the now moment. In Chapter 20, we will look further at some of these therapeutic techniques and determine why they do not work.

When To Look At The Past

It is always appropriate to look at the past when the now moment creates an emotional over/under-reaction. These emotional reactions can become positive triggers that assists you in making behavioral choices in your present moment. (The next chapter will help you determine how to look at your past.) For now, it is only important to grasp the concept of a now moment "trigger" being directly related to a past event.

What is happening when the now moment creates an emotional over/under-reaction, is that a button has been pushed on the computer called your brain. When that button is pushed, it is reminding you that something similar happened to you in the past, and you react as if the present is the past. Because we are not usually aware of this process, we tend to think that something is wrong with us because we are reacting so intensely to the present situation.

In reality, the trigger is offering you a gift - the gift of information which will help you decide what to do in the now. Your triggers are your keys to accessing your past, and you need the past to understand the present.

The following diagram will give you an overview of this process:

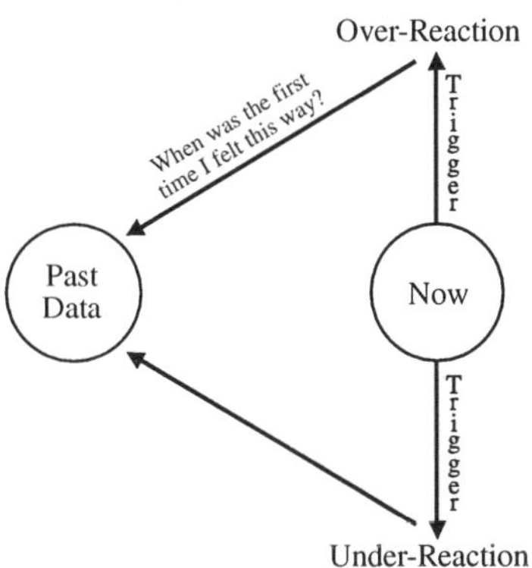

Over-Reaction

An over-reaction is a outward response that is more than the now situation calls for. Two examples are: 1) A man enters the room and says hello to you, and you snap back at him in a loud voice demanding, "What did you mean by that?" The man is taken aback and wonders what happened. You do not consciously realize that this person sounds like your uncle who used to spank you when you were a child. 2) The person you love begins to cry; you feel yourself tensing inside and you scream at her for not staying in control. All she wants is to be held. However, you trigger because when you cried as a child, your parents yelled at you for not controlling yourself when all you wanted was to be comforted.

An over-reaction is always a reaction that seems more than necessary for the situation. You will be more of an over-reactor if, as a child, you expressed yourself outwardly most of the time.

Under-Reaction

An under-reaction is a response that appears less than necessary for the situation. Inside, the person reacting is usually intense, but their outward behavior exhibits no visible reaction. For example, someone is slapping you and you stand calmly with no reaction at all. However, what is happening inside is intense anxiety and anger. Just like the over-reaction, when you under-react, the past is playing a major role in your response. In this example, you under-react because as a child you were beaten and told never to cry or the beatings would get worse. Now, as an adult, when you get slapped you simply stand and calmly take it.

You will be more of an under-reactor if as a child you held your emotions in most of the time. You will also be an under-reactor if you had a tendency to mentally leave the scene when something stressful was occurring around you.

Balanced Reaction

Not every event will produce an over/under-reaction. If an event calls for a specific emotional response, feel the emotion, express it, and continue on with life. However, if the emotion you are feeling is more or less than the event implies, then in all likelihood your past has surfaced in the form of a "now moment trigger." A balanced reaction to a life event is to respond appropriately to the now moment.

The gifts of over/under-reactions become clear when you learn and apply the *LifeScripting* process. It is important, when you look to the past, to keep foremost in your mind that looking with love is the key. In Chapter 15 you will learn how to look at your past, and in Chapter 16 you will learn what to do with what you find. For now, it is important to remember that the past can trigger your now moment responses. These triggers can occur at any given moment and need to be acknowledged, understood, and used for greater personal awareness.

How To Look At Your Past

With the knowledge of when to look at your past, the next step is learning how to access the past experiences which have created your belief systems. Once this information is on the screen of your mind, you will be able to make a conscious choice regarding your present behavior. Getting the past onto the screen of the brain is a very simple process. When you are having an over-reaction or an under-reaction to the now moment, simply pause and ask yourself the question, "When was the first time I felt this way?" When this question is asked, a distinct memory from the floppy disc of the child will emerge. This memory will provide all of the information you need to make a decision in the now moment. Do not judge the memory as not being significant, or think that the memory of a child has no relevance to your adult life. Remember, belief systems that were developed by the time you were six years old rule your adult behavior. Childhood memory is, therefore, the cause for all over/under-reactions, and these memories contain the information necessary for you to make a conscious behavioral choice in the present.

When you desire to access your memory, it is crucial to use the words, "When was the first time I felt this way?" This question probes feelings because as a child your beliefs were formed based on your feelings about love and belonging. Consequently, it is imperative to access the computer of your mind with the key words "feeling" and "first." The word "feeling" because the child felt, and the word "first" because your mind will then retrieve an event as close to the original belief system formation as possible.

It is important to understand that emotions are always involved in the process of over/under-reactions because the child, as well as the adult, is an emotional being. It is also important to adequately feel the emotion before asking, "When was the first time I felt this way?" The feeling must first be felt and dealt with, otherwise the brain will not be cleared to access the proper past data. While feelings are being felt the brain cannot simultaneously search for past memories because it is being over-loaded with the impact of the emotion. The brain is like a computer; it can handle many processes but never display more than one at a time. Therefore, each command must be handled before the next command can be processed.

Emotions are the key to unlocking the past and are gifts to all human beings. (Emotions will be explored in Chapter 19.) Unfortunately, most people have learned to judge emotions as good or bad, when in truth they are the balancing beams of the human system. In *LifeScripting*, emotions contain the accessing code to the beliefs of the past. With this viewpoint, emotions can be seen as the road map to understanding the real self.

To visually understand the concept of this chapter, refer to the diagram on the next page.

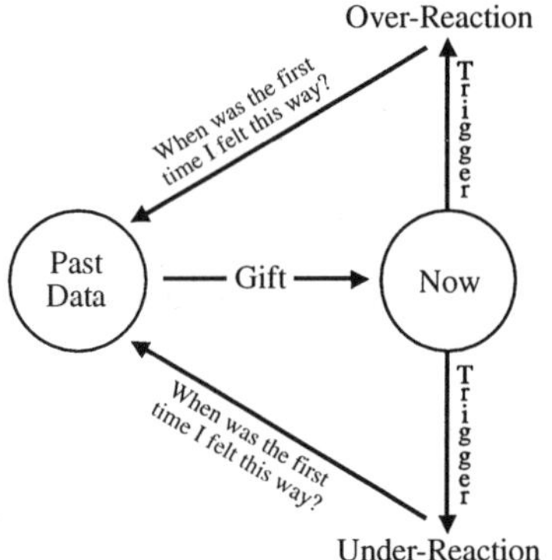

It has been said that all the answers for human beings are found within. Most agree, but this statement has created much confusion since people generally have no idea how to find the answers. The question, "When was the first time I felt this way?" is the key to unraveling this dilemma. Once you comprehend how to access the past, the next step will involve knowing what to do with what you find. That process is presented in the next chapter.

16

What To Do With What You Find

Once you understand how to access your past it becomes important to know what to do with surfaced memories. Specific steps to empower your life with your memory will be presented in this chapter. However, there are several guidelines that first need to be considered before approaching your past. They are:

1) When a memory appears on the screen of your mind do not become engulfed by the memory. Instead, watch the scene like you would watch a movie. This enables you to objectively understand the past experience in terms of what happened to form your beliefs. A helpful method to accomplish this is to approach all memory as you would approach the events of a child who has come to you with an issue. While helping the child, you would not panic or act as if you did not understand. Instead, you would calmly listen to the child and help the child understand what is happening in the situation. You would then provide the child with insights and options as to his behavioral choices. Finally, you would help the child determine what learning has occurred that can assist him with future decisions.

If you fall into your story and become engulfed by it, rather than viewing your past like a movie, you will create and experience the re-living of the scene. When that occurs, you will lock onto the past feelings and miss any valuable lessons the event is capable of teaching you. However, when you watch your past like a movie, you can objectively observe your part in the movie as well as the parts of others.

2) Be very careful not to judge the memory as good or bad. If you judge it as bad, the psychological message you give yourself is that you received a "bad life" and that you are not loved at the highest levels. This approach negates your feelings of personal worth and minimizes any chance for positive growth and development.

I am very aware that many times the events experienced by children are very intense, but to look back in a negative way only intensifies the situation for the adult. Remember, the past is over. But if the past is reframed, it provides you with major data and assistance for your adult life. It has been my experience, as well as the experience and observation of others, that the more challenges within a life the more the individual has to contribute to others in a positive way. It is psychologically healthy to approach your life looking for what you have learned, and how you can best share the value of your experiences with others.

It is important to remember not to fall into the story of another. This does not mean you cannot have empathy for another. Empathy is best defined as the ability to determine how another might feel based upon her view of life. True empathy does not include the message that life is wrong for anyone. Empathic people help others understand that all of life's experiences have value, and when properly reframed can become positive experiences for them as well as others.

3) When a memory appears, do not judge it as too big or too small. Remember, the memory is coming from a child's perception. To a child, a major event could be as small as the wheel falling off of a wagon. The event, no matter what the degree of intensity, holds the information needed in the now moment. All childhood memory should be viewed through the eyes and feelings of the child.

4) The more intense the feeling during an over/under-reaction the more intense will be the dynamics of the past memory and, therefore, the more powerful the message for your now learning.

5) Past memories provide you with valuable information regarding what to do, as well as providing you, at times, with information regarding what not to do. For example, my mother's bitterness used to frighten me because I felt I might become like her. With the power of reframing I have asked myself, "What did I learn from a mother who was often bitter?" The answer is very simple, I learned what bitterness can create, and as a result I determined never to become bitter.

6) When remembering your childhood, you may find that you only have a sense of the child and not an actual picture of an event. Do not judge how your memories appear for you. There is no right or wrong way for memory to appear. Memory may come to you in pictures, or it may come to you in feelings from your heart. Be with your past scenes in whatever ways they are available to you.

7) When you remember a past event, you are looking for information to help you decide a course of action in the now. It is not necessarily a message to change, but rather a message to choose.

8) Looking to the past is not about getting total awareness about your whole life all at once, but rather to understand a small piece of your life in the now.

9) Without memory, who or what would you be? Memory is a beautiful gift that allows you to know and understand who you are and what you believe. Memory enables you to remain in contact with yourself and your beliefs, and provides you with the opportunity to love. The purpose of memory is not to cause you pain, but rather to empower your life with the information the memory provides. However, you have the freedom to choose how you want to define and handle your memory.

10) If you feel you have no memory, be assured you do. There are many reasons for lack of a specific memory, which can include: a) It may not be the right time for you to remember because the memory does not serve you at the moment. b) Maybe there is little to remember about your childhood because one day was very similar to the next. c) Perhaps there was trauma and the child you were did what so many children do and mentally left the scene. When this disassociative behavior occurs, the memory tends to be vague or totally unavailable. Regardless of the reason for non-memory, do not be concerned. You will remember what is needed when it is the right time to remember.

What To Do With A Past Memory

When you have an over/under-reaction to an event and you ask the question, "When was the first time I felt this way?" a specific memory will be accessible to you. With the previous information in mind, it is now time to determine what to actually do with a memory once it is available to you.

Accessed memory will include characters and dynamics that match your present experience, or otherwise you would not currently be remembering that specific scene from your past. The first objective is to determine what is similar about the past and the present. Initially, you may choose to list on a piece of paper the characters and their behaviors from the past. At least do this exercise in your mind. Then ask yourself, "What was the role of each person, including myself? What did I learn from each of these individual teachers?" Other questions to ask include: "What is it about this memory that I need to know for my now moment decision? How does this memory serve me? How does it help me serve others? What did the child teach me?" Once you complete this process, list the characters in your present situation and see how they match the people from your past. Next ask yourself, "What am I learning from the people in my present experience?" With all this compiled information, you will have a clear understanding of what decision to make regarding your present situation.

The following two examples will assist you in further understanding this process:

1) Imagine you are at a meeting and a man offers you a job that includes a great salary, house, car, travel and expense account. You feel extremely intense inside about his offer, and you realize that you are having an over-reaction from your past. At this point, it is not appropriate to say to this man, "Excuse me, I am having an over-reaction to your offer and I know this means my childhood contains the answer as to whether I should sign your contract. Would you please give me a moment to explore my past?" However, what you can do is ask for some time before you make your decision. When you are alone ask yourself the question, "When was the first time I felt this

way?" Imagine now that a memory of your Uncle Tom appears in your mind. In this scene, your Uncle Tom promised to take you to Disneyland and provide you with everything you wanted to have while on the trip. With this accessed memory you now need to ask yourself several questions before deciding if you should sign the contract. These questions include: "What does this memory have to do with my present offer? How do the characters of my past and present match? Why is the present offer so much like the offer of my Uncle Tom about Disneyland?"

Whether or not you should sign the contract is dependent on whether Uncle Tom actually took you to Disneyland. If he did, then sign the contract because your belief that men keep their promises will win for you. If he didn't take you to Disneyland, then it is very risky to sign the contract because your belief will rule any interaction you have with men like Uncle Tom.

The tendency for most people would be to sign the contract and repeat the pattern from childhood that men are not there for them. This choice is made out of love for the child with the hope of changing the outcome. The truth, however, remains that if you repeat the same behavior, you will get the same results.

The reframe in this example is: If Uncle Tom did not follow through, then the child learned that interactions with men whose behavior is like Uncle Tom's will create negative consequences. Therefore, the adult needs to say "no" to the same type of situations. This decision-making process is not limiting but rather empowering. It enables you to have a much less stressful life because you will avoid situations that will create negatives. Conversely, you will choose only situations that work best for you.

It would also be valuable at this point in the reflection process regarding Uncle Tom, for you to look to your past to see if you have ever before repeated this situation. Determine what the end results were for you when you fell into the repetitive behavior, and apply that learning to the now situation.

I know you may be processing the example of Uncle Tom and saying, "I would sign the contract regardless of the past and break the negative pattern." I know this is a natural tendency because many times in the past I, as well as my clients, have attempted to break patterns with the hope of reversing past beliefs, thus obtaining immediate gratification. However, my experience has affirmed that even with total awareness and a desire to change the outcome, people time and again experience the repeated pattern and its predictable results. I now look at all the data from the past as a guidance tool for daily life. The past informs individuals of what does and does not work. Both have great value. When people choose not to repeat negative patterns, they have less aggravation, greater success, and more time to experience and enjoy what works best for them.

Even with the past information about Uncle Tom, if you choose to sign the contract, I suggest you become extra vigilant in monitoring the contract. I also suggest you become aware of the additional stress you will feel on a daily basis while you subconsciously wait for the situation not to work out!

2) The following is another example of how to look to the past for what to expect in the present. Imagine that you are driving your car and a tire goes flat. You experience an over-reaction of total panic about being alone on the street, even though it is daylight and you are in a safe neighborhood. You

realize you are having an over-reaction and ask yourself, "When was the first time I felt this way?" You immediately remember the time when you were a child and the wheel came off your wagon. You felt alone and afraid because you thought no one would come to help and you would get into trouble. You then remember your father found you, calmly helped you get the wagon home, and fixed it for you. What can you expect in this now moment scene? Because your dad helped, you can be assured that soon someone will arrive to help you fix the tire.

What if the memory of the wagon wheel had a different ending? What if you remembered that you were left alone, no one came to help, and you had to figure out how to get the wagon home without a wheel? You then recall the internal struggle of the child and remember that the child accomplished the task. What can you now expect to happen in the present situation? You will be confronted with solving the tire dilemma by and for yourself, but you will be able to accomplish the task.

I know this example will cause you to ponder and to ask the question, "How is it possible to have my past this deeply connected to my present?" I have asked this very question hundreds of times. I can only tell you that it has been my experience as a therapist, that every time I have looked to someone's past I have found how it precisely matches his present reality. Sometimes the match is very obvious and takes only a few seconds to discover, other times it takes some searching. But the match is always there and it is, absolutely worth the search.

Summary

When you access your past and it becomes available to you for information, there are three choices to help guide your present behavior:

1) You can repeat the dynamics of the past and experience the same results. If the results are something you desire to experience then this repeated behavior may be your first choice.

2) You can choose the opposite of past behavior and experience different results.

3) You can reframe the past situation for what it has taught you. When you reframe, choose the parts you want to keep and the parts you desire to change.

Using this portion of *LifeScripting* in your daily life creates total empowerment. If the child was the student and you are the expression for what the child learned, then go back and review the lessons of the child to create a more directed and meaningful adult life. The mind of the adult knows when to look at the past, and the heart of the child knows how to look. When you learn when and how to look at the past, and follow the guidelines for what to do with what you find, you will experience unlimited freedom because you will truly know "why you do what you do!" The result for you will be a life that flows because you are in control of your behavioral options. With this understanding of *LifeScripting,* you will begin to see purpose in every memory, and will come to love yourself in ways you have never before experienced.

Finding The Time Frames Of Your Patterns

With the knowledge of when to look at your past, how to look, and what to do with what you find, you can now add another dimension to your awareness. This dimension is the ability to discover the time frames of your major patterns.

It appears that many times we not only repeat an event, we repeat it within a specified time frame. Every person with whom I have worked, either individually or in a seminar, has found specific time frames to her life patterns. For example, Nancy came to me when she was about to marry for the third time. She said she was very concerned that her upcoming marriage wouldn't work since her two previous marriages had ended abruptly. Nancy had believed her past marriages were good, and yet both men left suddenly with no apparent explanation. They both left six years into the marriage. I asked her what happened in her life when she was six years old that pertained to her father. I asked this question because "Dad" represents to Nancy her beliefs about men, and those beliefs will determine what will happen to her in male relationships.

She said as a child she was very close to her father and that when she was six years old he suddenly died. The belief Nancy formed about men at the time of her father's death was, "men love me deeply but leave me in six years." Once she realized what was causing what in her life, she was able to work with her beliefs to make choices and take control of her life. Rather than letting life just happen, Nancy will now pay close attention to the sixth year of her relationship, and she can opt to negotiate and re-commit with her husband to complete another six years. She now knows that six years is a time for evaluation, choice and possible recommitment.

Another example of a specific time frame involves a man named Daniel who attempted suicide every five years. Daniel would maintain mental stability for five years, then sink into deep depression and talk about suicide. Knowing that Daniel's adult experience involves his beliefs from childhood, the question to ask is, "What happened to you when you were five?" - five, because that is the cycle of his adult suicidal experience. At five, Daniel was out playing in the snow without his scarf and hat. His mom asked his dad to take Daniel's hat and scarf to him. Daniel's dad walked out of the house, slipped on the icy steps, hit his head and died. The internal message for Daniel became, "I am responsible for my father's death and I don't deserve to live." Add to the loss of his dad, the fact that Daniel's father represented for him "What is a man?" and "Who am I?" and you can easily determine why Daniel believed he must die every five years. With recognition and understanding, this five-year cycle can become a time for growth rather than a time of confusion and destruction. It can be a time for Daniel to embrace the child and thank the teacher called Dad for his ability to teach selfless love. This experience can also be reframed as a gift to assist Daniel in helping children with the loss of a parent, especially in the area of handling any guilt that may occur.

To pinpoint time frames associated with events in your life, simply draw a straight line on a piece of paper. Have one end represent your conception and the opposite end represent today's date. On this line, place significant events that have occurred both directly to you and around you. Be as specific as possible. Also note the date and your age at the time of each event. Then ask the following questions, "What does each situation represent to me? How did I feel because of the event? What belief did I form because of this experience?"

These beliefs and feelings will trigger you when the time-lined event occurs again in your daily life. For example, if on your time line you noted that your parents divorced when you were eight years old, and if that event was difficult for you, then you will experience difficult endings in cycles of eight - every eight years, eight months, eight weeks, etc., or some combination of eight.

Another exercise to help recognize time frames is to time line the experiences you have had as an adult, then look back to the child's experiences for information about why you are repeating a pattern. For example, let's say as an adult you change jobs every year and a half. You would ask, "What happened to me at age one and a half? Was there a move, a loss, or a major change in my life?"

Time-framing your patterns will help you increase your self-awareness and lead to greater understanding about your life and purpose. Once you see your patterns emerge, you can then monitor what is causing what in your life. As a result, you will be more consciously aware when choosing your behavioral responses.

Relationships

With the ability to utilize your past for specific information about your patterns and time frames, an additional benefit is to apply these dynamics to interpersonal relationships.

Relationships seem to be a struggle for most individuals. This is certainly understandable once you realize that each and every individual has a totally unique belief system controlling his personal behavior. The purpose of this chapter is to assist you in looking at your relationships through the eyes of the *LifeScripting* principles. With the application of these dynamics in the context of relationships, a more positive and meaningful experience with others will occur. The 96 questions in Section II will further assist you in understanding the type of relationships you tend to form, and why you form them. You will also discover what type of relationships will work best for you, particularly in light of assisting you in becoming the person you desire to become.

LifeScripting Applied To Relationships

All relationships include two people. This obvious fact can be the source of great joy or the source of great stress.

To reduce the possibility of negatives in a relationship is to understand the *LifeScripting* process as it applies to both individuals.

To comprehend the variables of any relationship (spouse, friend, family, child, co-worker, etc.) is to look at the interaction process of two people who have different pasts and, therefore, different belief systems. Because of these individual beliefs, each person comes to a relationship with a different point of view, and yet each will erroneously believe what is happening in the now moment is based only on the present situation. They do not realize that their past belief systems, created by age six, will have a direct influence on their present lives together.

Most of their interactions, if kept in the now, will flow smoothly. However, there will inevitably be events that create triggers. When this happens, the person who is experiencing the trigger is reacting to the past and not to the present. This reaction usually leads to feelings of concern about the trigger and to the false belief that something is wrong with the relationship. The most common reaction is to then seek a way to fix the situation in the present. This approach misses the essential truth, that the now moment over-reaction is a gift with the purpose of helping the individual learn from the past. This information can lead to a deeper discovery of the self. It can also become a source of conversation that enhances communication and leads to a loving connection for the couple.

Positive results occur in all relationships when both parties are aware that their individual belief systems are the underlying cause of all over/under-reactions. The interaction between them is only the trigger and not the problem. With this understanding, they will no longer personalize, but rather welcome all over/under-reactions as gifts to better know themselves. The result can be sharing this knowledge with each other to enhance the relationship. Triggers will then be looked upon as the place of saying, "Thank-you for helping me discover myself while I'm loving you."

The story of Brian and Rachael will help you further understand the interactions of two people in a relationship. Imagine that Brian and Rachael have just fallen in love and are deciding if they should commit their lives to each other. Everything is wonderful during the initial stage of their relationship. What they do not realize is that their choice of partners is totally based upon the beliefs of the children they once were. Their attraction to each other is determined by how they viewed their mother and father, and how they interacted with each parent prior to age six.

Brian and Rachael, not knowing this, believe that magic happened as they said "hello" for the first time at the gas station. They started dating and now they are in love. No matter how "by chance" the meeting appears, the emotional connection happened because something about the other fits into each of their belief systems. It may be a feeling, a look, or a behavior that locks them into the recognition, but both have found a piece of their childhood belief in the other.

As their relationship progresses, moments of stress begin to occur. These normal life issues are handled with clear and loving communication. All seems well because the issues are about the present. Since there have been no over-reactions for Brian or Rachael, life seems not only good but almost effortless.

However, one day there is an over-reaction on the part of Rachael. Brian has not arrived home on time and she is convinced he has left her and that he no longer loves her. Her belief is triggered from a past childhood experience that involved Rachael's dad being late for her birthday party. As a child she felt abandoned by her father. She does not realize that her present over-reaction is about that event, and she reacts with hysteria. When Brian finally arrives home, he explains that he was delayed by a car accident.

If Rachael had the ability to go into her past and remember the scene that caused her trigger, she would have known that everything would turn out okay. She would realize this because in her childhood her dad did eventually come home. He was late because he was delayed at the office due to an unplanned business meeting. She would further recognize that the times she appears to be alone in life are the times she will have fear, but male support will eventually be there for her. She also needs to be aware that her relationship with men will sometimes include not having her needs met at the exact time she desires. It is at these times Rachael needs to let go of her panic and remember that all will work out well.

A graph of Rachael's interaction with Brian will be helpful for your visual understanding of what occurred for Rachael.

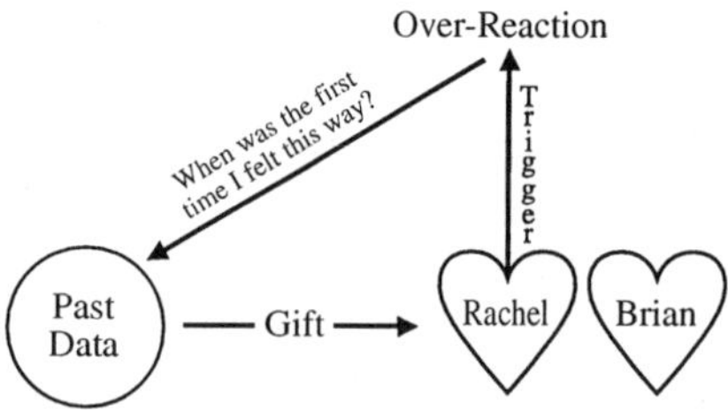

Since all relationships involve the reactions of two people it is also necessary to observe Brian's reaction to this situation. Brian internally feels Rachael's emotional trigger, and because of his childhood script about women, he also has an emotional trigger. His reaction is intense but appears as an under-reaction because he goes to the bedroom and withdraws to think about his feelings of being misunderstood and trapped. He does not know to look to his past for information about the situation. If he were to ask, "When was the first time I felt this way?" he would have remembered a six year old boy who came home late from a friend's house. The little boy had a reasonable explanation as to why he was late but his mother, in her concern, over-reacted with hysteria. Brian felt misunderstood by his mother and trapped by the situation. The little boy, like the man, went to his bedroom to re-group. What Brian needs to remember is that several minutes later Mom came into his room and talked to him, telling him she became hysterical because she feared something bad had happened. His mother further explained that she loved him so much she wouldn't know what to do without him. If Brian could remember this scene from the past he would know the outcome in the now. He would realize what the child learned for him is that women deeply care for him and will always be there no matter what the appearance of their exterior emotions. He would also know that hysteria is always about a woman's love for him and he would be able to accept the behavior for what it means.

The following graph will again help you visually understand the dynamics between Rachael and Brian.

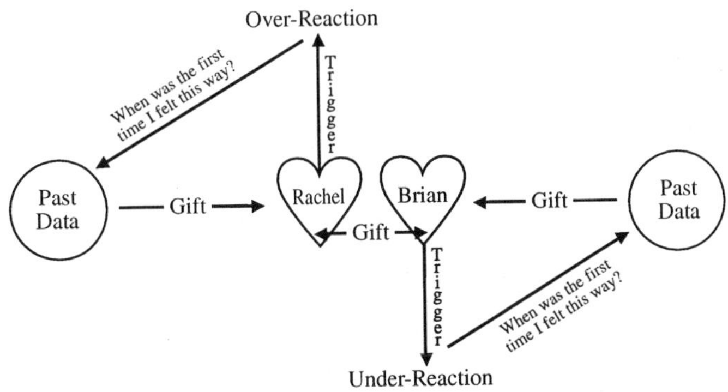

The example of Brian and Rachael is very simple in both its content and its application. It was kept simple so you would be able to not only visualize the dynamics, but realize the ease with which *LifeScripting* can be applied. You will now be able to take any situation in your life and apply the principles from this example to find out what is causing what in your relationships. You can then determine your future choices.

If Brian and Rachael were to continue on the path of misunderstanding, and were never guided to look at the past for valuable insights and information, they would follow the pattern of most and begin to look at their relationship for what was wrong rather than for what was right. Once this negative process starts, couples begin to feel their sense of love and belonging slip away. However, when the dynamics of relationships are viewed from the perspective of *LifeScripting*, events within a relationship become beautiful vehicles to know the self, and can therefore add to the love and strength of the relationship.

A Time To End A Relationship

Sometimes there is a need to end a relationship, and it is helpful to understand when that time has arrived. It is not time to end a relationship if the now moment triggers can be utilized to add love and depth to your relationship. However, if there are triggers within your relationship that never get resolved, it may be time to create change in your life. The unresolved triggers may well be an invitation to recognize that the relationship is not a positive life choice for you.

Remember, triggers provide information from past events and through the memory of the past you will have sufficient data for decisions in the now. To help you apply this concept to an understanding of when you may need to end a relationship, let's again use the example of Sarah, who was incested by her father. Imagine Sarah has grown up and looks for men like her father. She is now in a relationship with a man who, like her father, physically hurts her. Pretend Sarah knows the choices *LifeScripting* provides when she triggers. The man commits a hurtful behavior and she triggers. Sarah attempts to talk with him to alter the situation. He does not listen to her and does not pay attention to her needs. Nothing changes in terms of his behavior, and he continues to trigger her as the emotional trauma increases. Sarah realizes that without different behavior on his part she will continue to experience the same result. She makes a decision to leave the relationship.

Where Is The Evidence?

Do not leave a relationship too soon. It is important to establish solid evidence that it is necessary to leave a relationship before ending it. To help decide, ask the questions, "Where is the evidence that this is the same situation or person as in my past? Is this just an isolated event that resembles my past?" If there are only one or two ways a situation resembles your past, and the situation can easily be corrected, then it is important not to prematurely leave the relationship. However, if you ask the question, "Where is the evidence?" and there is sufficient evidence that the situation is the same as a past event which never resolved itself, then the triggers are warning you not to remain in the relationship.

Asking the question, "Where is the evidence?" helps put the relationship into perspective and keeps you from having one or two emotional situations dominate the entire picture of a possibly good relationship. All relationships require some fine tuning. The secret is to know what can be adjusted.

Additional Thoughts About Relationships

1) No one completes you. Connecting to another is an invitation to know yourself. Lovingly sharing this knowledge with another adds to the relationship.

2) The relationships you most struggled with as a child will be the type of relationships you will tend to repeat as an adult. Usually these relationships occur with the same gender. Example: If Mom was your major issue you will usually choose a woman like your mother with whom to work out the issue. You could also work the issue out with a male who has all the characteristics of your mother. When you answer the questions in section II you will discover your beliefs about all relationships.

3) When a repeated relationship appears in your life, ask yourself, "What did the child teach me?" Also ask, "What do I know because of this experience that will help me with my choices in the present?"

4) You have a list of what you want in another. She also has a list. Lists come from individual floppy discs. What is on your list? How much of what is on your list are you willing to give to another? Have you ever thought of asking what is on the other person's list? When we get upset, we tend to feel that our list is the only list that counts.

5) To find out what you love about yourself - think of how you introduce yourself in the beginning of an exciting new relationship. To what degree do you live the characteristics of that person on a normal daily basis?

6) At the beginning of a relationship, introduce yourself honestly because you will be held responsible for being that person throughout the relationship.

7) Love always wants to gravitate toward what it loves. Who and what do you love? How do you expand toward that love?

8) If you are trying to make a relationship something it isn't - it isn't!

9) Not everyone was born to have a mated relationship. Do not judge yourself, or another, based on the existence of a mate.

A further understanding of yourself and your relationships will be presented in Section II. You will greatly treasure the awareness of your beliefs in this area because this knowledge will enable you to make conscious adult choices in all future relationships.

The Beauty Of Emotions

Since triggers always involve emotions, a brief overview of emotions is valuable. There have been volumes written about emotions, however, for *LifeScripting* purposes, I will confine the role of emotions to a very basic awareness.

Most of us judge our emotions as good or bad. That judgement is usually based on our perception of the feelings we are having in any given moment. Yet what is really happening is that most of our adult emotional perceptions are coming from our childhood experiences about feelings. For example, if anger was never expressed in your childhood home, you may have concern when anger is expressed in your adult world. You will also tend to judge this emotion as negative. However, if anger was readily expressed in your childhood home you will generally express yourself freely when you are angry. If laughter was permitted in your childhood experience, then joy is easily expressed by you. But, if laughter was not a part of your beginning environment, that emotion could be difficult for you even though it is considered a positive feeling.

There is a simple exercise to determine which emotions you judge as positive and which emotions you judge as negative. List every emotion you experienced as a child. Next to each emotion note if it was considered a positive or negative feeling in the family, then write how you expressed each emotion and what happened when you experienced it. Now, review the entire exercise and you will clearly see the pattern you have formed for your adult emotional expression.

The psychological truth about emotions is that they are all positive because they are designed to aid in balancing the human being. The state of balance is called *homeostasis*, and it is attained by constant psychological and physical adjustments. If you are hungry you eat. If you are tired you sleep. If you are sad you cry. Your body and mind are designed to give you constant feed back as to what you need to maintain homeostasis. You only need to listen and then respond. Your emotions comprise a major part of the feedback loop that enables you to balance your system and maintain homeostasis.

When you experience an emotion, you are designed to feel the emotion and act upon it. When you respond to an emotion, the response neutralizes your being and enables you to continue with the next event. For example, if you feel the need to cry and you cry, you clear your system. This helps your total being maintain balance. Imagine needing to cry and holding in the tears. What happens to your body?

Emotions are beautiful gifts in your life. They are the vehicles you use to deeply know yourself. On a daily basis, your emotions speak to you about your values, your beliefs, and your behavior.

In *LifeScripting*, emotions provide the vehicles to find the events from your past that give you information for the present. Emotions are always involved when you over/under-react in the now moment. Emotions are not to be bottled up but felt, or the journey to the deepest part of yourself will be sabotaged. This is not to suggest that you feel and express your emotions in an inappropriate manner. Appropriate expression of emotion requires that you feel your feelings as close to the time of the event as possible. It is important to know that expression of emotion is about releasing your system. This release need not occur at the expense of another. There is a proper time and place to express all emotion. If you are feeling a feeling and it is safe to express it, do so. If you are in a space where expressing your feelings will create issues for you or another, then hold the feeling until you are able to express it.

Never stuff emotions as if you can forget them. When you stuff your feelings, that emotional energy has to go somewhere, and that somewhere is into your body's organs. Stuffed emotions create many issues for the body in terms of ill health. Our morgues are becoming filled with bodies that many times died because of stuffed emotions which were manifested in suicides, homicides, heart attacks, ulcers, etc. In no way am I suggesting that all such deaths are the result of stuffed feelings, but I am suggesting that many individuals die prematurely because of emotions that have overwhelmed the mind and body. We do not die from appropriately expressing our feelings, but many die from inappropriately stuffing them. Have you ever noticed that when people's lives flow smoothly they tend to remain healthy and experience less sickness and disease?

In *LifeScripting,* it is vital to recognize your emotions and feel them before going back to analyze your past. It is important to first feel your feelings, since it is impossible for the brain to emotionally feel and intellectually remember at the same time. Once you have experienced the feeling, ask the primary question, "When was the first time I felt this way?" Remember, this question assists in retrieving your past memory. The past memory will always involve similar emotions to the ones you are feeling in the present. Process the memory based upon the method you learned for reframing.

If an emotion is appropriate for the present event and is not an over/under-reaction, then it is not necessary to use the emotion to review your past. The only time it benefits you to use emotions as a key to understanding your past is when you are having an over/under emotional reaction (trigger) to an event in the present. At these times, your emotions become the vehicles and gifts that open the gateway to your past where you can discover your true self.

Emotions = Triggers = Information = Empowerment

Important Specific Emotions

Anger

The emotion of anger is important to understand since it seems to be an emotion controlling many lives in our modern world. The basis of all anger comes from the word should. Think about every time you have been angry. What did you feel should have been different? The list of shoulds is endless and includes statements such as, "He shouldn't have left me! She shouldn't have died! I shouldn't have been abused! The car accident shouldn't have happened! Mom shouldn't have beaten me!" Each "should" in your life blocks your energy and stops the joy you were born to experience. Shoulds can only close your heart. How long is your list of shoulds?

All shoulds are about the past because you cannot say "shouldn't" until something has already happened. To assist you in alleviating the anger caused by your shoulds, answer the question, "Can I change the past?" The answer is obviously no. All of us have tried and all of us have failed. You can, however, change how you view the past and open your heart to love by reframing your thoughts. With this new view, your heart will remain open and you will experience a more joyous, peaceful, and fulfilled life.

Changing one word in your vocabulary will help you change your life in the area of anger. Simply change the word "should" to the word "prefer." The word prefer reduces your anger and still allows you to have your viewpoint about what has happened. To accomplish this, you may want to talk to yourself by saying, "I prefer that hadn't happened, but it did. And if I believe my thinking creates my reality, how can I reframe this event in a positive way?" Prefer helps negate the anger, enabling your heart to open. This opening will take you to the abstract part of your brain where other options and perspectives exist.

Guilt

Guilt is another emotion that can create major trauma and paralysis unless adequately understood. Most guilt is not a natural feeling but rather a trained response. We have been taught to feel bad when we do not perform in the manner that others are asking or expecting. The result of this kind of guilt is that our system becomes imbalanced and our heart closes to love. There is a simple way to handle this type of guilt. Ask yourself, "If a child were faced with the situation that is causing my guilt, what would I say to the child? What course of action would I suggest the child take?" Take the very same course of action for yourself.

If guilt truly does belong to you because of something you have chosen to do, then endeavor to learn from the situation, correct what you can, and continue on. Remember, you cannot change the past, you can only use the past as a basis for change and further empowerment.

Depression

There are two types of depression, situational and chemical. We will not address chemical depression since its cure requires medication. However, we will address situational depression since it has been experienced by most people to some degree or another. Situational depression is simply feeling depressed because a situation did not unfold the way you had hoped. Generally, the result is that you feel disappointed. In other words, situational depression comes from wanting something you are not getting. The degree of your depression is directly related to how much you wanted that which you discovered you could not have. For example, if you want someone to love you, and you've planned your whole life around that love which the person chooses not to give you, your depression would be very deep. However, if you wanted to go to lunch with someone and he couldn't make the appointment, you might only be slightly depressed.

There are three options available when you are experiencing situational depression: 1) You can continue wanting what you do not have. This is a choice many depressed people make and the result is always continued depression. In the example of wanting someone who chooses not to love you, you can continue to want this love, however, as long as the person chooses not to return the love, the end result will be depression. 2) You can take action to get what you want. This will lift the depression as long as you believe the action is moving you toward your goal. If the action does not move you toward your goal, the depression will again re-appear. To illustrate this point, go back to wanting a person who isn't in love with you. You could take action to change his mind such as sending flowers, candy, or cards, or you could have a talk with him. As long as you believe this action will cause him to love you, you will not feel depressed. However, if your action does not obtain the desired results, you will again feel depressed. 3) The third option to lift depression is to change what you want. This does not suggest lying to yourself, it simply suggests understanding the truth about situations. Again the example of someone not loving you will illustrate this choice. You could now say to yourself, "Everyone has the right to choose who they love, and the person I love does not choose me. I will someday realize the gift in this experience, but for now I will fulfill my life by doing what works best for me. I will also focus on loving myself and sharing that love with others."

Situational depression is always the result of our expectations and the amount of energy and belief we invest in those expectations. If we do not get what we want, we can choose one of three options: 1) Continue wanting what we cannot have. 2) Take action to get what we want. 3) Change what we want. Sometimes it is appropriate to start with 1 and then move to 2. If things do not change, move to 3. The choice is yours - the results are predictable.

When emotions are viewed and used as positive gifts in your life, you will experience an inner peace about all that you are, have been, or will become.

What We Have Been Doing

Emotions are designed to be instruments of personal empowerment, particularly if they are approached in a positive manner. However, there are several therapeutic emotional release techniques that I believe have possible negative affects for the individuals engaging in them. With caution and respect, I would like to review several of these techniques to help you understand the potentially damaging effects, therefore assisting you with your future decisions.

In my opinion, there is only one way to decide if a technique has value to the person using it, and that is to determine if the entire process is based in love for all the participants. Please understand that whatever therapies you have previously used were right for you at the time you used them. Do not look to your past therapeutic experiences with regret but rather with a positive reframe. After all, we have to be where we were and are to get where we are going!

I do believe that most techniques have been designed out of a genuine concern for others, and with a hope that lives will improve. However, many times the deeper negative effects of the processes have been overlooked. I would like to point out a few of these potentially destructive methods to assist you in your future therapeutic choices.

Reversed Chair For Anger Release

This Gestalt technique asks you to mentally place your perceived abuser in an empty chair. With the perception that the person is present in the chair, you are asked to vent your feelings and thoughts at the chair. Many times the added dynamic of a batacka is used. A batacka is a hand held club that is foam padded and is used to hit the chair while you are venting your anger and harbored negative feelings. You are encouraged in this process to use anger statements like: "I hate you! You did it to me! I am angry at you!"

When a person is fully involved in this process, much emotion is generated and the energy released gives everyone the feeling that something good must surely be happening. When the emotions subside the participant usually reports relief, and often says something has shifted for them. Because of these expressed feelings, it is easy to believe that healing must have occurred.

With these seemingly positive results, what negatives could possibly be a part of this scenario? To fully understand, a deeper look at what is actually happening is necessary. This can be done by reviewing the parts of this process and their possible destructive consequences. Some of the negative dynamics of the reversed chair for anger are:

1) The person who experiences the process of placing another person mentally in a chair is either 100% involved

in the experience or is not involved at all. It is an all or nothing process. If the person is unable to respond 100%, she will report feeling awkward and unable to participate in the exercise. If the person becomes 100% involved, then she is no longer in the now moment but rather mentally back at the scene of the perceived trauma. Remember, thoughts create reality, so the person remembering the past scene is actually in the past scene. To recognize this truth, just think of a past emotional event and be 100% in the event in your mind. You will experience the feelings of that event as if you are actually a part of the event. What happens to the person in the reversed chair exercise is the same dynamic. The person mentally places herself in the past situation and feels the trauma again. In her mind she is truly living the experience one more time. When she returns to the present she feels a sense of relief. This is the same relief she felt at the time the original event ended. In my opinion, she confuses this feeling of relief with a perceived healing, rather than realizing her relief is the result of the scene being over.

To decide if this exercise is right for you, just imagine a child about five years old coming to you and saying that someone was hurting her. Would you say to the child, "Go back to the place where you were being hurt and figure it out"? Never! What you would do is be there for the child and spend time helping the child understand what happened and what she can do. You would also assist the person who hurt the child to get help so the individual would no longer hurt this child or anyone else.

2) Another dynamic to consider in this process is the idea that thoughts not only create your reality, but are sent out like radio waves affecting the people about whom you are thinking. While saying things like, "I hate you! I am angry!" etc., the words and thoughts are being sent out to

that person at 186,000 mps. In reality, those words and thoughts are felt by the sender and the accused. In my opinion, the result of this process is even more separation and tension between the individuals involved.

A student of mine had a realization of this truth when she recalled that every time she went to her former therapist and engaged in the reverse chair method about her father's abuse, her father got physically sick. Several times he actually felt sick enough to vomit.

3) An added negative in the reversed chair technique is that during the entire process the person is subconsciously telling himself that things weren't right in his life, and that life should have been different. This gives him a deep sense that his life was an accident and that at the highest of levels he is not loved. It also implies that he needs to fix what is broken. In my opinion, this process increases the potential for greater internal anger.

If the fundamental need in life is to love and belong, then this basic need must be satisfied in our interactions with the people who cross our life's path. The reversed chair anger technique tends to separate, rather than connect, the individuals involved in our life process. Anger and hate do not heal, nor do they move a person toward fulfillment in life. Anger and hate only lead to a closed and contracted heart.

To believe that one must first experience anger to arrive at love and wholeness is an obvious contradiction. If the goal is to love and to be connected, then the path to obtain this must be a loving one.

Re-Experience Your Feelings To Heal

Some therapies believe that in order to heal yourself from stuffed feelings you must go back to the original event to experience the feelings that were buried at the time of the event. This view suggests that stuffed feelings are impeding personal growth in some way. This is probably a valid assumption, but is the cure to re-experience the feeling? I believe not. What occurs when you re-experience your feelings is similar to what happens in the reversed chair technique. The result looks good but the internal message is negative.

So what does a person who has stuffed her feelings do? In the previous chapter you learned the importance of releasing your feelings. It was pointed out that feelings need to be released as close to the event as possible. This enables the system to balance itself in a healthy manner. What is a healthy release? First, it is necessary to remember that thoughts are things and that what you think creates your reality in the now. When you go back and feel the specific feelings of the past, these feelings are re-created inside your system once again. Consequently, they charge your system the same way they did the first time you had the experience. Once you realize that feelings are actually energy, then to facilitate release is to simply find a way to move the stored energy to the outside of your being. When this occurs it leads to internal balance and bodily homeostasis. This balance can be accomplished by physical exercise such as running, biking, fast walking, etc. It also can be accomplished by reframing the event and thereby re-channeling the energy to new thoughts and new responses. It is never necessary to relive the event to obtain internal balance because anger is not reduced by being angry about being angry.

To illustrate how feelings need expression but do not need to be re-experienced, imagine you are outside of a church and you are told a joke. How long will you laugh? You will laugh as long as it takes to release your system of the need to laugh. However, if you are told the same joke while sitting inside of the church while services are in progress, and the rule is "do not laugh in church," what will happen? You will undoubtedly stuff the need to laugh and that energy will store inside of you. With much self control you will contain your need to laugh. If someone should poke you, the laughter will again be something you will have to stuff and control. This process of stuffing could continue for the entire church service because the energy to laugh is still present and in need of being released. How can you release the energy? You simply go outside the church and laugh. How long will you laugh once outside the church? You will laugh until your system is totally released and the need to laugh has been satisfied.

When you leave the church and begin to laugh, you do not have to think of the joke or relive the experience. In fact, you may have even forgotten the joke. All that is necessary is to simply release the system by laughing. Once you have laughed, you can go back into the church and not have any urgency to laugh. You could even be poked by your friend and you will not have an emotional response because your system is now completely balanced.

All unexpressed emotions can be released without the need to go back and re-experience the original event. To fully balance the system, simply feel what you are feeling until the feeling is totally diminished. Once the feeling is released, reframe the event for its positive purpose in your life.

Passing Back Your Hurt

In this exercise, you are told that your hurt does not belong to you and you can be "healed" by returning your hurt to the person who gave it to you. The individual doing this exercise thinks of the person he believes hurt him and says things like, "I give you back your pain. Your pain does not belong to me. Take back your pain!"

Like the reversed chair of Gestalt, the intention of this therapy is to get the person deeply involved and filled with emotion. This exercise looks good while it is being performed because there is usually visible emotion on the part of the participant. However, when you look deeper you will find that the desired result of giving your hurt away can never be accomplished. It cannot be accomplished because of your ability to remember. You can scream and cry and say your experience does not belong to you, and even try to give it back to the person who hurt you. Yet when you close your eyes and remember, the memory is still a real part of your being.

Since the memory remains even after this process has been experienced, an additional issue is now created when you realize the hurt did not go away. You are now faced with deciding if the therapeutic exercise is at fault or if you are the problem. If you should decide that you are the problem, you then blame yourself because the memory is still there, therefore, you must have done "it" wrong. Consequently, you have further evidence that there is definitely something wrong with you!

It is imperative to understand that hurt can never be passed back, and memory cannot be erased. Memory needs to be accepted as a precious gift that aids you in knowing who you are, where you have been, and what you believe. To have memory of every part of your life is an invaluable aid when you ask the question, "What did the teachers of my life help me to understand and, therefore, to know?"

It is evident that nothing that has ever happened can be made to have not happened. Thus, you can only change how you perceive what has already occurred. Any attempt to pass your hurt back says your life was bad, that you were an accident, that you are not loved, and that you have to fix what is broken. The movie *The Never Ending Story* contains the only lasting solution to the issue of trying to make the hurtful parts of your life go away. The solution is stated when the little boy in the movie says, "You can't make the emptiness go away; you have to fill it with love."

Wave Good-bye To Your Family

In this exercise, you are asked to mentally wave goodbye to your family. This is supposedly accomplished by imagining the child you were, then taking the child out of the family house. As you leave the house you wave goodbye to those who hurt you (usually your mother and/or father). This exercise looks great because of the deep emotion and the desire to connect to the child. However, the internal messages are very much the opposite of the desired goal of connecting to yourself and to others in a more loving way. When you wave goodbye to your past, the internal message is that a mistake has been made in your life. The perceived mistake is that you have the wrong parents or are a member of the wrong family. With this conclusion as your base, you now feel you have to again fix what is broken. In this exercise, you are also given the subconscious message that you are now all alone, and that you have to erase and abandon all of the significance of the past in order to go forward with your life.

By answering a few logical questions, you will be able to internalize for yourself the destructive effects of this exercise. How do you wave goodbye to memory? How do you feel whole when the core of your life is being denied by waving good-bye to it? How can you feel complete by denying your parents as if they are not a part of who you are? How can you feel a part of the universe and feel loved, if the very family you grew up with is an accident that must be erased from your memory?

Summary

Therapists who assist others in the previously described exercises are usually well intentioned, though the results of these processes are usually counter-productive. To determine if a therapeutic exercise is one in which you wish to participate, simply define the basic desire you are attempting to fulfill. If your desire is an open heart, then the experiences you choose for wholeness must be loving by their very nature. To determine if a process is a loving one ask the questions, "Would I do this to a child I love? Would I say this to a child I love?" If the answer to either question is "no," then the process will not accomplish a loving result and is, therefore, not designed for you. If you answer "yes" to both questions, then the process is loving and will assist you in opening your heart to your life experiences. When you see your life through the eyes of love, your life becomes a message of how to be rather than a message of how not to be.

The Right Road

To have a fulfilled and happy life, it is necessary to be on the road of life specifically designed for you. The 96 *LifeScripting* questions in Section II will assist you in identifying your personal road in life. With the answers to the 96 questions as a base, there is also a daily method that will help you evaluate if you are on the right road for your life. The method involves awareness as well as the tracking of your personal energy. To help you understand this concept, I have developed the "Wrong Road Analogy."

Wrong Road Analogy

Imagine you and a friend are in Phoenix, Arizona and you decide to go play on the beaches of San Diego. You jump into the car and begin following a road map. After entering the freeway you see a road sign marked San Diego, 250 miles. What happens to you when you see this sign? You immediately feel excitement because the sign indicates you are on the right road, and you know if you keep going you will arrive in San Diego. As you continue on the freeway you see another sign that reads San Diego, 200 miles. Your energy at this point is even more intense because you realize you are getting closer to your destination. As you travel farther, you decide to pause at a rest stop where you and your friend have a snack and spend a few minutes talking. Eventually you get back into the car and head onto the road. Because you are not paying attention, you turn onto the wrong road, travel this road for a few miles, then see a sign that reads, "Barstow, California, 200 miles." Since Barstow is not where you want to go, what will happen to you when you see this sign? You will immediately feel panic and an energy tightness throughout your being. A decision now needs to be made, so you talk to your friend and decide that maybe you should just keep going, hoping that in a few miles you will see a sign for San Diego.

This decision is much like what happens to so many in life. People begin on the right road of life, but somewhere along the way they get distracted and make a wrong turn. They then try to convince themselves that if they stay in the situation it will become the road that will get them to where they originally wanted to go. It is at this juncture that therapists and stress management experts are often called. These helpers, out of genuine concern, oftentimes assist their clients who are on the wrong road (wrong job, wrong relationship, etc.) by suggesting they stay on that road and somehow make it the right road. (Please note, the road to Barstow is right for an individual, if Barstow is where she originally intended to go.)

Having made the decision to continue on the road to Barstow in hopes that it will become the road to San Diego, you and your friend travel a few more miles and see another sign that reads, "Barstow, 175 miles." Your energy tightens even more as you look at your friend and say, "It's obvious we're on the wrong road. The signs all say we are, and our tight energy says we are. What we really need to do is turn around." You both agree and you turn the car around.

As you start back toward the road to San Diego, your enthusiasm heightens and your tension lessens. Eventually you see a sign that reads, "San Diego, 180 miles." When you see this sign, you both breathe a sigh of relief. Knowing you are now on the right road, you begin to talk about what happened while you were on the wrong road. You realize that reframing the experience is necessary for peace of mind and learning. You both agree that everything happens for a reason and that your thinking is what creates your reality about any and all situations. Thus, it becomes your choice to discover what positives can be found in this experience. During the process of reframing, you talk about how the drive toward Barstow helped you appreciate more fully your original desire to be in San Diego. You discuss that perhaps there was a need to be on the road to Barstow that you may never understand, such as avoiding an accident. You also realize that you both were able to see a part of the country you would have never seen without the turn to Barstow. Finally, you recognize the gift of the road signs that helped you determine the right road. You discover this is also true in life. When you are on the right road in life, there is little or no tension. However, when you are on the wrong road, there is mounting tension and internal struggles - all signs that a change of direction is needed.

You, of course, also have the option not to positively reframe your turn toward Barstow and could choose to spend the rest of the trip to San Diego complaining about the road to Barstow. This is often the choice people make in life when they judge something as negative. They spend the rest of their lives complaining about how awful the experience was, resulting in a negative present moment. I do not mean to suggest that it is wrong to comment on an experience as stressful or disappointing. But to fill one's mind with negative thoughts and words about an already finished experience will greatly limit the joy of the present, not to mention how it will diminish the hope for future success.

Since you chose to positively reframe your thoughts about the road to Barstow, you and your friend can now continue on the road to San Diego and enjoy the fact that you are getting closer to your destination. Unfortunately, about 100 miles from San Diego you sense there is something wrong with the way the car is handling. You pull over to evaluate the situation, discover a flat tire, and contact a road service for assistance. They arrive and fix the tire and once again you are able to proceed on the road to San Diego. During this episode you experienced some tightness of energy. This time, however, you quickly recover because you knew you were on the right road and were simply having a small problem that could be easily overcome.

Helping with the flat tires of life is where therapists and stress management experts can work wonders in many lives. This is true because they are working with individuals who are on the right road and who simply need information and assistance to enable them to travel more smoothly. Therapy can also help tremendously when individuals are on the road to Barstow, if the therapy addresses how to get off the wrong road and get back onto the right road.

How do you know if you are on the road to San Diego or Barstow in your life? Your energy is your guide. Your energy is the road map that conveys messages about your life. If you feel an energy block and it does not release, but rather tightens as you move toward an event or person, then in all likelihood you are on the wrong road. Tightness, blockages, and energy losses are all signs that assist you in knowing you are going in the wrong direction. A client helped illustrate this point when she came into my office and in total pain and frustration said, "I pray and pray every night that my relationship with my boyfriend gets better, and every day it gets worse. Even God isn't listening to me." I suggested that perhaps her prayers were being answered because the situation was getting worse. She looked at me in disbelief. We talked about her perceived need to have what she thought she wanted versus her deeper need to follow the road that would take her to true happiness. She realized the energy blocks, which were not lifting, could be messages to adjust her life and inspire her return to her right road.

This example is not to suggest that you quickly or randomly leave relationships just because there is a small obstacle or disruption, but that you get totally in touch with your energy and happiness as key indicators in your life. You can learn how to monitor your life by paying close attention to any and all tension. When you feel tension in the form of an energy block, learn to pause and ask yourself, "What is it I need to know to decide what to do?" If there seems to be no method of releasing the block, then the block could be a gift designed to inform you that you are on the wrong road. If you stay on the wrong road, be assured you will arrive in the wrong place. In short, if you continue on the road to Barstow you will get to Barstow.

It is possible in life to have difficulty deciding what to do when you discover, or even suspect, that you are on the road to Barstow. This feeling of being stuck comes from being deeply invested in your own life as well as being invested in the many miles you have already traveled.

There are several processes that can help you know what to do when you get stuck on the wrong road: 1) You can imagine you are talking to your best friend and your friend is presenting your situation to you as if it is his situation. What would you advise your friend to do? Follow your own advice! 2) Imagine you are talking to a beautiful child. What you tell the child will affect the child's entire life. What would you tell the child to do if he were in the very same situation as you?

The 96 questions in Section II are designed to assist you in recognizing the right road for your life. Additional right road signs come from reframing every challenge you have faced, as well as from using the learning you've gained from every joyful experience you've have ever had. Additional assistance in discovering your right road can be found in the following ways:

1) JOY - Are you in joy? Find your joy and follow it.

2) PASSION - What is your passion? The word passion speaks for itself. When you divide the word it says it all. PASS - I - ON. To pass the "I" on. When you see someone with passion, she has found her deepest heart's desire and cannot stop until it's passed on. She is on fire in life no matter what the expression. It might be to quietly write a poem from the soul, or feed the hungry. Passion has no room for comparison since each person's passion is her purpose.

3) ENTHUSIASM - Be enthusiastic. The Greek word for enthusiasm is "en-theos" which means to be filled with God!

4) RELAX - How internally stressed are you? Internal stress is directly related to how far away you are from who you really are. Finding the right road for your life will greatly reduce your stress.

5) DO IT NOW - What is it you would regret not having done if you were to die? Whatever it is, do it today, or at least plan for it in the near future. Enjoy the process as well as the accomplishment. A friend of mine who was about to die said it best when she whispered, "I always thought there would be a someday."

When you make the process of tracking your energy a daily event, you will be greatly assisted in finding and enjoying the road that has been designed to take you to yourself and to your life's mission.

Action For Empowerment

Sometimes the obvious needs to be stated so it's not over-looked. In *LifeScripting*, taking action is a necessary part of achieving self empowerment. Acquiring new ideas, learning new processes, finding new direction, and realizing a new way of thinking are all valuable, but without action the desired goal of an empowered life will remain an illusion.

LifeScripting is not an excuse for behavior, it is an explanation! With this explanation, it is necessary to take personal action to change your life. Sometimes the action will involve behavioral changes that can be seen, and sometimes the needed action will be an internal process that cannot be seen. The necessary action will be dictated by the situation. The results you obtain in your life will be in direct proportion to the amount of action needed versus the amount of action taken.

Action Necessary For LifeScripting To Work

1) Learn and apply the concepts of *LifeScripting* presented in Section I.

2) Answer the questions in Section II.

3) Work with the beliefs you discover within Section II.

4) Pay special attention to triggers.

5) Reframe past events.

6) Complete the exercises in Section III.

7) Enjoy your life!

When you incorporate these seven action steps, *LifeScripting* will become a loving and supportive way of being with yourself and with others. You will look at all of life as an evolving picture that contains no accidents. You will see that everything is in process, and you will become committed to being fully involved in that process.

As you turn to Section II and discover your personal beliefs and life purpose, keep foremost in your thoughts that love is the key to all human happiness.

SECTION II

The Pieces Of The Puzzle Called You

WARNING: ATTEMPTING TO ANSWER THE 96 QUESTIONS CONTAINED WITHIN THIS SECTION COULD BE HARMFUL TO YOUR PSYCHOLOGICAL HEALTH AND WELL BEING UNLESS YOU FIRST READ AND UNDERSTAND THE LIFESCRIPTING PRINCIPLES DETAILED IN SECTION I OF THIS BOOK.

96 QUESTIONS
To Help You In The Discovery Of You

The 96 questions on the following pages will assist in helping you determine the core beliefs that are creating your adult behavior. Each of the questions has relevance to a specific belief you have about yourself. For the best possible experience, answer all 96 questions before reading the interpretation to the questions.

There are no right or wrong answers to these questions. Your answers pertain to your personal perceptions of the events and experiences that were a part of your life. Simply answer each question to the best of your ability with as much detail as possible. Do not judge your answers or try to interpret the questions as you answer them. Approach each question for the specific details of your life and for the information about the experiences of the child you were. Remember, do not "fall into" your story or "re-live" your past experiences. You are answering the questions only to obtain information. It is not necessary to re-experience the experience to accomplish this objective.

If you do not know the answer to a question, simply write, "I do not know." When each question is analyzed, the answer "I do not know" becomes valuable information about specific areas of your behavior. When answering a question with "I don not know," it is helpful to ask yourself, "If I could guess, how would I answer this question?" When guessing, write out the information and always note that the answer is a guess.

If a question troubles you, skip the question. The goal of this exercise is to have a rewarding, not troubled, experience. You can always return to the question at a later time.

Do not ask anyone for information about the questions until you have answered all of the questions for yourself. Your answers must come from your memory and your perceptions to validate your personal beliefs. You may later add to your answers by seeking information from others. However, when receiving information from others, always remember that their input is coming from their perception of the event, and, therefore, is not necessarily your reality.

If you were raised by someone other than your biological parents, initially answer each of the 96 questions with your biological family in mind. If your answers concerning your biological family create responses such as "I don't know," realize that "I don't know" will provide insights into specific areas of your life. After you have answered each question with your biological family in mind, answer the same question with regard to any others who acted in a parental capacity or who comprised your family during your formative years. For example, adoptive parents, grandparents, aunts, uncles, older sisters and brothers, foster parents, step-parents, adoptive siblings, step-siblings, etc.

When you answer the 96 questions, make sure you are in a quiet place and have enough time to become involved with the process. This experience is about you, so take it as seriously as you would if you were endeavoring to learn about someone you deeply love. If you want to answer the questions in several sittings, that is perfectly acceptable. Remember, for the best possible experience, do not skip forward and read the explanation to any question until you have completely answered all 96 questions. Since the child holds the key to your adult beliefs and behavior, most of the 96 questions are about the child you were. The beliefs you formed as a child occurred prior to age six, though many of the 96 questions will ask you to write about the child you were prior to age nine. This is necessary because most individuals have very little memory prior to age six. However, by age nine you were acting out the beliefs of the child. Thus, to talk about your behavior and feelings prior to age nine identifies the beliefs you formed in early childhood.

If any major events occurred in your life after the age of nine, please note those events because they also add to your belief system.

Keep in mind, as you journey into the memories of your childhood, that your experiences, when understood and reframed, will assist you in future positive life choices.

Note: There is not adequate room in this book to answer the 96 Questions. You will need separate paper or a notebook to complete your answers. Remember to give as much detail to each question as possible.

YOUR BIRTH

1) What do you know about your birth? Write anything you have ever heard or anything you feel.

2) Were you full term? Were you premature or late? What were the circumstances?

3) How long was labor? If you don't know, what would you guess?

4) Were there any complications during the pregnancy or your birth? What were they?

5) Was there any anesthetic used during the birth process? Did this anesthetic effect the baby? Were there any drugs used during the pregnancy?

6) What time of day were you born? What is your favorite time of day?

7) Were you nursed? For how long? Were there any events surrounding the nursing process? Example, did your mother want to nurse you, was she relaxed, etc? If you were not nursed, what was the reason?

8) How soon after birth were you held and who was the first person to hold you?

9) Were you a wanted pregnancy? How do you know or not know? Were you wanted by Mom? Were you wanted by Dad?

10) Were you a planned pregnancy? Were you planned by both Mom and Dad? If you don't know, what would you guess?

11) Did your mother want a boy or a girl?

12) Did your father want a boy or a girl?

13) Where was your father at the moment of your birth? If you don't know, where would you guess he was?

14) How was your mother during your pregnancy? If you don't know, what would you guess?

15) How was your father during your pregnancy? If you don't know, what would you guess?

16) How did your mother and father interact with each other during your pregnancy? If you don't know, what would you guess?

17) Do you know anything about your conception?

18) Were you loved at your birth? If so, by whom?

19) Were there any other family members or friends present or involved in your birth process? Who were they and what was their involvement?

SIBLINGS AND SELF

NOTE: If children other than your biological siblings were present during your formative years, include them in your answers to any questions that involve siblings.

20) What is your birth order? What are the names and ages of your siblings (include yourself)? Were there any deaths? Were there any stillborn babies or miscarriages? Were there any biological siblings not raised with you?

21) Who of your siblings is most different from you? How is he/she different?

22) Who of your siblings is most like you? How is he/she like you?

23) Briefly describe your other siblings as you saw them as children. Did you like or dislike them when you were a child?

Questions 24-84 need to be answered from the eyes of the child that you were prior to nine years of age (about 3rd or 4th grade). Go back as far as possible for your memories. If there were major memories after nine years of age, include them.

24) What kind of child were you prior to age nine? Give as much detail as possible to describe the character of the child you were. Include as part of your description the appearance, behavior, and the feeling of the child.

25) What was school like for you?

26) What was home like for you?

27) Did your family move frequently? What were these family moves like for you?

28) Did you like being a child? Why or why not?

29) Did you love the child you were?

Questions 30-61 require you to rank yourself and your siblings in terms of specific attributes. Rank yourself and your siblings in descending order for each attribute. Then describe your feelings about that attribute in relation to yourself as a child.

30) Who did you consider the most to the least intelligent?

31) Who received the best grades in school?

32) Who was the hardest worker? In what manner? Describe yourself in detail in the area of work.

33) Who helped around the house the most? Describe in detail how you helped around the house.

34) Were there any rewards for your help?

35) Who was the most to the least conforming and how?

36) Who was the most to least rebellious and how?

37) Who tried to please the most? Who did you try to please the most and why? Describe yourself in detail in this area.

38) Who was the most critical of others and how? If you were critical, what were you critical of? How did you express it? (Verbally, internally, etc.)

39) Who was the most considerate and how? Write about yourself in this area.

40) Where did the siblings rank in selfishness? What were you selfish about?

41) Who liked having his/her own way the most? How did he/she get it? How did you get your own way?

42) Who was the most sensitive and easily hurt? About what? How was it expressed? Make sure you cover in detail your experiences in this area.

43) Who showed his/her temper the most to the least? How was it shown and how did you feel?

44) Who had the best sense of humor? In what way?

45) Who was the most idealistic? Were you idealistic? About what? What were your hopes, dreams and desires? What did you want to become if all were possible?

46) Who had the highest standards of achievement? What did he/she want to achieve? What did you want to achieve?

47) Who had the highest standards of behavior and morals? What were your standards in this area?

48) Who was the most to the least materialistic? About what? What were you materialistic about?

49) Who was the most athletic and how? In what areas were you athletic?

50) Who was the strongest physically? How did he/she express it? How were you in the area of physical strength?

51) Who was the strongest emotionally? Where were you in terms of emotional strength? What did you consider emotional strength to be?

52) Who was the best looking? How did you feel about physical attractiveness?

53) Who had the most friends? What kind of friendships were they?

54) Who had the most long-term on-going friendships?

55) Who was the most spoiled? By whom and how? How did you feel about this?

56) Who was the most punished? By whom and how? How did you feel during this interaction? How were

you punished? Give details and recollections. (If punishment was intense for you, do not fall into your story. Simply watch your past like a movie and state what happened.)

57) Of the siblings, who took care of whom?

58) Who of the siblings played the most with whom?

59) Who of the siblings got along the best?

60) Who fought and argued the most? How did he/she fight and argue? Who won?

61) Were there any major events in your life after the age of nine? What were they and how did you feel about the events?

PARENTS

NOTE: If during your formative years you were raised by someone other than your biological parents, first answer questions 62-83 with your biological parents in mind. Once completed, answer each question again with regard to any other parental figure.

62) Who was your father's favorite? How do you know?

63) Who was your mother's favorite? How do you know?

64) How old are your mother and father? If either parent has died, describe the details. How old were you at the time of the death?

65) Are your parents still married? How long have they been married? If there has been a divorce, how old were you when they divorced? Are there any remarriages and do you like the people involved?

66) What kind of person did you perceive your father to be prior to you being nine years of age? Give as much detail as possible.

After writing about the character and memories of your father, answer these additional questions concerning him.

a) What kind of interactions did you have with your father?

b) Did your father say "I love you?" How did you feel?

c) Did your dad hug you? How did you feel?

d) Did you feel loved by your father?

e) Did you love your dad?

f) Did you like your dad?

g) Did you feel comfortable around your father? Why or why not?

h) Did your father have any addictions? What were they?

i) Was your dad physically attractive to you?

67) What kind of person did you perceive your mother to be prior to you being nine years of age? Give as much detail as possible.

After writing about the character and memories of your mother, answer these additional questions concerning her.

a) What kind of interactions did you have with your mother?

b) Did your mother say "I love you?" How did you feel?

c) Did your mom hug you? How did you feel?

d) Did you feel loved by your mother?

e) Did you love your mom?

f) Did you like your mom?

g) Did you feel comfortable around your mother? Why or why not?

h) Did your mother have any addictions? What were they?

i) Was your mother physically attractive to you?

68) Who of the siblings is most like your father? How? How are you like your father?

69) Who of the siblings is most like your mother? How? How are you like your mother?

70) What kind of relationship did you witness between your mother and father when you were a child?

71) What kind of affection did you observe between your mother and father when you were a child?

72) Do you feel your mother loved your father? How did you come to this conclusion?

73) Do you feel your father loved your mother? How did you come to this conclusion?

74) Who told you about sex? What was your experience with this information?

75) How old were you when you had your first sexual experience? Was it pleasant? Why or why not?

76) Is sex okay for you now? Why or why not?

77) Who made the decisions in your home, your father or mother?

78) Did your mother and father ever argue openly? What did they argue about?

79) How did these arguments progress from beginning to middle to end?

80) How did you feel about these arguments? What did you do when they occurred?

81) Whose side did you take and why?

82) Did your parents agree or disagree on the methods of raising the children? If they disagreed, what did they disagree about?

83) What parent wanted the most for your life? What did your mother want for you and what did she do about what she wanted? What did your father want for you and what did he do about what he wanted? How did you feel?

84) Did any other people ever live with your family? Describe him/her/them and your relationships to them.

ADDITIONAL INFORMATION

85) Relax and allow your mind to recall three early memories prior to nine years of age. Do not judge the intensity of each memory. Allow the memories to appear on the screen of your mind one at a time. What

age were you during each memory? What happened in detail? How did you feel at the time of the memory?

86) Did you have any re-occurring dreams as a child? What were they? How did you feel at the time of the dream?

87) What was your favorite fairy tale or story as a child? What character did you relate to the most intensely? Why?

88) Who were your heros? Why?

89) If you could be any animal right now, what would that animal be and why?

90) What was your concept of God as a child?

91) What is your concept of God now?

92) Close your eyes and imagine yourself in a white room. There are white walls, a white floor and a white ceiling. You are in the room alone and there are no windows or doors. Write three words that describe how you feel in this room.

93) What were your thoughts about money as a child? How did you obtain money? What did you do with money?

94) What do you believe about money now?

95) If you put a neon sign above the door of your family of origin to let people know what to expect inside of the house, what would the sign say?

96) If you could design your life right now with no limits, what would your life be like for you? There is only one condition; you must be willing to live what you design.

What The 96 Questions Mean To You

The process of determining your belief system is much like putting together a jig-saw puzzle. The information in the first 22 chapters serves as a "board," or foundation, upon which you can construct your puzzle. The answers to the 96 questions are the individual pieces of the puzzle that you will be placing upon the "board." Each piece must be placed in a very specific way, since the exact position of each piece will determine how the total picture emerges.

During the process of interpreting your answers, please be gentle with yourself. There is no need to try to understand all of your life in one day. If the explanation to a specific question confuses you, or it does not seem to apply to your life at the present time, simply set the question and answer aside like you would a piece of a real jig-saw puzzle that doesn't quite fit. At a later time, when the piece seems to fit, place it into the overall scenario of your life.

While interpreting your life, remember to apply the basic tools of *LifeScripting* to the process. It is also helpful to keep in mind the questions that will assist you in reframing your experiences. These questions are:

- Why was I given this experience?
- Can I change what happened?
- What is right about this picture?
- What did this situation teach me?
- Who are the teachers in this memory?
- What did they teach me?
- How can I serve others with what I have experienced?

As you analyze your answers to each of the 96 questions take the time to determine how the information applies to your life at present, and also how it has related to your life experiences in the past. Once you comprehend how the answer to each question has become a part of your belief system, then take the next step and begin to use the information to help determine your future behavioral choices.

Each question and answer will contain examples to assist you in understanding how to apply the information to your daily life. Be aware that the examples are given only as a means of assisting you in learning how to apply your answers to your personal life. No two lives are the same. Your life, therefore, can only be interpreted by your perceptions of your experiences. Your perceptions are what determine your personal behavior. Look to each word in your answers for precise information about yourself. Ask yourself, "How are my answers similar to who I am and how I perceive the world today?"

At first, the process of understanding and interpreting your answers may seem awkward. But as the process unfolds it will become easier and, over time, automatic. Ultimately, you will be able to interpret your life beyond the 96 questions in this book. The goal of *LifeScripting* is for you to look to your life, not to a book, for who you are and where you are headed. The end result for you will be true empowerment from within.

LifeScripting Questions Explained

As you answered the *LifeScripting* questionnaire, you noticed four highlighted sections. Each section addressed an overall belief that was formed during your childhood. Each of the questions within the section combines to form the specific pieces of data that contributed to your basic core beliefs. On the following pages, each overall belief will be explained, then each contributing piece of that belief will be addressed.

Pay close attention to any questions answered, "I don't know." These are specific areas where you may find yourself unable to understand your adult behavior. The answer "I don't know" is similar to someone attempting to access a particular file on a computer and discovering a blank screen because that file does not exist. A LifeScripting example of this would be: you are a woman answering the question, "Where was your father at the moment of your birth?" and you answered, "I don't know." As an adult, you will find yourself feeling, at the deepest levels, that you "do not know" where men are for you when you are making major life choices, analyzing relationships, trying to solve problems, etc.

Keep in mind that no single question or answer represents the entirety of your beliefs. There can be several questions that contribute to a specific belief. For example, you will learn that your overall belief about men, regardless of whether you are a man or a woman, came from your belief about your biological father. This belief about men was developed as a result of more than one interaction with your father. To help you understand this concept, remember that within the 96 questions there were many questions about your father. More than one question was necessary since your relationship with your father plays a major part in determining who you are. Some of the questions about your father included: Where was your father at your birth? What were your interactions with your father as a child? How did you see him as a person? Did he say I love you? etc. This data about your father, when combined, determines the belief you formed about men. It is, therefore, important to realize that focusing on just one question and one answer to determine the complete picture of your life, could create a distorted view of your total beliefs. To have the deepest experience with *LifeScripting*, remember that each and every piece of your life contributes to all that you are and all that you will become.

While interpreting your answers to the 96 questions it is important to remember that you will generally behave in either the same or opposite manner of your childhood experiences. If the childhood situation was pleasant, then your tendency will be to repeat the situation as an adult. If the situation was difficult for you as a child, then your adult tendency may be to push the situation away. Another option, if the situation was difficult, would be to bring the same situation into your adult life in an attempt to fix the past for the child. Looking at your present behavior will assist you in understanding the specific contract you formed with the child you were. The goal of *LifeScripting* is to simply identify your present behavior in order to assist you with conscious choices for your future.

When you are initially attempting to understand the dynamics of your past, sometimes it is helpful to draw a picture of the people who were involved in each significant past event. By drawing the characters as they were in any given scene, it becomes easier to imagine what the people involved in the experience might have been thinking and feeling at the time of the event. This process will greatly assist you in reframing your experiences not only for yourself, but for others.

A drawing of your birth could be as simple as:

This example is a mom with a baby in womb (you) and a dad. Add brothers and sisters or any other important characters as they pertain to your family at the time of your birth.

Your drawings can be any expression you desire. My drawings are often as simple as circles with the initials of the characters in them. With your drawings as a guide, imagine, as the questions unfold, what was happening for you the child at the time of the experience. Also imagine what the child would have said if the child could have spoken about what they were feeling and thinking. An additional benefit to this exercise is to imagine what each person in the past situation was thinking and feeling.

Before studying the explanations of the 96 questions, be aware that your story speaks to you and only you. The questions, explanations, and examples are provided only as guidelines to assist you in interpreting your own life. The beginning questions are more intense in their presentation of information than the later questions. This is necessary to initially assist you in learning how to interpret a belief. As the questions unfold, you will find yourself almost knowing the meaning of the question before you read the interpretation. By the end of the 96 questions, you will have become proficient at interpreting your life events. You will also be able to assist others in discovering more about themselves by asking them the same questions.

YOUR BIRTH

What Is The World Like For You

The information you gathered by answering questions 1-19 (which pertained to your birth) will give you an overview of your beliefs about the world, and how you perceive you fit into the overall process called life. In short, this section creates for the child the point of view for "What is this world like for me?" The formation of this belief began as early as conception. As an embryo, you registered perceptions from your surroundings and formed impressions about life. While a fetus, the fact that you did not have developed brain cells or reasoning ability is irrelevant to your belief system formation. You will recognize this to be true, as question by question your early beliefs unfold, and you begin to recognize how these beliefs apply to your present life.

QUESTIONS 1-19

1) What do you know about your birth?

This question will help you understand how you feel about life in general and the role you believe you are to play. It is the basis for how you approach the world. Your answer to this question forms your belief for what you feel you know, or need to know, in your private and public life.

If the baby you were could have spoken at the time of your birth the baby would have expressed what the world appeared to be like at that moment. The story of your birth is uniquely yours and it provides you with information about your life experience and your future life choices. Therefore, the interpretation of your personal answer to this question is what is valuable for you. The following examples are provided only to assist you in how to possibly interpret your unique answer.

Examples Of Answers

A) "I know nothing, I was never told anything." Most often this person will feel, at a deep level, that he does not "know" what others "know" and that he is never quite given the information needed. Conversely, he may have a deep need to know everything about important situations and may spend great amounts of time and energy seeking out or asking for data. (Remember, the adult will do the same or opposite behavior based upon the situation.)

Reframed: This individual will either become a person who does not question life and does not require deep understanding of situations, or will become a person with an insatiable need to know the details of any important life situation. Both behaviors have value in life, if they are positioned correctly. The first behavior works well in a position where the person is directed by others. The second behavior works well in a position where the person would seek out information for, and coordinate the details of, a company.

B) This person answers the question, "What do you know about your birth?" with only data such as the time, date, and location of her birth. This adult will place primary importance on the basic details of life. Details such as where do I live and where do I work, must be settled before she can relax and branch out in life. When entering a new situation, this person will tend to be more concerned about the basic details of the situation, and less concerned about knowing the people involved in the situation.

C) If an elaborate story about the entire event of birth is told, take the parts of the story and see where they fit in the behavior of the adult. For example, Janet was born in the middle of a tornado and the hospital was spared. Mom, Dad, and all personnel were very concerned. As an adult, Janet finds herself in situations where everyone around her is in some kind of turmoil, but her life is always calm amidst the stress of others. Remember, when interpreting the result for the adult, look at what the child was doing in the situation. The child in this case was fine and simply approaching birth. The people experiencing and viewing Janet's birth were the ones in stress. Reframed: This event has created an individual who can and does handle stress in a very calm manner. People look to Janet to be the calm force within stressful situations.

Another example of an elaborate story that will assist you in understanding how detailed this question can be, is to view the birth of Cathy. Two weeks before Cathy's due date, her uncle had a tragic boating accident that resulted in his drowning. Cathy's mother, because of her grief, went into labor and Cathy was delivered early. Cathy was taken to her uncle's funeral. She became the beautiful reminder of new life amid the sadness. Imagine Cathy being passed around and admired as people were crying and grieving. If baby Cathy could have talked, what would she have said about this event? What belief would the event be forming? Cathy's adult behavior vividly portrays the belief of the child. As an adult, Cathy frequently finds herself in situations where others seem to be dying in some way. They are either dying emotionally, financially, or physically. In these situations, Cathy always assumes the role of saviour. Her presence and efforts become the reasons others are okay. However, this approach to life has caused Cathy much stress since she's always felt responsible for fixing everyone. When she looked at this event through the eyes of *LifeScripting,* she reframed it as a gift from the classroom of her childhood. She realized that one of her many jobs in life was to lovingly provide for others during their times of sadness and grief. Her role is to assist them in once again seeing the beauty of life. She also realized that in her private world she needed to recognize and avoid the type of relationships that involve troubled or dependent people.

D) "I was adopted. My adoptive parents told me my biological mother was unmarried and young. Her parents insisted she give me up for adoption." Because this individual's biological parents were absent, this person will have a sense of wondering where he really belongs in life. This concept can be more clearly understood if you put words to this newborn's perception at birth. When the baby was taken away from the mother the baby most likely would have said, "Where are my mother and father? Who are these loving strangers holding me?" For further insights into the resulting behavior of this child, add any details to this adoptive story which may have impacted the inner world of the baby. Since the biological mother relinquished her baby because of pressure from her parents, this person will tend to exhibit one of two behaviors: 1) The individual would easily give up and believe others could readily discard him. 2) He will never give in to the requests of others and stand tall for the child who was given away.

Reframed: This individual could realize that nothing in life is an accident and believe he was placed in the perfect environment for his learning. He could also know that others will always be there in times of need, just as his adoptive parents were there for him. Ultimately, he may realize his internal confusion about human connection could be directed toward a connection greater than that which is experienced on a human level.

The beliefs and behavior that result from Question 1 are as individual as the stories contained on each questionnaire. Your answer contains the beginning of your view of the world and your relationship to it. Look at your answer and ask, "How does this information relate to my belief about life? How does it relate to how I interact in my life?" Use the information you gain about yourself from this question and apply it to understanding your past behavior and future choices.

2) **Were you full term? Were you premature or late? What were the circumstances?**

This question involves your sense of time, and being on time.

If you were born full term, you will tend to arrive on time to events with little stress. If you were late, your natural tendency is to be late. If you were premature, you are either early for events or you have a need to always decide for yourself as to when you will arrive, and/or when you will complete a project. If you were induced, you may dislike being pushed by anyone or anything.

There are exceptions to everything, but the specific details of the birth always contain the answers. For example, Bob was always early for events. The assumption was that he was a premature baby, but in truth, Bob was a late baby.

Since he was behaving opposite to his actual birth, he decided to ask his mother for more information about the situation. She said that at that time she was concerned about him being late. Consequently, she talked to him in womb saying, "Hurry up and be born, I'll be much happier when you are born." Bob is now early for events to please others. If left to his own clock, he would take his time and be late just like the baby was late.

Place yourself in positions in life where your belief and behavior about time will create balance for you. If you were a late baby, realize that you will work best in a job that does not require precise time frames. If there is a need for you to be on time, realize the stress this may cause you, and adequately plan so you can be on time. If you were born on time, then place yourself in positions where time frames are important. If you were premature, your ability to control your own time is an important consideration when deciding employment options.

3) How long was labor? If you do not know, what would you guess?

The length of your labor has to do with how long you labor over issues, problems, projects, events, etc. If your labor was long and difficult, you will tend to make projects long and difficult. If labor was short and fast, you will do things quickly with very little labor. If labor was normal, you will do assignments and projects in the allotted time with no stress about completion. If there was no labor because of a planned C-section, you will want to be in situations where labor is not required. If you do not know how long your labor was, you may feel tension when deciding how long it should take to complete a task.

Reframed: If you are on a team or involved in a project, look to the gift of your labor for your contribution to the team. Those who had long labors have endurance when it is needed. Short labored individuals are the people who can complete projects quickly when necessary. If you do not know how long labor was, you can easily take instructions about when to complete a project. You will also follow through on a schedule once you are briefed and directed. If you did not know how long labor was for you, you can gain insight into the possible answer by simply watching your past behavior patterns in the area of laboring over issues and events. Remember, the adult is behaving in direct response to the child's experience.

4) **Were there any complications during the pregnancy or your birth? What were they?**

This question addresses the area of complications in your life and your reactions to them. If there were no complications during your pregnancy or birth, then you desire a life with few, if any, complications. If there were complications during your mother's pregnancy or your birth, the same types of complications will appear in your adult life.

For example:

A) Your mom became toxic and they were concerned about you because of this condition. As an adult, you tend to find yourself in places where the situations around you feel like they are toxic. If you were healthy in the womb and not affected by your mom's toxic condition, then you will face intense situations but always find yourself okay in the end. If the opposite scenario was true and you were affected by your mom's toxic condition, as an adult you will tend to get involved in situations where the behavior of others will influence you in a negative way.

B) Mom was in a car accident in which you were pressed against the steering wheel of the car. You felt the jolt and felt Mom's tension and concern for your life. As an adult, you are extremely cautious and find yourself surrounded by people who are constantly concerned about you. Reframed: You can now recognize the types of situations in your life causing the 1+1s that = 2 in the area of personal complications. With this knowledge, you can now position yourself where your behavior can best serve yourself and others.

C) A baby is born with the help of forceps. Think what this was like for the baby. If the baby could talk, the baby would say, "Stop pulling me and pushing me at the same time." This adult will tend to over-react to being pushed or pulled by others in his life. He needs to put himself in places, for the love of the child, where being pushed or pulled by others is not a part of a daily routine. Also note that this individual can and will deliver if pushed or pulled, however, he will tend to become stressed in the process.

D) A baby is born in the breech position. As an adult, this person does things different from the norm. This adult will seem to do things almost upside down and backwards. She may at times believe she is slower than the average person at grasping concepts because she only arrives at conclusions after much thought and deliberation. The reason for this behavior can be understood when we look at what was going on at birth for the breech baby. Breech babies usually have more of a struggle with the birth process. They are born feet first and eyes last. They see things only after much time and effort has been expended. Their feet must first be solidly on the ground before they can "see" the picture. Reframed: Breech babies are the people on a team who look at things different from others on the team. They can and will give a whole new perspective to a situation. They do not routinely accept life as it is presented to them. They are more deliberate and precise. They also tend to have a script of, "I'll do it my way."

E) The exact circumstances surrounding the birth of a C-section baby are what will determine the behavior of the adult. If a C-section baby was involved in a long, stressful labor before the C-section occurred, as an adult he will tend to get involved in laborious and stressful situations. He will also tend to feel he is not okay during these situations. This adult will also expect quick solutions after long labor. This occurs because the C-section caused a quick solution to the long labor of the baby. If the C-section was a planned event to keep the baby from facing stress, then this adult will look for someone to intervene on his behalf. He will want others to make decisions that result in a stress free life for him.

An interesting note: C-section babies tend to love water. They take long showers and baths and generally love the pool or jacuzzi. It seems they want to go back to the water of the womb since leaving the womb was a very abrupt experience for them.

Additional Information

If the complications of your birth were with your mother and not with you, then life will tend to be complicated around you rather than because of you. If the complications of your birth were with you, then it will seem that you complicate things and issues. Others may also see you as the reason for their complications. Reframed: Are you someone who can handle complications because that is what you learned through the child's experience? How can you take your ability to handle stress and apply it to your family or work situation? If you are someone who did not have complications at birth, you will experience few complications in your adult world. How can you consciously add this positive energy to your family and the world in which you live?

5) **Was there any anesthetic used during the birth process? Did this anesthetic affect you, the baby? Were there any drugs used during pregnancy?**

The answer to this question will help you understand the need to use, or not use, outside sources or comfort when life is stressful for you.

If there were no drugs used during your mother's pregnancy or delivery, you will not have a tendency to seek the use of drugs or other escape alternatives to avoid the reality of life.

If drugs were used you will, at times, have a feeling of wanting something, or someone, to take away "the pain." The tendency for you to want to escape when you are stressed or facing life decisions could also be present. This does not mean you will necessarily be a drug user. It simply means that the tendency to avoid pain and stress with alternative methods will be present.

If specific drugs were used during your mother's pregnancy, or at your birth, then it is advisable to learn about the effects of these drugs and realize what part they could play in your life. Educating yourself and making healthy choices based upon that information will help guide and empower you. It is also advisable to determine if any family members had issues with drugs or alcohol since this tendency could be genetically passed from generation to generation. Knowledge and awareness will provide valuable insights for your future decisions.

6) **What time of day were you born? What is your favorite time of day?**

Your favorite time of day is the time each day when the world feels just right for you. This favorite time is usually the time of day when you were born if no anesthetic was used.

If anesthetic was used during your birth process and it affected you, then the time of day you were born is usually the time of day you feel most groggy. Your favorite time, or at least your most awake time of day, will be the time when the baby emerged from the effects of the drugs. If you have a time of day that is always groggy for you, and it correlates with your birth time, the chances of anesthetic being used are extremely high.

If you know your favorite time of day and the details of your birth, you can reframe each day to maximize the best usage of your time. For example, if you were born in the morning and no anesthetic was used, do the majority of your production in the morning. If, however, you know you have a groggy time of day because of anesthetic used at your birth, then at that time of day either take a break or realize you will need to push yourself because your internal timing is off.

Alice is an example of this. She was born at 8:10 a.m. under heavy anesthetic. Every day she wakes up groggy and does not fully awaken to life until about 5:00 p.m. (probably the time the baby awoke). Alice functions best with a job that involves an evening shift because she performs to the best of her ability at that time of day.

7) **Were you nursed? For how long? Were there any events surrounding your nursing process? Example, did your mother want to nurse you, was she relaxed, etc? If you were not nursed, what was the reason?**

This question has to do with your feelings about intimacy. It also has to do with your ability to achieve intimacy. The dynamics involved in the answer to this question result in major consequences and behavior for the adult. If you remember the story of Eddie in Chapter 5, you will begin to recall the impact of nursing and bonding. During nursing all five senses are receiving information. The baby and the mother have a connection that is indescribable, particularly if the mother is positive about the process. This event creates a deep sense of oneness between the baby and the mother, and is, therefore, the future connection to intimacy. Intimacy is best defined as one's ability to see, feel, and experience the presence of love with another. Intimacy includes the ability to feel you are loved by another, as well as the ability to give love to another. This process creates not just intimacy in committed relationships, it also creates intimacy regarding the love of others.

I believe that one of the basic reasons for the over-abundance of self-help books which attempt to assist us in finding intimacy with ourselves and others stems from the fact that for several decades the nursing process was taken away from most mothers. If the babies born to these mothers could have spoken at the time of their birth, and in the immediate hours that followed, they would have said, "Where is my mother? Someone hold me! Where do I fit?" These babies are now part of a generation desperately searching for the self. They are both reading and writing the books that attempt to solve the very issues that were spawned from an era where nursing was many times absent from the birthing process. The popular books that contain subjects such as *Who am I? How do I find love? How do I get him/her to commit? Why do I feel alone when I am with someone?* etc., can all be placed under the title "*Were You Nursed*?" And if you were nursed, was it a loving and connected process?

If intimacy has been an issue for you, like it has been for so many, you should now have greater insights into the dynamics you have been experiencing in this area of your life. Remember, there are no accidents, and even supposing there were, your life is as it is. In any case, reframing this experience is the gift that can best empower your life regarding your feelings about intimacy.

Reframed: If you were nursed and it was a connected process, then you have the capacity to experience closeness and intimacy with others. You can also give the gift of connection to others at the deepest of levels. If you were not nursed, you now understand why the feeling of being close may have alluded you, regardless of your intent. Perhaps one of the reasons you were with a mother who did not nurse you is so you would search for "self," and as a result learn to connect to more than yourself. You can share this connection with others because you understand how someone could feel less than connected in her life.

It is helpful for you to look at the details of your personal nursing process so you can have a clearer understanding of your adult behavior. The following stories of clients will provide you with insights that may assist in your personal interpretation.

A) Jack was concerned because he only felt connected within a relationship for about three months. He said, "After three months the relationship feels like it just dries up." When we reviewed Jack's nursing experience, we learned that it contained the exact dynamics of his relationships with women. His mother nursed him for three months and then her milk totally dried up. As a result, Jack lives that dynamic over and over in his interactions with women. Knowing this, Jack now recognizes what causes what and experiences relationships that last beyond three months. He accomplishes this by negotiating with the person every three months for an additional three months of connection. This example is not to imply that the ending of nursing will always create time frames around endings of relationships. However, it does imply that any intense dynamic related to the nursing process has the potential to affect behavior. In this case, the situation felt like an abrupt ending for Jack, and he consequently formed the belief that women abruptly go away in three months.

B) Another example of confusion resulting from nursing is the case of Rose, the baby of a mother who consented to nursing her because it was "the thing" to do. As a result, Rose was nursed in the arms of a mother who was annoyed by the entire process. She was also with a mother who did not want a child. As an adult, Rose believes others do things for her only because they feel they must. During intimate moments, she also believes the other person is not really there for her. With this insight about her nursing process, Rose can now choose one of several behaviors. She can continue believing people are not there for her and experience that result. Or she can find, for the child, someone who is truly there for her. When this occurs, she can intentionally create bonding with the person to fill the need of the child who never felt bonded. This "right" person can be found by asking specific questions of those she dates. Rose needs to ask if the person was nursed and if his mother wanted that experience. She also needs to ask if he was wanted by his mother and father. If the person answers yes to these questions, that person has the capacity to form close relationships. Rose can then be assured that connection will always be present in her relationships. The next step for Rose is to ask the question, "How can my nursing experience serve me and others?" The answer is contained in Rose's feelings about her life. Now that Rose is aware of what connection and intimacy truly are, she will never again settle for a relationship without these ingredients. She also realizes she can assist others who feel disconnected by helping them find the source of their true feelings.

If You Were Not Nursed

If you were not nursed, it is helpful to understand the reasons. Discovering the reasons will provide you with insights concerning your feelings about your connection to others. For example:

If your mother did not nurse you because she had worked outside the home, you may tend to feel others have to take care of their needs before being there for you.

If your mother did not nurse you because of social pressure, you may feel people close to you tend to listen to others before they acknowledge your needs.

If your mother did not nurse you because your dad didn't want her to do so, this dynamic could create in you a feeling that women must obey men at all cost.

If your mother did not nurse you because it was easier to use a bottle, this could create a feeling in you of not wanting to inconvenience anyone. It could also create behavior that prompts you to always want to take the easy way out.

Remember, in *LifeScripting* it is important to look for the possibility of the opposite behavior occurring. For example, if your mother didn't want to nurse you simply because it was inconvenient, that may create the need for you to become a person who always recognizes and takes care of the needs of others. This opposite behavior occurs because no one recognized or acknowledged your needs. As a result, you learned the feeling of separation. Because you understand the dynamics of separation, you can easily assist others in not feeling separated.

Additional Information About Nursing

Bonding can also occur with a bottle fed baby if she is held in a connected manner. The baby's head must be turned toward the mother so eye contact can occur as the baby is fed. Eye contact for the first two months is crucial. Also vital for bonding is a heart to heart connection.

If you feel you were not nursed and bonding did not occur, there is still hope when you reframe your experience. Realize what the experience teaches you and what you can share with others as a result. Also know that there are processes that can assist you in creating the bonding connection. One of these processes involves eye contact. Since eye contact creates bonding, it can help you feel connected. Start with yourself by looking into a mirror. Look deeply into your eyes. Spend time looking into your eyes as if looking into the eyes of a baby, sending the same love you would send to a child. Do this as frequently as necessary until you feel deeply connected to yourself. Once this connection occurs, you will begin to notice that you feel more connected to others. You will also notice that eye contact with others is much easier for you.

Section III of this book will also help you enhance your ability to bond by outlining several additional exercises to assist you in obtaining a deeper connection to yourself. I know these processes work because I have had countless reports from individuals regarding their new found ability to feel and express intimacy after completing the exercises.

8) How soon after birth were you held and who was the first person to hold you?

This question assists you in understanding your need to quickly connect, or your frustration when you feel you have to wait for what you want.

The first person to hold you and have eye contact with you is the person you will be most connected to in life. This is particularly true if that connection was positive. If the connection was not positive, then this is the person with whom you may have the most difficulty forming a connected relationship.

If because of circumstances you were not held by your mom or dad after birth, those specific circumstances will appear in the same form throughout your life. For example, if you were born ill or premature and were isolated in an incubator for a period of time, throughout life you may find yourself feeling isolated from your loved ones. You will tend to feel this isolation even in the presence of others. To understand why this feeling could occur, take a moment and speak for the baby. What would a baby say after birth if the baby were immediately separated from his significant others? The baby would probably say, "Where is my mom? Where is my dad? Why am I with strangers away from my mom's familiar heartbeat? Why do I feel so alone even though I am being held? Who are these people and why are they touching me and using all of this equipment on me?" With these questions as the basis for a belief system about life, it is easy to understand why this adult may tend to feel isolated. The amount of time the baby was in the incubator will also determine the length of time the adult will feel disconnected. As an adult, an incubator baby may also tend to need private time when experiencing stress. This occurs because the baby was away from its significant others during the stressful incubation period.

Reframed: This adult would be excellent at working alone. He would also benefit from time alone and may find himself making his best decisions in isolation. On the other hand, he may do the opposite behavior and dislike being alone, finding himself unable to function without assistance. Either method of behavior can be used for personal empowerment, particularly when the individual understands why he does what he does and places himself correctly in life.

9) **Were you a wanted pregnancy? How do you know or not know? Were you wanted by Mom? Were you wanted by Dad?**

This question pertains to your feelings of being wanted in the world.

If you were a wanted child, you will have a general feeling of being wanted in the world. If you were wanted by both your mom and dad, you will feel wanted by both men and women. If you felt unwanted by both Mom and Dad, you will have a sense of not being wanted anywhere. For example, you go to apply for a job and regardless of your preparation and training, you have a deep feeling that "they" will not want to hire you. If you felt unwanted only by one parent, then that is the gender you believe will not want you. For example, if you felt Dad didn't want you, in situations involving men you will feel unwanted. If you felt Mom didn't want you, in situations involving women you will feel unwanted.

10) **Were you a planned pregnancy? Were you planned by both Mom and Dad? If you do not know what would you guess?**

This question provides information about your belief in the area of planning your life as well as your belief regarding the need to be involved in a plan.

If you were planned, you will look for and need a life plan. You will also feel most comfortable in work situations that involve long-term plans. When you are involved in a relationship, you will want a plan about the relationship. If you are applying for a job, you will first want to see how you fit into the company's plan. You will also believe you will be hired because you fit into the already existing plan.

If you are a woman and your mom planned you but your dad did not, you will always take charge of any situation involving your life. You will not be dependent upon the assistance of a man. If Mom planned you and you are a man, you will find yourself consulting women about your life plans. The same dynamics apply with regard to men if Dad planned for your birth.

If you were not planned, then you probably have confusion as to what the plan is for your life. You may also do the opposite behavior and become obsessed about a life plan. Unplanned children often become very precise and deliberate in their behavior styles. They want all the details of life in place so they will not surprise anyone or "rock the boat." This behavior is the result of the baby feeling she created stress for her parents. The resulting adult behavior is to avoid inconveniencing anyone.

To know what fits best for your life, look at your answer to this question. Think about the behavior you've had in this area of life and determine how your answer matches your behavior. Reframed: If you need a plan, you are a person who can produce and direct yourself and others in establishing and implementing a plan. If there was not a plan for your pregnancy, you may want to position yourself where a plan is not always required of you. If you were not planned, and as a result have developed great spontaneity, you can use that gift in your interaction with others.

11) Did your mother want a boy or a girl?

This question has to do with your comfort about your gender when interacting with women.

If your mother wanted a girl and you are a girl, you are comfortable about your womanhood and will tend to be comfortable around women. If your mother wanted a girl and you are a boy, you may tend to feel you are not totally accepted by women. You will behave in one of several ways to compensate for this feeling. You could become very "macho" to prove it's okay to be a boy, or you may act somewhat feminine to compensate for Mom's desire for a girl.

If Mom wanted a boy and you are a girl, you may feel you are never quite okay in the eyes of Mom. You may also generalize this feeling to other women. This disconnect from Mom could also cause confusion about yourself since Mom represents to you the beliefs for, "What is a woman?" and "Who am I?" If your mother wanted a boy and you are that boy, then you are comfortable being a man around women.

12) Did your father want a boy or a girl?

This question has to do with your comfort about your gender when interacting with men. If your father wanted a girl and you are that girl, you will have a sense of being comfortable and connected to men in relationship to your femininity. If Dad wanted a girl and you are a boy, you will act out with one of several behaviors. You could tend to be overly masculine to prove to Dad that it is okay to be a boy, or you could attempt to replace the girl he did not have with feminine behavior.

If your father wanted a boy and you are a boy, you will generally have a solid connection to your manhood. If Dad wanted a boy and you are a girl, you will lean toward one of two behaviors. You could become overly feminine to show Dad that being a girl is all right, or you may become a "tom-boy" in order for Dad to have the boy he desired.

The reaction of each parent to your gender is an important factor when understanding how you interface with men and women. Keep in mind that "your story" informs you of the personal beliefs running your behavior and your choices. Additional life experiences with your parents will also add to the basic belief you formed prior to your birth. For example, you are a boy and both your dad and mom wanted a boy, but as you grew in age you did not align with your father and struggled in your interactions with him. Since Dad represents to you "What is a man?" and, "Who am I?" your disconnection to Dad will cause you to feel unsettled inside. Because of this inability to connect to your father, you will in all likelihood commit to becoming the opposite of him.

Please remember it is important to keep all parts of your life experiences in mind when interpreting any one of the questions. Additional circumstances can and will affect the overall picture of your behavior. Approach each piece of your behavior as if it is just that, a "piece" of the puzzle called you.

13) Where was your father at the moment of your birth? If you don't know, where would you guess he was?

If you are a woman, this question provides information about where men are for you, especially when you are making life decisions. If you are a man, this question provides information about where you feel you should be for women, particularly while they are in the process of making life choices.

Dad's presence, or lack of presence, in your life is vital to the formation of your belief about yourself and your relationship to men. Most tend to believe that the mother is the driving force in a baby's life since the baby is formed in her womb and she is, in most instances, the primary care-giver. But the truth is both parents are vital to the child's belief formation since it takes both a man and a woman to create a child. The connection to each parent is, therefore, a connection to half of the self. How you relate to each parent plays a vital role in the perceptions you have of yourself. If you are out of balance with one or both parents, you will forever feel an imbalance within yourself. Additional insight into your parental relationships will be presented in questions 62 through 84.

For Women

If you are a woman, the answer to this question sets the foundation for where you believe men are for you at important moments in your life. Some scenarios that may help clarify this concept include:

A) Dad was in the waiting room, concerned and waiting for the report. As a result of Dad not being in the room at the time of your birth, you will tend to feel men are somewhere close when you need them, but never completely there when you are making decisions about life issues. You will often feel you must make your life decisions alone and report to a man later. Reframed: With this information, you can now understand any past frustration you may have had with regard to any man helping you make your life choices. You also know that you can, and many times will, make life decisions without leaning on a man. However, you can be assured that men will be close, concerned, and waiting with interest for the report about your life.

B) Dad was not at the hospital. As a result, you will tend to feel that men are totally unavailable to you at the times you make life decisions. It is important to understand the reason that Dad was not at the hospital because it will set the pace for why men tend to be unavailable for you at important times in your life. For example, if Dad was at work you could form a belief that a man's work is more important than you are. If Dad was with his friends then you could believe that a man's friends take priority over you in your relationships. If Dad was drinking, then you could find yourself in relationships where a man's habits take him away from important times with you. Reframed: You are your own person. You do not need to look for a man to help when deciding what to do with your life. Realize that this reframed power does not mean you cannot have a loving relationship with a partner. You need only to recognize that you have the ability to stand alone in making your personal life choices.

C) Dad was in the birthing room and supportive of Mom. Because of this connected experience, you will feel men are supportive of you and are involved in your important life events.

With an understanding of the programming this question addresses, it becomes easy to appreciate why many of today's women feel men do not understand them or recognize their needs. For generations, fathers were not allowed to be a part of the delivery process, and much of the time they were not even encouraged to actively participate in the process of the pregnancy. Consequently, female babies were feeling a disconnect to men and male babies were born not understanding how to connect to women. When you comprehend the far reaching effects of the disconnect between fathers and children, the tension between the sexes is much easier to understand. Women fight for equality with the very men they do not believe will be there for them, all because their fathers were not present at birth. This tension is compounded when we realize that men from the same generation of disconnected babies have no idea how to be there for women, because their fathers were not there for their mothers or them at the time of birth. This situation has occurred, not by individual choice, but by the prevailing trend within hospitals to immediately separate babies from their parents. By giving the birth of babies back to the families (as many doctors and hospitals are now doing) a major step can be taken toward the healing of male/female issues. This healing can also lead to a general healing within society.

For Men

If you are a man, where your dad was at the time of your birth represents where you feel you should be for a woman in terms of her decision making and life choices. This belief is formed because Dad represents to you "What is a man?" and therefore, "Who am I to myself and to women?" If Dad was supportive of Mom and at your birth, you will feel this is also your role with women. If Dad was not at your birth, you may find yourself unavailable to women when they are making major decisions. You may also choose the opposite behavior and attempt to always be there for the women in your life. Your adult choices in this area will be determined by your mother's response to your father's absence as well as by your degree of attachment to your mother. For example, if you were deeply attached to your mom and you observed her sorrow about Dad's absence in her life, you could make a commitment to never hurt a woman like your father hurt your mother.

Reframed: When deciding where the dynamics of Dad fit for you, simply look at the information you wrote about your dad and apply it to your life. Ask yourself how this information applies to your behavior. Try to determine how dad has influenced your feelings about yourself. Also ask yourself how you interact with the women in your life based on your perceptions of dad. Use this information for greater self understanding as well as power in deciding future behavior.

14) How was your mother during your pregnancy? If you do not know what would you guess?

Look again at the picture you drew of your mom and dad with you, the baby, inside of your mother. For the entire nine months of your mom's pregnancy, her thoughts, feelings, nutritional balance, stress levels, movement, heartbeat, etc., were your world. How Mom was feeling and what Mom was doing set the pace for your belief about the world and who you are in it.

If the in-womb baby could speak, what would the baby tell you about the world and the environment he was experiencing? How similar is this to your view of the world today? Always remember, adult behavior is either the same or the opposite. The following are some examples of in-womb experiences and how they influence adult behavior:

A) Jeff's mother was calm and looking forward to his arrival. His mother ate correctly and had regular checkups to monitor his progress. She also enjoyed her relationship with Jeff's father. As a result, Jeff requires a calm environment. Jeff also needs to feel he is a part of all that is occurring. He has a routine in his life and experiences very little stress.

B) Stacy was in the womb of a mother who was in total conflict with Stacy's father. Her father drank to excess and when drunk, beat her mother. Stacy's adult life is filled with conflict, and she has found herself in several relationships where she has been beaten by men while they were drunk.

C) David's mother had many physical difficulties during David's entire pregnancy, though David was physically fine during that time. David now finds himself nurturing people who are having physical problems.

D) Julie's mother was emotionally stressed during her pregnancy. Julie finds herself in friendships and relationships that are excessively emotional.

E) Janet, like Julie, had an emotionally stressed mother during her in womb experience. She also saw her mother stressed during her childhood. As a result, Janet made a commitment that this behavior would not be a part of her adult life, and she makes great effort to create a calm and peaceful world for herself and others.

How is your in-womb experience similar to the many and various parts of your adult behavior? Reframed: How can this information and experience serve your life and the life of others?

15) How was your father during your pregnancy? If you don't know what would you guess?

Again, your dad represents the concept of "What is a man?" To a male, this equates to "Who am I?" and "How do I relate to women?" To a female, Dad represents both the belief of "What is a man?" and "What is a man to me?" How Dad reacted and responded during your mother's pregnancy helps set in motion how you interact with men and what you believe about them for the rest of your life.

If you are a woman and Dad was available and attentive during you mother's pregnancy, you will want an available, attentive man in your life. If you are a man and this behavior was present, you will find yourself available and attentive in your relationships with women.

If Dad was working, preoccupied with his life, frequently leaving the pregnancy up to Mom where Mom did not resent his behavior, as a woman you will want a man who takes his work very seriously. If Mom had difficulty with Dad's absence and behavior, then you may find yourself resenting men for not being there for you. If you are a man who experienced these dynamics while in the womb, you may find yourself having the same drive about work as your father. If Mom felt no resentment toward your dad, in your relationships women will accept your work role with no stress. However, if your mom resented your dad's time away from her, then you may find yourself in situations in which the women in your life resent your absence.

To reframe this event just ask, "What has the child's experience created for me, and how can I choose to do the same or the opposite behavior in my life?"

16) How did your mother and father interact with each other during your pregnancy? If you don't know, what would you guess?

How your mom and dad interacted during your pregnancy initiates your belief for "What is a relationship?" Every time your mother and father interacted while you were in your mother's womb, you were there to experience the process. You were also connected to your mother's feelings about your father during these times. After your birth, your role became one of an observer of their relationship rather than a participant.

Some examples of in womb experiences are:

A) Gene's mom and dad were loving and gentle with each other while he was in the womb. Consequently, Gene wants his relationships to be loving and gentle.

B) Nancy's dad and mom shared time together talking and planning. As a result, this is the type of interaction Nancy prefers in her adult relationships.

C) An inmate's father was abusive to her mother while she was in the womb. The abuse was so extensive that at one point he took her mother into the woods and held a gun to her head threatening to kill her. As an adult, this inmate constantly finds herself in abusive relationships. In one relationship, the abuse escalated to the point of having a gun put to her head with the threat of death, just like her mother was threatened by her father while she was in the womb. Reframed: This inmate now knows the kind of men who will cause negative events in her life. Because she can now recognize these men, she has the option of saying no to them. Ideally, she will now choose a man whose behavior is the opposite of her father's. This will insure the safety of the little girl she once was. Because of *LifeScripting,* she also realizes that her father was the teacher who taught her what type of men she is to avoid.

17) Do you know anything about your conception?

If you answered "yes" to this question, you will tend to be an individual who looks for the deepest details of life. The situation of your conception creates a beginning feeling about life, and can add to the details of who you are and why you choose to behave the way you do. For example:

A) Jean knows she was conceived in love. She finds herself most comfortable in loving situations, especially when she is intimate with someone.

B) Holly's mother was having a difficult time becoming pregnant and was instructed to use the temperature method. Her parents were also instructed to use unique physical positions to better insure pregnancy. During a major rain storm, Holly's mother discovered that her temperature was at its correct level and her parents engaged in the instructed, unusual sexual position. Thus, Holly was conceived. As a adult, Holly has often wondered why she finds herself extremely amorous on rainy days, and why she also enjoys and agrees to any physical activity that involves unusual positioning.

C) Robin was conceived while her parents were sleeping in her aunt's bed which her mother described as very lacy, feminine, and beautiful. Robin loves her bed and insists that it be lacy and feminine.

Most people do not know the details of their conception so to answer this question ask yourself, "If I were to guess about my conception what would I guess? How does this answer apply to my life today?"

18) Were you loved at your birth? If so, by whom?

Being loved at birth creates a feeling that the world is a loving place. It also creates a belief that you are connected to the people in your world. If you were loved by both your mother and father, you will feel a deep sense of love from both men and women. Being loved at birth also equates to the love of self. If you felt loved by Mom but not loved by Dad, or vice-versa, the person you felt most loved by will be the person, as well as the gender, with whom you are the most comfortable.

19) **Were there any other family members or friends present or involved in your birth process? Who were they and what was their involvement?**

If there was extended family involved in your birth process and that involvement was positive, then the connection of extended family is important to you. You will feel off balance when there isn't support from others in your family. If, however, the extended family interaction was negative, you will find yourself feeling pressure when interacting with those who comprise your extended family. The exact dynamics of the interactions during your birthing process will tend to be the same as your present experiences. For example:

If your mother's mom was supportive and assisted with your birth at the hospital and at home, you will find yourself with the presence of a supportive female every time you are in need of assistance. If your father's mother was present and created much stress for your mother, you may tend to have stress with your spouse's relatives when you face intense life events.

Integrating The Parts Of Your Birth

You may want to pause at this point and integrate the information you have just been given before moving on to the next portion of the puzzle called you.

To better integrate the parts of your birth, invest some time looking at the overall picture of your present life in terms of the beliefs you have discovered about yourself and the world in which you live. How do the circumstances into which you were born coincide with what you are experiencing as an adult? Take time to realize the gifts in your life as a result of your experiences from childhood.

Recognize how these events have helped you become who you are. Who were your primary teachers and what do you now know because they were in your life? How will you use this information to more wisely choose your future behavior? Will most of your choices be the same, or does opposite behavior seem more appropriate?

Remember, you are the baby and the baby is you. Thus, connection to information from the child can empower and direct your adult choices and behaviors. To not recognize the child is to deny your life. To recognize the child is to connect head/heart, adult/child, and create a conscious and whole human being capable of living at the highest of levels.

The first 19 questions and answers about your birth have relevance to your belief formation for "What is the world like for me?" The next section relates to your interactions with your siblings which formed your beliefs for "Who am I as I interact in the world?" and "Where do I personally fit in the world?"

SIBLINGS AND SELF
Who Are You In The World

Your interactions with your siblings created your beliefs in relation to where you will place yourself with other people. Your siblings were the teachers who helped you understand what to expect from your peers. Remember, beliefs are formed by age six and what you believe is what you will live. It is because of this early belief formation that your childhood brothers and sisters (or lack of them) are the peers from whom you learned the elements of how to be in the world. Consequently, much of your adult life will involve a repetition of the same dynamics you experienced with your siblings during your childhood. Your interactions with your siblings also formed your belief for how the world will accept you as a person.

There are many facets that comprise this portion of your belief system. As you experience questions 20-61, remember your life is a series of puzzle pieces all of which make up the total you. None of the pieces stands alone. They all interlock to form the complete picture called you. It is helpful to approach this portion of the questions as if looking for the qualities that would best create an ideal job description for you. For example, if you feel you are intelligent but not a hard worker, the job that will most effectively utilize your skills will include the use of your mind without manual labor as part of the process. There are multiple skills that will be addressed in this section so it is important to carefully address one question at a time. Once all of the questions have been analyzed, develop an overall view of the information you have acquired about yourself by asking, "If I were to give this person (me) the perfect job, what would that job include?" Be as specific as possible.

When you reframe the entire picture of your childhood and your interactions with your siblings, you will begin to value the incredible gift of these childhood teachers.

Remember, in life we learn from all events. We learn from what we enjoy and from that which is difficult. All experiences provide us with insight for our future choices and behavior. If you enjoyed something as a child, repeating the experience as an adult will give you the same pleasure. Likewise, if you had difficulty with something in childhood, repeating that situation will give you the same disappointing results. Through *LifeScripting,* you have been given the tools which will enable you to reframe any situation and turn it into joy, peace, and a sense of accomplishment. Invest the time necessary to gain insight from each of the questions about yourself and your siblings. If you should find yourself getting tired as you address question after question, take a break and return to the process when you are refreshed. Keep in mind that each and every question provides you with valuable information in a specific area of your life. When all the information from your answers is combined and placed in proper perspective, you will have a deep understanding of your past, present, and future behavioral choices.

If you have no answer to a particular question, you will understand why you may have difficulty or discomfort in that area of your life. It is much like pushing a button on a computer and getting no data on the screen. No data equals no past experiences from which to draw information. If there is no data, then those areas of life are places where you may sense an inability to interact with others or to emphatically decide about life. Take each question seriously regardless of how extensive your answer.

If you are an only child, some of the questions may seem to not apply. However, it is important for you to answer each question even if your answer is, "N/A (not applicable)." You will soon discover the questions you answered in this manner pertain to specific areas where you may have had difficulty relating to others. For example, the question regarding which sibling is most like you has no specific answer since you had no siblings. However, when you examine the meaning of this question, you will discover why you have always felt you are not like anyone else in this area.

If you were not raised with your biological siblings, it is important to look at any interactions you may have had with non-biological siblings as also providing data for how to place yourself in the world.

Remember as you review your answers to questions 20-61, each question is a piece of the picture, not the whole of your personality.

20) What is your birth order? What were the names and ages of your siblings (include yourself)? Were there any deaths? Were there any stillborn babies or miscarriages? Were there any siblings not raised with you?

I have personally come to understand birth order not through reading, but through my experiences with clients. As a result of these experiences, I believe the best way to gain insight into an individual's birth order is to simply ask what his/her position in the family created for him/her. Only through the eyes of the individual comes the belief about him/her fitting into the world. To know about your birth order and the influence it had upon your life, ask yourself the question "What was it like for me to be in my particular family position?" The following information will help you further understand birth order for yourself and others:

A) Drawing a picture of your family is helpful when analyzing your birth order. Pictures of stick people or circles with initials will suffice. You may want to draw solid lines between siblings who got along, and broken lines between siblings who were possibly at odds with each other. Who in your life today is like these childhood characters? How do your interactions with them compare to your childhood interactions? These answers will give you a clear picture of how you tend to position yourself with your peers. It will also give you a picture of how you position yourself in business.

B) Another helpful insight regarding the dynamics of birth order is to imagine what it was like for each child arriving into an already existing family scene. The first child sees life as being only about himself and his parents. The second child has the view that life is about a sibling and parents. The view of the first born about the birth of the second child is very different than the view of the second child about the first. The first child is aware that the second child was not always present in that first child's life. If a third child is born, this child feels that life is about two siblings and parents. The other two siblings know they were in the family first and approach their new sibling with that knowledge. As you add more siblings you can see the added dynamics begin to unfold. Also add to the scenario of the expanding family the changes that have occurred in the thinking and feelings of Mom and Dad as more children are added to the family. Each family member experiences the changes in all other members as the dynamics within the family intensify with each new arrival.

C) To help you understand what it's like to be an "only child," hold up one finger on your hand. How many fingers do you see? That is the underlying script of the only child. The only child has no sibling interaction. As a result, he tends to do best in positions of control and independence. He tends to work well alone or when directing others from a distance. Only children are usually treated in one of two ways by their parents. They are treated either as total adults or as helpless children. The adult the only child becomes will respond to the world in the same way the child was treated.

D) Twins are affected by birth order as well. The first born twin generally takes the role of leader and the second born twin generally takes the role of competitor. If the second born twin outperforms the first born twin, these roles may reverse. The degree of competition between twins is also related to gender. Same sex twins tend to have the same competitive issues as same sex siblings. Twins of the opposite sex tend to have fewer issues about competition. Twins usually have a deeper connection to one another than sequential siblings because they shared the womb.

E) Siblings who are five or more years apart, generally do not have as deep an affect on each other as siblings born closer in age to each other. This happens because they are separated both in school and in their interactions with peers. If the older sibling takes on a caretaker role, he may find himself in that role with others once he becomes an adult. The younger sibling, comfortable with being taken care of, may find that as an adult, he will tend to look for someone else to take care of him. If the older sibling resents the younger child, as an adult he will probably find himself in roles with younger adults who he resents. If the resented child recognizes the resentment from the older sibling, as an adult this individual will feel resentment from others as he interacts in the world.

The combinations are limitless. Only your story will provide you with answers. Remember, what you lived as a child is what you will re-live as an adult.

F) Same sex siblings who are born within a short period of time from each other, will generally feel competitive toward each other. The younger sibling will look to the older sibling and observe how that sibling is getting attention. In all likelihood, she will try to out-do the older sibling in that area. If she succeeds, the older sibling may give up and become the best in another area of life. If the younger sibling cannot overshadow the older sibling, then the younger sibling will tend to give up and become something very different than the older sibling. For example, an older sibling is good in sports and the next same sex sibling attempts to overshadow her. If the second sibling cannot accomplish the task, she may become the opposite of a sports figure, perhaps a computer expert. The same could happen for the older sibling if she is overshadowed. She could give up sports and become involved in computers.

Reframed: The interactions with your siblings established a job description for you in your adult world.

If you were to be involved in sports, computers, art, music, writing etc., then the interactions with your siblings were the perfect interactions to create that reality for you.

G) If there was the death of a child in your family, you need to become aware of what that death created for you while realizing the effect the death had upon your mother and father. If the death occurred before your birth, you may have experienced a feeling throughout your life that you had to be more than yourself to make up for the loss of your deceased sibling. If the sibling who died was the same sex as you, you may feel a double need to perform. If the sibling was of the opposite sex, you may tend to feel that you can never be good enough because after all, you are the wrong gender. If the death occurred after your birth, then ask yourself what memories you have of the sibling and the sibling's death. Recognize from this experience how your life has been altered or influenced.

Many of my clients have reported major life changing perceptions based upon the death of a sibling. For example, Bill was born after the crib death of his sister. Bill is one of four living boys but the only boy born after the death. He has difficulty believing he will ever be good enough and works extra hard to prove his worth and establish his identity. Reframed: Bill knows he will always go the extra mile for others and try to make up for things that others have not completed. He will also do what is necessary to keep those around him from experiencing pain. Another interesting piece of Bill's *LifeScript* comes from the fact that his mother spent much time during his childhood attempting to understand the death of his sister. She believed that the medical answers were insufficient to explain the death of her baby daughter. Bill is now in medical school.

An additional example comes from my life. When I was seven my mother gave birth to my brother Steve. Steve lived for three minutes. The affect of Steve's short life on mine has been profound. As a child I wanted Steve in my life so I would have someone to nurture. His death created a physical void for me, and yet at the same time opened my life to a much greater spiritual vastness. Steve became my angel who was always there for me and oftentimes became my aide to a greater awareness of God. To this day, I wear a baby ring on a chain around my neck in honor of his presence in my life.

H) Miscarriages and stillborns are viewed in birth order much the same as a death. The affect upon your life will be a result of the timing of the event. If the event occurred before your birth, the effect will be different than if it occurred after your birth. Much of the affect upon you will be based upon your mother and father's reactions to the experience.

I) If you had one or more siblings who were not raised with you, it is important to recognize their affect upon your life. Were you connected to them in any way? Did you feel the loss of their presence? Were you okay with them not being in your life?

The story of Jennifer will help you appreciate the significance of an absent sibling. When Jennifer was seven, her sister Tracy was born. Jennifer loved Tracy and spent hours nurturing and taking care of her. At the time of Tracy's birth, Jennifer's mother and father were separated. Tracy's father was not Jennifer's father. Jennifer's mother and father were arranging a reconciliation and one of the conditions of their reunion was that Jennifer's mother give up Tracy. Jennifer was totally unaware of this situation and was sent to her father with the promise that her mother would soon join them. When her mother arrived, she did not have Tracy. Jennifer could not believe her sister was not with her mother.

She was informed that Tracy had been placed with another family. Jennifer begged her mother to go and get Tracy. She promised that if Tracy came back she would care for her and be the mother. Jennifer was told Tracy would never return. Throughout her youth Jennifer longed for her baby sister and vowed to someday find her.

Reframed: This event, though traumatic, has helped create the beautiful adult Jennifer has become. As an adult, Jennifer often intervenes for the unification of siblings. She also diligently works to connect parents and children. As a result of her childhood need to raise Tracy, Jennifer also had a deep desire to have a child and raise her baby alone. By doing this, she could prove to the child she was that she could have truly been Tracy's mother. Jennifer is now the wonderful single mother of a beautiful little girl. Jennifer proves on a daily basis that she alone can lovingly raise a child. She does this not only for her biological child, but for the little girl she was. (The child who was never given the chance to care for Tracy.) Shortly after the birth of her daughter, Jennifer's ongoing search for Tracy ended. Through great effort she and Tracy were reunited. They have become great friends as adults.

Your birth order position has a major influence on how you position yourself with your peers both in business and in your private world. This awareness can assist you in all of your future life choices concerning personal placement.

21) **Who of your siblings is most different from you? How is he/she different?**

This question is not designed for you to describe your sibling, but rather to help you define yourself. When describing what is opposite about another, you are really defining your own behavior. For example, if you said, "I am opposite of my brother George because he is insensitive and withdrawn," you are saying you are sensitive and open.

Look at the picture you verbally portrayed of the sibling who is the most different from you and recognize what it says about the qualities you believe you possess. If you said, "I was different from all my siblings," then you will tend to feel different from the people around you in most areas of your life.

If you were an only child, the fact that you cannot answer this question provides you with data about how you interact in life. Because there was no comparison with others as a child, you will tend not to evaluate yourself based on your interactions with others. You will only evaluate yourself from your own perspective.

22) Who of your siblings in most like you? How is he/she like you?

Once again, this question adds information to the unfolding picture of yourself. The qualities you listed that were like you with regard to your sibling are pieces of who you believe you are. When you say you are like someone, you are really making a statement about your own character.

If your answer to this question was, "No one was like me," then you will tend to feel set apart and different from others.

If you are an only child, you will again find yourself without an answer to this question. The lack of an answer suggests that you will generally not evaluate yourself in terms of others. You may find yourself most comfortable standing alone.

23) Briefly describe your other siblings as you saw them as children. Did you like or dislike them when you were a child?

The description of your siblings helps you understand what types of people with whom you will find yourself interacting in the world. People comparable to your siblings will appear time and again in your life. Your brothers and sisters provide you with the basis to determine what you like and what you don't like about the people in your world.

How many people in your present world are like your siblings? Who triggers you and how can you best reframe these experiences when they occur?

If a particular sibling is still an active part of your adult world, you may not have a need to replace him/her with someone similar. If siblings are not active in your life, you will probably find people very much like them as replacements. These replacements will appear either at work or among your friendships. For example:

A) Linda had an older brother who dominated and controlled her by threatening to tell on her for the smallest of things. Linda seems to always position herself with male supervisors who hold the smallest things over her head and who threaten to go to her boss if she does not conform.

B) Sam had an older sister who took care of him and always included him in her activities. As an adult, Sam is very comfortable around women and finds himself in situations with women supervisors who assist him and who always include him in their plans.

24) What kind of child were you prior to the age of nine? Give as much detail as possible to describe the character of the child you were.

The child you described in this question makes up the deepest part of the adult you've become. Every characteristic is a vital part of the real you. Look at each word you used to describe yourself as a child and apply that information to the adult you are. Spend the time necessary to understand all the facets of your personality that are parts of this child. Are you honoring this child in your life? A major *LifeScripting* principle is: the more stress you have in your life, the further away you are from the child you were. This distance creates your stress because it keeps you from utilizing the valuable lessons learned in your childhood. To reduce the stress in your life, simply return to the information from the experiences of the child.

Children are wonderfully different and those differences are their gifts to themselves and others. It is in remembering the child and honoring the lessons of the past that you will find direction and purpose for your life. Only the child knows who you really are and what you are truly designed to become. Reframe each part of your description of the child by asking, "What did the child want me to know through my childhood experiences? How can I become the vehicle for the child's learning?"

For example:

A) Derek said, "I was a quiet child. Not because I was afraid but because I saw things from an inside perspective. I was happiest in my room reading and being alone. I had one close friend. I loved playing outside by myself." Derek is an adult who will do best in a quiet environment not only at home but at work. He can be left alone and will be comfortable with just one friend.

B) Kathy said, "I was an active child. I loved having a lot of people around. I enjoyed creating activities such as carnivals for the neighborhood kids. I would invent ways to make money and then turn that money into new ways to make more money. I loved people and I loved life." As an adult Kathy creates many projects that involve money. She is active both in the world and at home. She feels best when she shares her energy with many people. If Kathy were ever to be confined in a highly structured office or in a closed environment she would experience great stress in her life.

C) Myles said, "I was a happy child and full of life until my parents divorced when I was seven. It seemed after the divorce I felt sad and didn't seem to fit anywhere." Myles now finds himself entering situations enthusiastically then notices drastic changes in increments of seven (seven years, seven months, seven days). The time element of seven tends to happen for Myles because he was seven when the dramatic event of divorce occurred. Myles would do well in places were there is great energy needed for a defined period of time, like starting a business, for example. Once the business is established, he may want to move to the next project. He would also do well helping others who are experiencing life changes. Because of his experience, Myles has skills to help people develop new perspectives by helping them understand how to remain focused while experiencing change.

Again, remember that the story of your childhood contains the details for your adult life. The more you can remember and write about the child you were, the more you will know about the adult you have become.

25) What was school like for you?

This question will help you understand several aspects of your life - firstly, how to approach education, and secondly, to recognize how to position yourself in the business world.

When we send our children to school, it is much like sending the adult to the world of business. The event of school is usually the first time the child leaves home to enter the larger environment of the world. The child's interaction in this setting will greatly determine his future interaction in the world beyond his home. I sometimes see children going to school and visualize them carrying a briefcase instead of a lunch pail.

Every detail you wrote about your school experience has meaning in your adult life. The events that particularly stand out for you about school will re-appear in your adult life at some point in time. If they have not already repeated themselves, look to the future for the re-appearance of these events. To assist you with your interpretation of the overall effect of school on you the child, look to the following examples.

Those who saw school as important and worked hard at education will approach their jobs in the same manner.

If school was a place to play, the same approach will pertain to one's life outside the home.

For those who felt trapped in the school setting, entering the structured world of business will create a feeling of entrapment.

To reframe this experience is to ask, "What did the child want me to learn from his attitude about school?" As a result of your answer, where can you best position yourself in the working world for your greatest satisfaction and accomplishment?

26) What was home like for you?

Your beliefs about your childhood home will dominate your adult home environment. You will either repeat what you experienced as a child or you will attempt to do the very opposite. Examine your home environment as an adult. How is this environment like the child's environment? If you are in stress about your home, ask yourself, "How far away from the child's beliefs and desires have I strayed?"

If you had a quiet and orderly home and this environment was comfortable for you, as an adult you will require the same type of home environment. If, however, as a child you dreamed of something that would change the sameness of your quiet and orderly childhood setting, then as an adult you will find yourself more comfortable in an environment that incorporates the changes desired by the child.

If your home was chaotic and messy and you disliked the chaos, as an adult you will want order, cleanliness, and peace.

If your home was filled with emotional turbulence, as an adult you will find yourself in one of two settings. Either you will repeat the situation in an attempt to fix it, or you will avoid emotional stress in your home.

If you never invited anyone over because you were embarrassed by what was happening in your home, as an adult you will tend to have a very private home life. You could also do the opposite and have a home that is perfect so you can entertain anyone at anytime.

If your home was filled with people and you loved the excitement and interaction, you will desire a lot of activity and personal interaction in your adult home.

27) **Did your family move frequently? What were these family moves like for you?**

This question will help you understand your need to have a stable home address or your need to frequently move.

If you never moved when you were a child and you liked the stability of not moving, you will seek and endeavor to create that stability in your adult life.

If you longed to move but never did, you will want to experience moving as an adult. In all likelihood you will enjoy the process.

If you moved frequently as a child and did not like moving, you will not want to move as an adult. If you moved frequently and liked moving, then you will want to move often as an adult.

28) Did you like being a child? Why or why not?

Your answer to this question will help you understand the ease or the stress involved in remembering your childhood experiences.

If you liked being a child, it was probably an easy process for you to answer the questions in this book. You will also find that as an adult, when you are asked a question about your childhood, you will easily access data and feel pleasure as you respond. On the other hand, if you did not like being a child, answering the questions in this book was probably a challenging experience for you. You may also find it is difficult to reminisce about your childhood.

If you had difficulty being a child because you always felt you were really an adult trapped in a child's body, then *LifeScripting* and the concept of gathering data from childhood will be a welcomed gift. You will enjoy going back to childhood with your adult mind and greeting the child's matching mind. Regardless of your adult feelings about childhood, the child learned for you. Since all childhood learning impacts your adult life it is wise to know the smallest of details about the child's life.

29) Did you love being the child you were?

This question helps you understand your deep feelings of self-love, or your perceived lack of self-love. Remember, you have always deeply loved yourself even if you have not consciously recognized that fact. Everyone has loving contracts with the child he/she was. This question provides insight in helping you understand the ease with which you can recognize those contracts. It also provides a recognition of your existing love of self.

If you answered this question with a "yes," it has never been difficult for you to accept the concept of self-love. If you answered this question with a "no," then accepting the concept of self-love has been a struggle for you.

A beautiful exercise to help you establish immediate love for the child you were is to imagine yourself sitting under a tree, relaxing and enjoying the day. A child approaches and sits next to you. This child looks very much like you did when you were a child. You look into the child's eyes and magically see in their eyes every feeling she has ever had. Can you love this child? If this child were to tell you about her life experiences, even if they were unpleasant, could you unconditionally love this child? Would you console and comfort her? There is no difference between this child and the child you were. The very same love you have for this child is the very same love you can consciously have for yourself. All you have to do is decide to love yourself as you love this child.

Ranking Your Siblings And Yourself

In this portion of the questions, you were asked to rank each of the following attributes from the highest to the lowest for all of your biological and non-biological siblings. You were also asked to include yourself and explain why you felt this way as a child.

The answers to questions 30 through 61 provide the specific data of how best to place yourself in the world. As a result of your answers, you will understand why you have felt and interacted as you have in the past. The answers to the individual questions, when placed in the proper perspective, will provide a clearer picture of the real you. With this picture, you will be able to understand how best to establish yourself in the world for the maximum amount of tranquility and accomplishment.

If you are an only child, it is important to address each question from your personal perspective. Give as much detail as possible in each area. It is also helpful to look at each question in terms of your relationships, or lack of relationships, with others. Each question has as much vital information for you as it does for those who had siblings. For example, you did not play with siblings but you regularly played with two or three neighborhood children. Consequently, you find you are comfortable interacting with people both at work and in your neighborhood. At the same time, you find yourself desiring a quiet work space and home environment.

30) Who do you consider the most intelligent to the least intelligent?

This question indicates the view you have regarding your intelligence. Intelligence is defined in this question solely by your perception of intelligence. It could mean tested intelligence, natural ability, perceived intelligence, or any combination thereof.

If you said you were the most intelligent, you will present yourself to the world with your intelligence. You will require a position in life that involves the use of your mental capabilities. Because you saw yourself as number one in intelligence, you will want to be viewed by others as number one in this area.

If you viewed yourself as second in intelligence, but you felt able to hold your own, you will believe that someone else in your home or in your world of business will be more intelligent than you. However, you will believe you can intellectually hold your own.

If you did not feel intelligent, you will find yourself at times feeling less then adequate in the area of intelligence. It is important for you to find an employment position where intellectual pressure is not a part of your job description.

If, as a child, you had a learning challenge, reframe your childhood challenge for your adult empowerment. For example, you are dyslexic. As a child, you were not aware of this challenge because it was not detected. As a result of your dyslexia, you felt you were not intelligent so you learned to observe every detail of life just to get by. Reframed: You are a person who has a great sense of detail. You do not miss anything. You are of great value in areas where those qualities are necessary and appreciated.

As you spend time contemplating your feelings regarding the intellectual level of the child you were, you will find a direct correlation to your thoughts and feelings about your intellectual ability today. To avoid stress in your life, do not place yourself in areas that do not honor your belief about your intelligence. When you are placed in areas you believe require more intellect than you think you possess, you will become stressed. Likewise, if you are placed in areas where you are not required to intellectually preform at the levels you believe you can, then you will also become frustrated and stressed. The value of this question is to provide you with an indicator of where to best position yourself in life regarding your intelligence.

31) Who received the best grades in school?

School grades represent rewards for effort. Your grades indicate the rewards you have come to expect for the effort you expend.

If you worked really hard and consequently received the best grades, in life you will work hard and expect the reward to match the effort.

If you worked hard and did not receive good grades, you will work hard in life and not expect to be greatly rewarded. If you worked hard and got good grades which you felt were never good enough for your parents, then you will feel that no matter how hard you work it will never be good enough in the eyes of others.

If you didn't work hard and still got good grades, you will find yourself in positions where little effort is required for great reward.

If you didn't work hard and grades were unimportant to you or to your parents, you will find yourself with a nonchalant attitude about the correlation between work and reward.

Reframed: How can this area help you better understand yourself? How can this information about yourself help you understand others and their efforts in life?

32) Who was the hardest worker? In what manner? Describe yourself in detail in the area of work.

How you worked or didn't work as a child is how you will work or not work as an adult. It is important to position yourself in the area of work according to what the child taught you.

If you worked hard and loved to work, find a position that enables you to work.

If you worked hard but disliked the work, then find a position where your work gives you pleasure instead of dissatisfaction.

If you did not work hard, you are an individual who must find a position where hard work is not a part of the job description.

If as a child you worked hard and desired time off once in awhile, as an adult you will work hard. However, it is important to remember to give the child the desired time off.

The specific areas in which you worked also have significance regarding the direction of your adult life. If you worked hard in a particular area and enjoyed it, then that area still creates joy for you. For example, if you loved to dust and vacuum, as an adult a great stress releaser could be to dust and vacuum. If you worked hard in an area that did not give you pleasure, then that is an area in which you should not involve yourself as an adult. For example, one of the many jobs that my mother required of us was to regularly work in a huge garden. For me, the garden felt like a built-in prison. The condition of the garden was always hanging over our heads. Before we could be granted privileges, the garden had to meet my mother's standards. The garden was also used as a place of punishment, where weeding was required as a sentence for a perceived crime. Obviously, as an adult, I do not enjoy gardening or yard work. Reframed: One of my jobs is certainly not to be a gardener. I appreciate the hard work of others in this area, but I know it is not a place of joy for me.

An opposite example of a childhood interaction about gardening, is Jim. In his childhood, Jim saw his mother and father enjoying yard work. If the job required a man's strength, his father would have his mother sit on a chair close by and talk to him as he completed the task. As Jim aged, he was included in the process of working in the yard and he enjoyed the interaction with his family. Reframed: One of Jim's true joys is to work in the yard. He feels connected to those he loves by inviting them to watch and share in his efforts. Jim assists others with advice about yard care and helps others in completing difficult gardening tasks.

33) **Who helped around the house the most? Describe in detail how you helped around the house.**

How you helped, or did not help, in the house of your childhood, is how you will help, or not help, in your adult home. You will enjoy the same experiences the child enjoyed. You will not enjoy the same experiences the child disliked. You will find yourself most comfortable doing only those tasks the child loved, and you will feel stress when doing what the child disliked.

If you did not help around the house, then as an adult sharing in the household tasks will probably be difficult for you.

If you wanted to assist in specific areas and were not allowed to, then as an adult these areas are the places that will give you the greatest pleasure if you pursue them. For example, if you wanted to cook but Mom did not allow you in the kitchen, then cooking could be a profession/hobby that could give you great pleasure.

Reframed: Look to the interactions of your childhood for insights into the area of working within the house. What do you now understand about your past interactions that will help you as an adult? Where can you best position yourself in your present home environment to create the least amount of stress and the greatest joy for yourself and for others?

34) Were there any rewards for your help?

The rewards given to the child for expended effort will become the adult requirements for work that is accomplished.

If the reward matched the work, you will require equal and just compensation for your adult accomplishments.

If there were no rewards for your efforts, then the child taught you to work hard and to not look for rewards as your compensation.

If you did very little work and received major compensation, as an adult you will expect to be rewarded greatly for very little effort.

Your personal story sets the stage for you. Look to the dynamics of your childhood and determine how they match what is now happening for you in terms of your feelings, behavior, and need for compensation. The following story from my childhood will assist you in understanding the concept of reframing in the area of work/reward.

When I was a child, my mother created an allowance system where you could end up owing her money at the end of the week. Mom posted a list of jobs and we were allowed to choose the jobs we wanted to perform. After completing a task we would initial the square next to the listed job. If Mom perceived that the job was done correctly, we were given a penny. If Mom believed that the job was not completed to her standards, then we owed her a penny. Many times at the end of the week I owed my mother money. Week after week I would continue to try to please my mother, never considering the possibility of just not working. To add to the dilemma of my debt to Mom, I was also required to give a dime to God every Sunday. At the end of most weeks I not only owed Mom money, but I also owed God money. Fortunately, at times my dad would bail me out by creating fun jobs for me to do which would provide enough money to pay Mom and God.

Reframed: Since the child was serving Mom and Mom represents "What is a woman?" and "Who are women to me?" the child taught me to serve women (Mom) and not to look for money as compensation. In fact, she taught me there would be times when I would be serving women and it would cost me money. The child also taught me that when the pressure mounted financially, a man would assist me by creating a fun job that would provide enough money to pay all of my debt. The money would also allow me to make a contribution to God. This has been my adult experience in many instances. An incident that matches this learning is the work I do in the prisons. I began my work in prisons as a volunteer, providing the materials needed for the inmates from my own finances. As time passed, a non-profit organization headed by a man saw my dilemma and created a wonderful plan that compensated me monetarily for this work. I love my prison work, and I know that the child is the one who taught me that one of my many jobs is to serve women, no matter what the cost. Mom taught me not to look at money as my compensation. I also learned that if I do the work required of me, a man's planning will, at times, assist with any financial needs.

35) Who was the most to the least conforming and how?

This information guides you in knowing if you are comfortable or uncomfortable conforming. It also informs you if you tend to look to others for direction.

If you were a conforming child, it is easy for you to become part of a system or a family. If you were a conformist, as an adult make sure you place yourself in environments worthy of your conforming nature. If you place yourself incorrectly, you will find yourself being taken advantage of or becoming what the situation requires. As a person who conforms, you can become a great asset to teams that require dedication and follow through. Again, make sure you place yourself on a team where the goal is compatible with what you desire to accomplish. This will enable you to comfortably dedicate yourself to the task.

If you were a non-conforming child, you need to find adult positions where non-conforming behavior is accepted. Examples of non-conforming positions include politics, trouble shooting, negotiating, being an entrepreneur, etc.

If as a child you conformed in some areas but not in others, place yourself in the areas where the child felt most comfortable. For example, while at home you conformed to the desires of your mother and father, but at school you challenged teachers and often received disciplinary action. As an adult you will like a tranquil home, but you function best in a challenging work environment where people do not always agree with your ideas.

36) Who was the most rebellious and how?

This area forms your belief for how you will behave to get your needs met. It determines the limits to which you will go, particularly when you believe you have a personal cause or need.

If you were not rebellious as a child, then you will have difficulty being rebellious as an adult.

If you were rebellious as a child, you will be an adult who is capable of making a statement about your needs in life.

The areas in which the child rebelled will be your adult areas of rebellion. These areas can be great gifts to you if properly reframed. For example, if the child challenged authority, the adult can use this skill to challenge the status quo and promote positive change within systems. If the child wrote on walls, then the adult might want to find a cause and write for people who can effect change. Use your reframing skills to find your power and enhance your adult behavior in this area.

How you observed your siblings behavior in this area is also important. If the behavior of your siblings was acceptable to you, then peers acting in the same manner will provide comfort for you. But if your sibling's behavior made you uncomfortable, when you are with similar acting adults you will find yourself feeling uncomfortable. Your ability to properly place yourself as an adult is best enhanced when you understand your reactions to your siblings.

37) **Who tried to please the most and how? Who did you try to please the most and why? Describe yourself in detail in this area.**

This question indicates how you interact with others in your adult life and what role is the most comfortable for you.

If you tried to please, you will be a person who does not rock the boat when others are involved. If you did not try to please, then you will be an individual who is her own person at all costs.

Who you tried to please will indicate who has the most influence upon you in your adult life. If your mother was the person you tried to please the most, you will have a need to please women who are authority figures in your world. If you tried most to please your dad, then men will be your focus. If it was a sibling you tried to please, you will find a peer with whom you interact in very much the same manner.

Look to your adult behavior for parallels to the child's experiences.

38) **Who was the most critical of others and how? If you were critical, what were you critical of? How did you express it? (Verbally, internally, etc.)**

Your ability to have a critical eye comes from your answer to this question. The things about which the child was critical are the things the adult will criticize.

If you were critical of other people's clothing, as an adult you may want to consider some form of fashion consulting.

If you were intensely critical of the behavior of others, reframed you could make a good detective or trouble shooter within a company.

If you were critical of the way people verbally expressed themselves, you could work well in the area of writing or teaching.

If you expressed criticism openly, you may want to position yourself where you can openly express your point of view.

If you kept your criticism to yourself, you will need to place yourself in positions where you will not be required to speak out regarding what you see and believe.

If you were not critical as a child, you will not be critical as an adult. You will tend to be a person who enjoys the status quo, with no interest in changing people, organizations, or structures.

39) **Who was the most considerate and how? Write about yourself in this area.**

Look closely at your answer and carefully consider the details you wrote regarding yourself in this area. How are those details like the behavior you exhibit as an adult? If this behavior worked for you in childhood, you will probably be comfortable and successful repeating it as an adult. If your behavior in this area created childhood stress, you may want to ask yourself what you learned from the child that will assist you in developing opposite behavior.

If you believed you were extremely considerate as a child, then you will be a considerate adult. If you thought others were more considerate than you and you liked their behavior, then you will find yourself in situations where the same kinds of interactions will dominate. If you were not considerate and felt comfortable with this behavior, that same behavior will dominate your adult world.

Also look to your childhood feelings about consideration, or lack of consideration, with regard to others. How do these feelings apply to your interactions with others in your adult life? For example, you had a sibling who was never considerate of others and you felt stressed by his behavior. As an adult, you will want to place yourself in positions where this type of behavior on the part of others is seldom exhibited.

40) **Where did the siblings rank in selfishness? What were you selfish about?**

What you were selfish about as a child are the things that are important to you as an adult. It is necessary for your happiness to provide yourself with what was important to the child.

If you were selfish about your toys, as an adult things will be important to you. If you were selfish about your time, then time is your valued possession. If you were selfish about your space, your space will then be an important ingredient for your adult comfort.

If as a child you saw others as more selfish and you did not like their behavior, you will see the same interaction occurring in your adult world. You will probably find yourself having the same reaction to the behavior that you initially had as a child. It is, therefore, important to recognize this behavior in others and position yourself where this behavior does not occur.

If you were not selfish in any manner, you learned as a child not to have demands for yourself. Consequently, it is important to position yourself in places where this quality is a genuine asset. Examples of this positioning include areas where the needs of others take precedence over your needs. These areas could include social work, volunteer work, nursing, working with children or teens, etc.

Understanding yourself in the area of selfishness will give you valuable information about your personal desires. To reframe selfishness is to realize the rewards you can provide for yourself based on the desires of the child you were. If the child needed time, provide yourself with time. If the child needed things, provide yourself with things. If the child was selfish about space, provide yourself with adequate space.

41) **Who liked having his/her own way the most? How did he/she get it? How did you get your own way?**

This question has to do with your beliefs about how to obtain what you desire. Read each word you wrote in your answer and review how your answer applies to your past experiences. The various combinations of answers for this question are limitless. Some combinations include:

If you liked getting what you wanted and you figured out the best possible way to accomplish this, then in most adult situations you will find yourself figuring out the best possible way to get what you desire.

If you liked having your own way and you got it by throwing a tantrum, as an adult you will find yourself repeating the same behavior. This past learning can be reframed by making sure that what you want is best for you. Once you confirm that your desire is best for you, endeavor to obtain it in a mature, persuasive manner. You might also consider speaking up for a cause and helping others obtain their desired results.

If you liked having your own way but found yourself never getting your way, then you are a person who can easily give into the needs of others. To reframe this childhood learning is to recognize that you can be there for others by placing them ahead of yourself. As an adult, it is also important to make sure you occasionally provide yourself with some of the things the child desired.

Look to the behavior of your siblings in the area of how they got their way. Did you like or dislike their behavior? How does this apply to your feelings about the behavior of others in your adult life? How can you use this information to reduce stress when positioning yourself with others? For example, Mel had a brother who always got his way by using his physical strength to overpower others. As a child, Mel felt fearful of his brother and disliked his behavior. As an adult, Mel needs to recognize situations that could lead to being overpowered by others. He needs to avoid these situations and seek out tranquil associates and environments.

42) Who was the most sensitive and easily hurt? About what? How was it expressed? (Make sure you cover your experience in this area.)

What you were sensitive about as a child will be what you are sensitive about as an adult. How you expressed your sensitivity and hurt as a child is how you will tend to express yourself as an adult. If you were sensitive when others criticized you, then personal criticism will tend to be a difficult issue for you.

If as a child you went to your room and felt bad when you were criticized, as an adult you will tend to leave the scene of criticism and prefer to be by yourself. Reframed: Know that you prefer to place yourself in situations where you are not openly faced with personal criticism. Accept the role of helping others who are criticized by letting them know you understand how they feel. You will also be a loyal friend who will be there for others.

If you were sensitive about your weight, then weight will be an internal conflict for you. To reframe this issue, ask yourself what the child was teaching you about your body? How can this knowledge best benefit you today? With this information, how can you assist others who have weight issues?

If you were sensitive about people being cruel to others and you cried because you wanted them to treat each other in a loving manner, you are a person who can assist others in being kind to one another. It is also important for you to stay out of environments where elements of cruelty prevail.

If you were sensitive to the mere look on someone's face and you altered your behavior accordingly, as an adult you will find yourself interpreting the expressions of others and reacting on self-deduced assumptions. Reframed: You will be sensitive to even the unspoken needs of others. You will be able to tell instinctively and without words what others are feeling. You will also be able to anticipate how to be of assistance to them.

If you were sensitive about not being heard, as an adult you will be someone who can speak up for others when they are not being heard.

The areas in which you were and are sensitive determine the areas in which you can express love for yourself and for others. Look to what the child taught you about yourself and apply those insights to your capability to love yourself and others. Your siblings and their interactions in this area also gave you valuable data to add to the picture of what you learned about the role of sensitivity in your life.

43) Who showed his/her temper the most to the least? How was it shown and how did you feel?

Your experience with anger as a child created your adult beliefs regarding anger. These beliefs apply to both your belief about yourself and your belief about others.

When you were a child, if you had difficulty dealing with the anger of others, as an adult, when someone expresses anger you will have the same feelings and reactions as the child. If anger was never expressed by anyone in your home, then as an adult you will function best in environments where anger is not an issue.

If anger was a regular part of your childhood, as an adult you will find yourself in situations where you are often dealing with anger. If you expressed your temper as a child, then as an adult you will find yourself with the same behavior when you are upset. The exact situations that triggered your childhood temper will trigger your adult temper. How you felt and responded will also be the way you feel and respond as an adult when you are angry.

Reframed: You can now look at the behavior which created intense feelings for you as a child and find a way to use that same energy in positive ways that will affect the lives of others. For example, if as a child you became furious when you felt pushed around by other children you could, as an adult, assist others who are being pushed around. To assist your reframe, ask yourself questions such as: "What did the child really want me to learn? What can I do as an adult to help this child accomplish the desired result? How can I assist others in this area?"

If as a child you did not feel anger, you will not experience much anger as an adult. This does not mean you are stuffing your feelings, it simply means you learned how to accept life for what it was. As a result, you did not experience unresolved issues. Remember, emotions are gifts designed to balance your life and your body. Emotions such as anger are healthy if expressed appropriately. Refer to Chapter 19 to review how best to handle the emotion of anger.

44) **Who had the best sense of humor? In what way?**

This information helps you understand the part you play in your desire and ability to interface in the world with laughter, humor, and lightheartedness.

If you were the child who made people laugh, one of your adult jobs is to share that aspect of yourself with others. If you were the one who laughed with others but did not create the laughter, that will be your nature as an adult. If you had siblings with a sense of humor and you liked that aspect of their character, you will find yourself with the same types of people in your adult environment. If you did not appreciate your siblings' sense of humor, when you find yourself with adults who are similar, you will become agitated and uncomfortable. If the child you were loved to laugh and you are not laughing as an adult, how can you get yourself back to the child?

45) **Who was the most idealistic? Were you idealistic? About what? What were your hopes, dreams and desires? What did you want to become if all were possible?**

Your answer to this question, is a key factor in assisting you to understand your personal purpose in life. The core of your life's purpose and your self expression can be clearly seen in your answer. You will be a passionate and empowered adult when, in some form, you become what the child dreamed of becoming. Following your life's dream creates positive energy and happiness. The path to true happiness is, therefore, through your knowledge and awareness of what the child wanted. You had the perfect childhood and were given the perfect childhood dream to inspire you to become all you were meant to become. As an adult, the further you are away from your childhood dream the more stress you will experience in your life. This stress is the message and the gift informing you that you are on the wrong road in your life. To reduce the stress is to return to the dreams of the child. It is never too late to rejoin and honor the child.

Make sure you spend adequate time reviewing your answer to this question so you can fully understand where to place yourself in the life you were designed to live. If you are far away from the dreams of the child, do not despair. Simply design a plan that will allow you to systematically fulfill all, or some portion, of that dream. For example, if you dreamed of being a doctor and you are now sixty years old, it is unlikely you will apply to medical school. However, you could volunteer at a hospital and assist those who have medical needs.

Some examples that may help you interpret your life's dream are:

If one of your favorite childhood games was playing school where you always played the teacher, as an adult you need to involve yourself with some form of teaching others.

If you put together plays in the backyard and dreamed of being an actor or actress, as an adult you need to involve yourself in some form of theater/drama to feel complete. If you feel it is too late to arrive on the Hollywood scene, find a little theater or college and participate in their programs.

If you came from a totally stressful environment where your dream was mostly fanaticizing about life being different, as an adult your job is to create a personal world with little or no stress. It is also your job to reach out to others who are experiencing the same types of stress you experienced by assisting them in overcoming their stress.

If you dreamed of having a family and a peaceful life, it is your mission to create that in your adult world.

If you wanted to help others in a specific way, your purpose is to find a method to fulfill that dream in your adult life.

If you dreamed of solitude and quiet, that is a necessary ingredient for your adult happiness.

If your ideals seemed limitless and you desired everything possible, as an adult you must be multi-faceted in expression, service, and accomplishment.

If the child was not idealistic and accepted life as it was, then you were trained by the child to become a now moment individual. Consequently, it is important for you to place yourself in an environment where the present moments are comfortable for you. Also make sure you are never pressured into major commitments about the future.

Please be aware that there are no right or wrong ideals. No one is better than another because of the size or scope of his dreams. We are all in this life together and the objective is to weave our personal thread and live our personal purpose. By doing this, we find our place in the tapestry of life. I have worked with people who have had major and multi-faceted visions and I have worked with those who have had very simple ideals. They all have equal joy in their hearts when they accept and honor the part they are to play in the total picture of humankind.

An example of a very simple and yet profound ideal is the life of a 55-year-old woman who flew from the East Coast to Phoenix to experience *LifeScripting*. She not only traveled many miles but invested a significant amount of money to find out why she was feeling so off balance in her life. She had spent her life as a housewife and mother and had loved that experience. However, her friends were now telling her that the key to her future was to have a career so she could experience a greater sense of accomplishment. The peer pressure was so intense she was feeling negative and unsettled about herself. When I asked her what she dreamed of as a child, she said her only dream was to be married and have children to nurture. Her dream included having a home and taking care of her husband and children by cooking and baking. She is now a grandmother and enjoys doing this for her grandchildren. I advised her that her best service to herself and to the planet, was to reduce her stress by returning to her dream. This could be accomplished by being there for her children and grandchildren. I suggested she invite the friends who were putting pressure on her to come to her home to enjoy her fresh baked cookies. She has written several thank you notes to tell me her life is again filled with joy and purpose.

If your childhood was filled with many challenges and your dream was to have a life that included the exact opposite of what you were experiencing, as an adult your joy will come from creating a life free of challenge. You will also experience joy when assisting others in the areas in which you were challenged. For example, one of the many stresses of my childhood was watching the negative interaction between my parents. I used to watch them fight and say to myself, "If only she would _____ , or he would _____ , then this fight would not be occurring." As a result, I have a natural ability to assist couples who are having difficulty interacting. I help them sort out the behaviors causing their separation and I help them develop behaviors that will bring them closer together. As a child did I say, "Gee, I want to be a therapist?" Of course not, I didn't even know what a therapist was. However, as an adult I have looked to the child's experience for my adult job description. It has thus become obvious that the field of therapy is a wonderful place of expression for the learning of the child.

If you were a child who didn't have a specific dream and you did not face challenges, look to your life for what was good and right. Use this information for your adult job description. Help others find the peace and joy you have always experienced.

The identification of your purpose is the first step to lasting joy. Taking action to accomplish your purpose is the next crucial step. Appropriate action toward your dreams contains built-in bonuses for your life's joy. When you are on the right road, you will experience positive energy flow and receive universal cooperation. The only person who can stop the child's dream is you. Ask yourself, "What would I say to a child if she told me her hopes and dreams for the future? How would I tell her to move toward her dreams? Would I ever call her dreams foolish or unobtainable?" Do not judge your experience in the area of your own childhood dreams, just accept the child's dreams as your true purpose. Then proceed to the best of your ability to turn these dreams, into your adult reality. When you follow your dreams you not only serve your life but you serve all of humankind because you are weaving your thread for the benefit of all.

46) **Who had the highest standards of achievement? What did he/she want to achieve? What did you want to achieve?**

This question adds to the information about your goals and purpose. What you wanted to achieve as a child is important to achieve, in some form, as an adult. The answer to this question also helps you understand the requirements and standards you have set for yourself in life. To be happy, you will need to achieve in the areas of the child's desire.

If the child wanted to achieve recognition in academics, the pursuit of education is crucial.

If the child wanted to attain the attention of one or both of your parents, the need to perform for people in authority will be a frequent occurrence in your life. Caution: If you need attention from those in authority, make sure you place yourself with the appropriate people in terms of values.

If the child wanted to obtain the best grades, then working hard to achieve excellence is necessary for you in all areas of your life.

When you were young, if you felt others always achieved more than you and you were left on your own, go to the place where the child first felt pain about being left behind. Ask yourself, "What did I really hope to accomplish if all things had been possible?" Pursue those desires in some form for the sake of the child. Also know that as a result of being left alone, you are probably an individual who works well in that type of setting.

Regardless of the standards you have set for yourself, it is important to remember that it is never necessary to achieve what others desire for you. It is only necessary to achieve what you desire for yourself.

47) Who had the highest standards of behavior and morals? What were your standards in this area?

This question is designed for you to better understand your beliefs and standards in the area of personal values. This question is not religious in nature, although for some it may become one. Each individual will define "behavior" and "morals" from his/her own history and point of view. It is from one's history and point of view that each person develops a personal code of ethics. What is your code of ethics? How has this code of ethics dominated your past behavior choices? How do you want your ethics to be incorporated into your present life?

If you grew up in an environment where your family lived with the ethic of kindness and caring for others, these values will be a part of your interaction with others.

If you were raised with the ethic of every man for himself and no signs of caring were demonstrated, then this may have become a way of life for you. If as a child you disliked this ethic and wished it had been different, you may desire to create the opposite of what you experienced.

If you grew up believing you must maintain the ethic of being sensitive to others, this quality must be a part of your adult behavior for you to be happy. If, additionally, your family members were sensitive to others, you will want to place yourself in environments where this quality is valued. If you regularly attended church and your family values were based upon religious beliefs, those values must be a part of your adult life for you to feel balanced. To maintain a sense of personal worth, it is important to consciously incorporate your values into your everyday life.

48) Who was the most to the least materialistic? About what? What were you materialistic about?

This question helps you determine the value you place on material things. The value you placed on specific things as a child will determine the things you place value upon as an adult. To obtain balance as an adult, it is necessary to provide yourself with what was important to the child in this area.

If as a child you placed value on your things, as an adult you will value your personal possessions.

If the child placed value on clothing, as an adult you will feel best if you provide yourself with wonderful clothing. You could also incorporate this into your career choice and utilize this love of clothing as possible employment in the field of fashion.

If you were not materialistic as a child, then material possessions are not important to you.

If as a child you felt stress because of the lack of material possessions, you may find yourself striving diligently to provide yourself with possessions.

49) Who was the most athletic and how? In what areas were you athletic?

How you feel about the necessity for exercise and movement of your body is affected by your answer to this question. Have you ever wondered why it is so easy for some people to exercise and yet so difficult for others? The answer lies in the physical activity of the child.

If you were an athletic child, you will feel most balanced and happy if you are an athletic adult. If you were athletic and are not active as an adult, then you will have difficulty feeling good about yourself because of your lack of physical activity. If you were not athletic or active as a child, it will be difficult to be active as an adult. This does not mean you should never attempt exercise since it is important to health, but it will explain why exercise can be difficult for you. If as a child you expressed yourself athletically by being part of a team, then some form of group sport or team exercise is important to you as an adult. If you regularly participated in individual athletic events such as tennis, track, swimming, etc., you will tend to seek out isolated exercise or individual sports.

To better understand how this past information can assist you in the area of helping others, look for the areas of activity where you felt joy. Share this information and joy with others by coaching a team, training individuals, writing articles or starting a club.

50) **Who was the strongest physically? How did he/she express it? How were you in the area of physical strength?**

Physical strength has to do with your personal beliefs about your physical capabilities. Look to your answer for the information you need in the placement of yourself in the area of physical exertion.

If you felt physically strong as a child, it would be advisable to place yourself in positions where this characteristic can be utilized. If you felt you were weak physically or if physical strength was not important to you, then it is prudent to place yourself in positions where physical strength is not required.

If you had a sibling who used his physical strength to control you and you struggled with this interaction, you will find yourself in similar situations as an adult. You may want to identify those situations and realize what is causing what. With this information, you will now be able to choose situations where this behavior does not occur. You may also want to assist individuals who are being physically controlled by others to help them recognize different options.

If you were the one controlling others with your physical strength, you may want to reframe this behavior and use your strength to now assist others in a positive way.

51) Who was the strongest emotionally? Where were you in terms of emotional strength? What did you consider to be emotional strength?

Your feelings about emotions as a child are your beliefs about emotions as an adult. The things that created emotional responses for you the child will be the things that create your adult emotional responses.

If as a child you felt deep emotion but did not express what you were feeling, you were trained by the child to withstand much and withhold your emotional responses. Reframed this can become your power. As an adult, you will be able to endure emotionally demanding situations without the need to express your personal emotional responses. This will serve you well in settings where it is best not to visibly demonstrate emotions. Conversely, it is also important and healthy to express your feelings when you are in an appropriate environment. For example, if you are working with people who are sick and dying, it is important to provide the patient with your emotional strength and support. It is equally important and appropriate to express what you are feeling when you are alone or with those who understand.

If as a child you felt deeply and were able to freely express your feelings, you will be an adult who easily expresses feelings. You are also an individual who can assist others in expressing their feelings. Since emotions are a primary balancing mechanism, it is vital to spend time understanding what the child taught you regarding your emotional needs. If as a child you were emotionally stressed by what was occurring in your world, go to the child and ask what the child needed at that time. As an adult, make sure these needed ingredients are a part of your life.

All emotions are positive. They inform you of what is happening in your mind, heart, and body. To obtain balance, emotions should not be stuffed but should be addressed, felt, and expressed. Proper mental balance includes the ability to appropriately release your emotions. Appropriate release is owning an emotion by feeling it for yourself. Inappropriate release is to disown an emotion and release your feelings at someone else.

52) Who was the best looking? How did you feel about physical attractiveness?

Each individual is deeply affected by their feelings about their body and sense of attractiveness. Therefore, the issue of where you fit in the world in terms of physical appearance is important to understand.

Recently, the view of the physical self has been greatly influenced by campaigns of the mass media that inform us as to how and what we "should" look like. It is important to recognize how much you have personally believed these campaigns. Each person needs to establish for herself a balance about her appearance that comes from within. It is certainly okay to dress well, but if your clothing, cosmetics, or body become who you are in your own mind, you may want to consider additional options regarding your personal balance.

If as a child you felt physically attractive, as an adult it is important to maintain that viewpoint of yourself. For you, it is vital to continue doing the things necessary to maintain what you believe constitutes physical attractiveness.

If you felt unattractive as a child, you may still experience those feelings about yourself. You can assist others when they feel less than attractive because you have an understanding of the depth of their feelings.

The following three exercises will assist you in accepting and loving your physical appearance.

The first is to imagine that you are God. As God, you are choosing the ingredients necessary to make the perfect you. Remember, as God you can see the entire picture of your life as it spans from conception to death. Because of this all encompassing view, you understand the many components necessary for your long-term learning and character building. One of the components is to choose the body that would best serve your entire life's purpose. As God, why would you decide on the body you have? How does this body serve your total life and learning? As an adult, are you maintaining this perfect body with proper exercise, rest, and nutrition?

The second exercise is to imagine yourself sitting in a beautiful tranquil setting. As you contemplate the beauty around you and realize the perfect order in the universe, a child comes onto the scene and sits beside you. This small person has several bodily challenges. One challenge is a large birthmark on the side of his face. Another is that he is overweight. The child tells you how terrible he feels when he looks into the mirror and when others tease him about his appearance. What would you tell this beautiful child? Would you say, "You are ugly and God obviously made a mistake"? Or would you help the child see the beauty in his body and life? Would you help him recognize how he can use his uniqueness to do something special for others?

The third exercise utilizes a mirror to help you reconcile any physical characteristics you believe are negative. Stand in front of a mirror and look into your eyes. See your eyes as you would see the eyes of a child. Think of everything you have judged as wrong about your body. Now try to tell this beautiful child looking back at you what you believe is wrong with him/her. Do this by listing all the things you believe are wrong with you. Could you actually tell a beautiful innocent child what you have been telling yourself? You are that child. So ask yourself, "If there are no accidents, how are my face and body perfect for who I am and for what I am to accomplish in this world?"

Your Physical Reframe:

If you are in a beautiful body, how are you going to use this asset to assist yourself and others? If you are in a package that is less than what you consider beautiful, how does your body add to your life and to the lives of others? If your body has experienced physical challenges, how are these challenges assisting you in learning about your purpose for yourself and other?

If you desire to achieve the best body possible for yourself and you believe adjustments could be made, then again approach yourself as you would a child. If you were with a child who was overweight, you would not lecture or scold her, you would simply assist her with loving direction toward healthy food and exercise. You would also help her become educated in the area of nutrition and body enhancement. To reach your desired goal about your body, take this imaginary child by the hand and do for yourself what you would do for this child.

Since your body is the only vehicle you will ever have, it is vital that you take care of it so you can accomplish all you have been destined to accomplish.

53) Who had the most friends? What kind of friendships were they?

This question tells you the number and type of friendships you need to feel balanced as an adult.

If as a child you were reserved and only had one close friend, and this was comfortable for you, you will find yourself most comfortable with one close friend.

If you had many and varied friendships, you will be most comfortable with many and varied friends.

If you made friends easily but often moved and had to constantly change your friends, as an adult, part of your job description is to make friends easily and let go when necessary. If the child was uncomfortable with the frequent moves and the need to always make new friends, then for the comfort of the adult you may want to establish long-term friendships and remain in a permanent location.

Remember, what the child loved, needed, or desired is your instruction for becoming a balanced adult.

54) Who had the most ongoing friendships?

This question will help you understand your need, or lack of need, for longevity in friendships.

If as a child you made and kept long-term friendships, as an adult, establishing and maintaining long-term friendships is vital to your happiness.

If you maintained friendships only for the period of time they worked then easily let go when they were finished, you will find yourself behaving in the same manner.

If you felt you wanted meaningful friendships but just could not create them, you must fill the need for meaningful friendships in order to become balanced.

With the information about your need for long-term friendships you will be able to better understand your pattern of behavior in this area. You will also be able to understand the behavior of others with regard to friendships, consequently honoring their personal choices.

55) Who was the most spoiled? By whom and how? How did you feel about this?

How you were or were not spoiled will provide you with information about your need to be spoiled as an adult. The areas in which you were spoiled will assist you in understanding where you can expect to be spoiled as an adult. Who spoiled you has relevance as to who will spoil you in your adult life.

If you were spoiled, as an adult you can expect to receive the same type of treatment you received as a child. Knowing who spoiled you will also help you understand where to look for adult preferential treatment. For example, if your dad spoiled you by buying you things, you will find yourself in situations where men provide material things for you. If your dad spoiled you with his time, you will feel best spending time with male relationships.

If someone outside of the family spoiled you, someone outside of your immediate family will spoil you as an adult.

If you were not spoiled, then you were trained to become an adult who does not look to others to provide the extras of life.

How you felt about being spoiled or how you felt when you saw others being spoiled indicates what you will feel regarding the same events when they occur in your adult life.

Reframed: Ask what the child learned for you in terms of how to interface in the world. As a result of your past experience in the area of being spoiled, what skills do you now have to share with others? For example, as a child you were spoiled by your mom because she gave you extra treats when you performed well. As an adult, you will find yourself getting extra bonuses for a job well done. It is important to realize that you must place yourself in positions where rewards are tied to job performance.

56) **Who was the most punished? By whom and how? How did you feel during this interaction? How were you punished? Give details and recollections.**

Punishment has to do with your belief formation regarding how much pressure and stress you can handle in adverse situations. When pressured you will respond in one of three ways: 1) You will do the same behavior done to you as a child. 2) You will find yourself in situations where the same behavior done to you as a child is being done to you as an adult. In these situations, you will generally respond the exact way the child responded. 3) You will live a commitment to never allow, or do to others, what was done to you the child.

Look to your specific answer to obtain the information you need to understand your belief in the area of stress and pressure. Ask yourself, "What did the child learn for me? What can I handle in areas of pressure because of my childhood experiences of punishment? What can I expect in the area of stress and how am I prepared for these situations?"

For example:

If you were never punished, pressure is not something you can handle nor is it something you should expect.

If you were severely punished, you can take major amounts of pressure in life. Please recognize that if you were severely punished it is not necessary to ever relive the scenes of your punishment. It is only necessary to review the movies of the past for the information you need to understand your adult behavior choices. It is also important to realize your ability to help others who may have experienced the same situations you have experienced.

Who punished you will also help you understand from whom your adult pressure may come. If a man punished you, most of your pressure will come from your interactions with the same types of men. If it was a woman who punished you, then most of your adult pressure will come from interactions with that type of woman. If you were punished by both men and women, you will find pressure from both males and females who are similar in type to those who punished you.

How you reacted to the punishment of yourself and others will help you better understand your adult reactions to stress. For example, after punishment, if you withheld your feelings and didn't cry until you got to your room, as an adult, when something occurs where you feel punished, you will hold in your reaction until you are alone. Reframed: You have been trained to be an adult who can withhold personal reactions to situations. When alone, it is important to respond to your feelings to create balance within your body.

Your degree of service to others is an important by-product of your experiences in this area. What you felt about punishment of yourself or others speaks loudly regarding your empathy for others, particularly in terms of being there for others with understanding. For example, if you were beaten, you know what it feels like to be beaten.

As a result, you can now assist others who have been beaten. You can also assist others who are being beaten by helping them reframe the situation.

If you were not punished but saw others punished and had intense feelings about the event, as an adult you will have empathy for others in similar life situations. You can use this awareness as a basis for service by doing for others what the child wanted to do for the people in your childhood. This question provides extensive information about what to expect in your future regarding stress. Spend the time necessary to review your past and apply it to your future.

57) Of the siblings, who took care of whom?

The answer to this question will help you understand how you interface with others. There are three basic methods of interfacing that are determined by this question: 1) You will be taken care of by others. 2) You will take care of others. 3) You will be independent of others.

If you were taken care of by your sibling or siblings, as an adult you can expect someone to always be there for you when you have a need for assistance. Those assisting you will be of the same type as your siblings. If you took care of others and felt joy in the process, one of the jobs you will love as an adult will be to assist others. This is a gift to yourself and to others. It is important to keep in mind that to truly assist others includes support and encouragement. It does not include doing for another what he should and could do for himself. If you were not taken care of and you did not take care of others, then you are to be independent in this area.

To be most comfortable and effective with others in this area, look to your answer and determine which of the three methods is best for you in placing yourself with others.

58) Who of the siblings played the most with whom?

Your sibling interaction in the area of play trained you to interact with your peers with comfort or discomfort. Those interactions also taught you how to play in the world. You will find yourself most comfortable in situations that resemble the family dynamics of your early years.

If you played with a particular sibling and you liked the interaction, you will need to find someone who resembles that sibling for interactions that result in fun.

If you played with different siblings at different times, as an adult you will need varied interactions with several types of individuals.

If as a child you did not play with anyone and you were comfortable with that, then play is not something you require. However, if you did not play but had a desire to play, as the adult you will find balance by playing for the child.

59) Who of the siblings got along best?

Your interactions in this area trained you in methods of how best to get along in the world. You will tend to have adult alignments similar to the alignments of the child.

If you got along well with all of your siblings, then you have been trained to get along well with your peers. If you got along with one of your siblings but not the others, as an adult you will find you will get along well with people who resemble your favorite sibling. You will also discover you do not get along with peers who resemble your difficult siblings.

Reframed: Who in your adult life resembles your siblings? How can your interactions with each sibling teach you to better interact with the individuals who resemble your sibling?

60) Who fought and argued the most? How did he/she fight and argue? Who won?

Your sibling interaction in the area of arguing, and winning versus losing, prepared you for your ability to interact in this area of your adult world.

If you fought and won, know that you will exhibit the same behavior it took for you to win as a child. If you did not fight when an argument was pending, you will not fight when there is adult pressure or conflict. If you fought but felt you always lost, then as an adult you will fight, feeling you will inevitably lose.

Reframed: What were the lessons of the child in this area? Look to both the comfort and discomfort of the child for information about yourself. If the child was comfortable, repeat the behavior. If the child was uncomfortable, then remember what the child would have preferred to have occur. To honor the child, try to accomplish what was needed in childhood for the adult you have become. How can you assist others in your life with the information from this question? For example, you grew up in an environment where your siblings argued and you felt totally uncomfortable with their interaction. As an adult, you can help others learn conflict resolution thereby enabling them to resolve their problems without the need to argue.

61) Were there any major events in your life after the age of nine? What were they and how did you feel about the event(s)?

Most beliefs lock in by the time we are six years of age. However, if there are major emotional events past six, additions to our beliefs are created. To recognize if any event was significant enough to be added to your already existing beliefs, simply look at the event and ask, "Is this a new event in my life or have I previously had this experience in any form ?" If it is a completely new event, it must be integrated into your belief system and reframed for your power.

For example:

If you never experienced loss as a child but at age 15 your parents divorced, how did this affect your life? How can this event help you help others who are experiencing loss?

If as a child you never experienced trauma but at age 21 you were attacked, how has this affected your life? Once you work through your feelings about the attack, how can you assist others in the area of reframing trauma?

The possibilities for reframing new events into belief systems are as limitless as the events that can be described by you. Remember to use the tools of *LifeScripting* while realizing the situation cannot be changed. However, your thinking about the situation can be changed. It is your adult thinking which creates your present reality. Ask yourself, "What did I learn from this event? How can this event add to my character? How can the situation not only assist me but serve others?"

If there were no major events after age nine, then realize most of your adult life will be a repetition of the life of the child you were prior to age six.

Suggestion

You may want to take some time, before moving to the next group of questions, to look at the various facets of your sibling interactions. This will enable you to further determine what these interactions have created for you the adult. Look to each question for as much information as possible. When you feel you understand the information, combine the pieces of data into an entire picture of who and what you are when "acting out" in the world. Again ask yourself, "If I were to give a job to the person who has been revealed in this section, what job would I give her?"

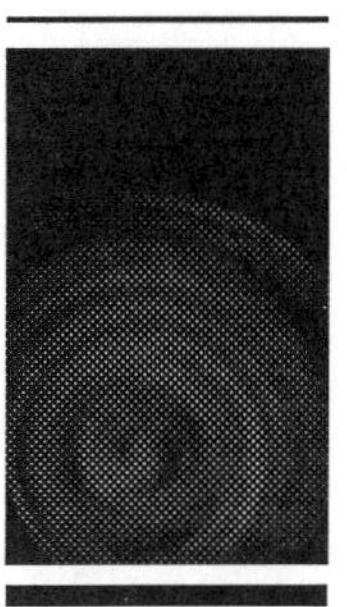

PARENTS

What Is A Relationship To You?

Your childhood interactions with your parents formed the basis for your beliefs about men, women and relationships. Your primary beliefs in these areas originated from your interactions, or lack of interactions, with your biological parents. If adoptive parents, step-parents, foster parents, grandparents, etc., were involved in your formative years, they too will have impact. However, that impact will be influenced by your already existing belief system with regard to your biological parents. Additionally, you will be influenced by the relationship, or lack of relationship, between your biological parents and your non-biological parents.

It is vital for your psychological balance to understand the depth of your connection to your biological parents. With this understanding, you will have a clearer picture of how to achieve and maintain balance within yourself and within your relationships. The following diagram will provide a visual of the dynamics of this connection.

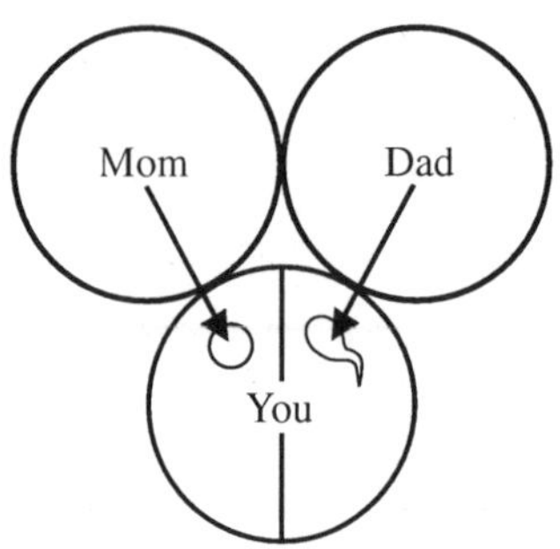

As an individual, you are half of your mother and half of your father. This is true because it took Dad's sperm and Mom's egg to create you. Because of this fact you will forever be a part of each of them. Until you come to an understanding of the role that each of your biological parents played in your life, you will not feel balance within yourself. If you are having issues with your father, the part of you that is about your dad will not be balanced. If you are having issues with your mother, the part of you that is about your mom will not be balanced. The only way to achieve internal balance is to discover for yourself what each parent has taught you through your experiences, or lack of experiences, with them. When this understanding occurs, you will begin to recognize why each parent is the perfect parent for you. If you have had challenging interactions with your parents, and those challenges still continue, it is not necessary to physically associate with them to obtain internal balance. However, it is important to mentally associate with them in a balanced manner. This can be accomplished by understanding and reframing the role of each parent as they pertain to the classroom of your life and belief formation.

When a child observes his father, he represents to the child "What is a man?" If the child is a boy, the father also represents "Who am I?" If the child is a girl, the father represents "Who is a man to me?" In Western culture the father also represents to the child "Who is God?" This occurs because we call both Dad and God "Father" and "He." Therefore, as adults when we say the word God what actually appears on the screen of the adult mind is the programming for the words "he" and "father." These words match the belief for "Who is Dad?"

With this awareness it is understandable why some participants in Twelve Step Programs have a difficult time when asked to turn their will and lives over to God as they understand Him. The person turning her will and life over to God needs to realize that the programming for "Who is God?" matches her programming for "Who is Dad?" If Dad was loving, then God is loving, and this step of the program is an easy step to accomplish. If Dad was a challenge, then God is a challenge, and the steps to God become difficult for the individual.

To visually demonstrate the connection of the child to the father, let's look at half of the original diagram concerning your mom and dad.

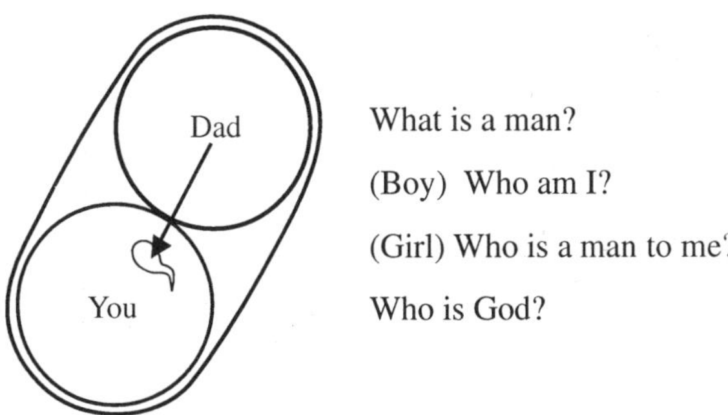

As a child prior to age three, every situation that included or excluded Dad created for you the depth of your belief in the area of your relationship to men and God.

With this in mind, consider the magnitude of the influence of your biological father.

For the child, Mom represents "What is a woman?" If you are a girl, your mom represents the concept for "Who am I?" If you are a boy, your mom represents, "Who is a woman to me?"

To visually demonstrate this connection, let's look at the other half of the diagram involving your mom and dad.

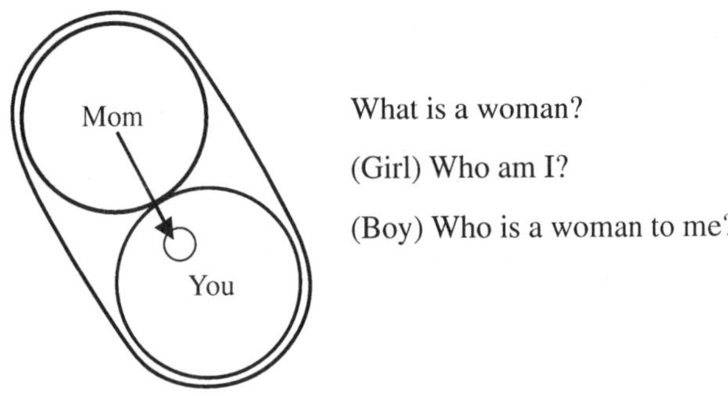

Before looking at your responses to the questions which represent your beliefs about men, women, and relationships' several possibilities need to be addressed that can affect the interpretation of your data. First, look to the information within your answers for how you are the same as your parents. Then look for how you are different. Realize also that if you did not interact well with a particular parent, oftentimes you may emotionally push that parent away by saying, "I refuse to be anything like him or her." In pushing away, you run the risk of losing the value of what that parent is teaching you. If you push a parent away, that parent will also have most of your attention. This is much like ignoring someone at a party. You must constantly be aware of the person you are ignoring because you have to know where he is and what he is doing in order to ignore him. Therefore, who really has all of your attention?

When you truly understand and believe that your parents are your valued teachers, you will be able to reframe every situation and recognize what you learned from them. You will also begin to look for what you believe is right rather than focusing on what you believe was wrong.

When you reframe the role of your parents in your life, you can truly put the two diagrams of Mom and Dad together to form a heart. This heart will then become the core of you.

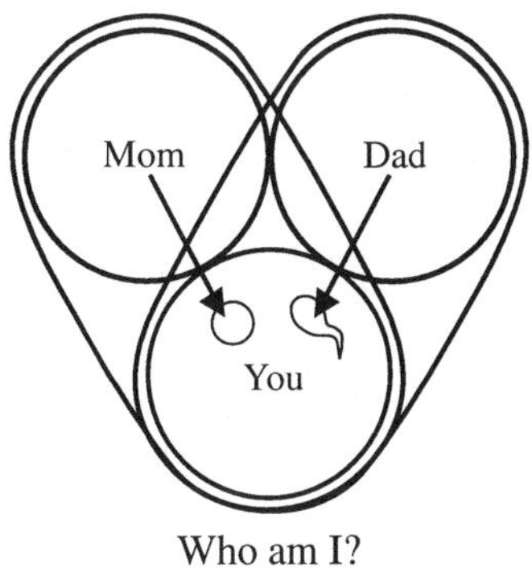

Who am I?

Until you move from your head to your heart, it is impossible to see the positive aspects of your life experiences. This move, when accomplished, will establish a place of honor for your parents as your perfect teachers. Without your parents, you would not even be alive! With this awareness, the appropriate response to your parents should be, "Thank you for giving me my life!"

The questions that follow will provide you with specific details of the learning you received from your perfect parents.

Remember, if non-biological parent figures were involved in your life, they too will add to your knowledge base about relationships. However, your deepest beliefs are a result of your answers about your biological parents.

62) **Who was your father's favorite? How do you know?**

If you are a woman, this question assists you in understanding where you believe you fit with men. If you are a man, this question will assist you in understanding your viewpoint of self.

If you believed you were the favored child of your dad and you are a man, you will place yourself as number one in your life. If you are a woman and were favored by your dad, you will expect the men in your life to see you as number one.

If you were not number one in your father's eyes and you are a man, you will not put yourself as number one in life. This is not a negative. The child you were simply taught you to see others as more important in terms of their needs and priorities. If you were not number one with your dad and you are a woman, you will find yourself in the same position with men in your adult world.

Reframed: The position of the child in relationship to Dad is the best position to place yourself with men to achieve all you can become in a relationship. For example, if your dad did not focus on you as number one, then you do not require total attention from the man in your world. This allows you to do many things on your own without spending major amounts of time focusing only on your relationship. Think of how your interactions with your father in this area apply to your adult life. How do they best serve you?

If you were raised by a father figure other than your biological father, look to your interactions with this individual for what you learned about your placement with significant male figures in your life.

63) Who was your mother's favorite? How do you know?

This question assists you in understanding where you best fit with women.

If you were your mother's favorite and you are a woman, you will put yourself as number one in your life. If you are a man and you were number one in your mother's eyes, you will want to be number one with the women in your life.

If you are a woman and were not number one in your mother's eyes, then as an adult you will not see yourself as number one and will place greater emphasis on others rather than on yourself.

If you were not number one to your mother and you are a man, you will not feel that women see you as their first priority. You could also attempt the opposite behavior and demand the number one position. If you demand the number one position, you will most likely have a feeling inside that women still do not place you as number one, regardless of how it appears.

If you had a sibling who was number one to Mom and you resented this interaction, as an adult you will find someone very similar in your life who you resent for her status with others.

If you were raised by a mother figure other than your biological mother, look to your interactions with this individual for what you learned about your placement with significant female figures in your life.

Your personal story tells the details of your life in the area of positioning yourself with others and self. Take a moment to synthesize your understanding regarding your placement with both of your parents. How does this placement affect your positioning in the world? What did the child learn for you?

Some examples:

A) You are a man and were number one with your father, but felt your mother loved your younger brother more than she loved you. As an adult, you easily put yourself first. However, in relationships you struggle with believing that your partner sees you as number one. Inside you feel that someone else will come along and take your place, just like your brother took your place with your mom. Reframed: You know to place yourself as number one in life. However, where you place yourself must obviously create value for yourself and others. In relationships you can reduce your internal struggle by not demanding that others be all things to you.

B) You are a woman and were number one to Dad but not number one to Mom. As an adult, you easily feel connected to men. However, you struggle with feeling number one to yourself or to the women in your life. This occurs because your mom did not place you first and she represents "Who am I?" and "What is a woman?" Reframed: Know that men will always be there for you. It is important not to focus your need for support on women. It is also best not to focus upon yourself.

C) Both Mom and Dad saw you as number one. As an adult, you feel confident and supported by yourself and others.

D) You did not feel number one in the eyes of either parent. As an adult, you have always felt you are on your own in life. Reframed: You know that the child taught you to take charge of your life and accomplish your goals in a self-motivated manner.

64) How old is your father? How old is your mother? If either parent has died, describe details. How old were you at the time of the death?

This question establishes a point of reference as to the age difference between child and parent. The teachings of younger parents tends to vary widely from those of older parents. How you felt about the age of your parents can also determine your feelings of comfort with them. For example, having older parents could cause embarrassment for you at functions where the other children's parents are younger.

If a parent has died, it is important to recognize the impact of that event upon your life. It is also important to understand how the death of a parent can sometimes bias your answers about that parent. This happens for several reasons: 1) You may have bestowed "sainthood" upon a deceased parent. As a result, you will remember only what fits that view. 2) You could slant the memory of a parent because of personal regret or lack of closure with that parent. 3) You may have had a difficult time reconciling the death and therefore cannot get to the true memory of the parent.

If you believe the death of a parent created a clouded view for you when you answered the questions regarding that parent, then attempt to answer the questions again. When you answer the questions for the second time, keep only the view of the child in focus.

65) Are your parents still married, how long have they been married? If there has been a divorce, how old were you when they divorced? Are there any remarriages and do you like the people involved?

Your answer to this question forms your belief in terms of how long you believe a marriage should last. It also helps you develop an understanding of your feelings regarding divorce and remarriage.

If your parents are in a long-term first marriage and are happy, your belief will be that marriage is forever. You will also believe that marriages should be compatible, since your parents modeled this.

If your parents are in a long-term first marriage and are stressed in their relationship, you will tend to believe you also must be married forever no matter what the cost or circumstances. You could also have decided, by viewing their relationship, that you would never remain in a stressful marriage. But if you divorce, you may tend to feel failure simply because your parents never divorced.

If you experienced the divorce of your parents, you will react in the same or opposite manner should you personally experience a divorce. In the event of your own divorce, your reaction to the divorce will be based upon your feelings about your parents' divorce.

If your parents have remarried, your feelings about their new partners will add information regarding your comfort level with your parents and their partnership choices.

To better understand your personal beliefs in this area, simply observe your past behavior and thoughts about the concept of marriage.

66) What kind of person did you perceive your father to be prior to you being nine years of age? Give as much detail as possible.

This question is very detailed and contains the core of your beliefs about men. It determines for a man, "Who am I?" and it answers for a woman, "Who or what is a man to me?" It also determines for most, "What do I believe about God?" (Your beliefs about God will be further detailed in questions 92 and 93.)

Look closely at your description of your biological father. How does this description match your present belief about men? Look to your words describing his character such as strong, intelligent, absent, weak, fun loving, sensitive, etc., and realize these are words that best describe what you believe a man to be. If you are a woman, how does your description of your father match the relationships you have with men? If you are a man, how does this description match your belief about yourself? Remember, you will create the same or the opposite behavior.

If in your formative years you were raised by a non-biological father, applying the questions about your father to this individual will provide you with additional information about men. However, your core belief, since Dad is half of you, is "Men are like my father." You will, as a result of what you felt about your biological father, choose the same or the opposite behavior. Look closely at your answer before reading the following scenarios for assistance.

For Women

If you loved your father and liked who he was, you will have a belief that men are wonderful. You will tend to find someone like your father for a relationship. (Note: I have often observed that having the perfect father can create a dilemma for some women. What happens in these cases is that Dad becomes the child's everything, and to find someone like him creates a feeling of dethroning Dad. To avoid dethroning Dad, these women may choose someone opposite of their father, and as a result, their lives tend to become turbulent.)

If you struggled with your dad and his interactions with you, you will generally find yourself struggling in the same type of adult male relationships. Remember, you will look for someone just like your dad because your goal is to love the child and prove to her you can fix a man like your dad. To assist yourself in reframing this dynamic with men, remember that your dad is the perfect teacher to teach you who "not" to be with. If someone like your dad enters your life, say, "Thank you for the reminder," and move on. Always remember to reframe any and all perceived past negatives. Make sure you look for the good interactions with your dad to see the gifts he provided in your life as well. Ask yourself what gifts your father's presence provided in terms of obtaining knowledge that can help you serve others?

If your dad was absent in your life, you will feel that men are absent in your adult life. Reframed: Dad could be the perfect teacher to assist you in understanding that your purpose is probably not to focus on men, but rather to concentrate on the gifts you have for yourself and others.

If your father died when you were a child, you will find that men leave you or are not present long-term in your adult relationships. The circumstances of your dad's death and your attachment to him will determine the dynamics of your adult relationships. For example, you were very close to your father and he died of a painful, terminal illness when you were seven. You will find yourself very connected to the men in your life but will have a deep sense that something awful is going to take them away from you. To reframe, this event it is important to pay close attention to the number seven and consciously renegotiate with people every seven years for an additional seven year connection. Your father also was a gift to teach you that men love you and are there for you.

If you never knew your biological father and you had no other father figure, you will be an adult woman who does not look to a man for connection or direction.

A helpful exercise in assisting your understanding of the role of male relationships in your adult life is to list on paper the dynamics of each male relationship you have had. Describe the character and behavior of the person as well as the positives and negatives within the relationship. Compare this description to your beliefs about your father. When you have completed your comparison to your father, compare your male relationships to each other and look for any common threads. What can you learn from this exercise for your future choices?

For Men

If your father was someone you admired and with whom you felt a connection, you will feel a need to become all you believe he was. Because of this connection, you will also tend to have a strong sense of self. However, if for some reason you should not live up to your image of your father, you will feel a deep sense of failure. Reframed: Your dad is the perfect teacher to assist you in becoming and sharing his positive qualities with others. His teachings will also assist you in sharing these qualities with your children.

If you struggled with your father's behavior, as an adult you will find yourself struggling at times with your sense of self. Sometimes when you detect that you are acting like your father, you will not feel comfortable with yourself. Because of your struggle with your father's behavior, you could also have formed an internal contract to never be like your father, therefore doing the opposite behavior of your father. Reframed: Dad is the perfect teacher to instruct you in what "not" to do. As a result of knowing your father, you could also have the capability to understand people who have an inability to connect to males. You may become excellent at assisting others in the process of connection to themselves and to the world.

If your father set standards you found impossible to keep, yet kept trying to meet to get his approval, as an adult you will tend to struggle to become good enough while simultaneously feeling you will never succeed. Reframed: Your father taught you to always work hard and never settle for less than the best. This quality can be a gift to yourself and others, particularly if you relinquish the need for approval from others.

If your father was absent, you will tend to struggle with the question, "Who am I?" Reframed: The resulting gift of this lack of connection with your father could lead to a deep search within yourself that will result in a spiritual connection far more rewarding than the human connection with your father. You will also be able to assist others in their search for themselves.

a) **What kind of interactions did you have with your father?**

If you are a woman and had positive childhood interactions with your father, the same type of interactions will create closeness with men in your adult life. If you are a man and had positive childhood interactions with your father, the same type of activity will give you the greatest pleasure as an adult.

If your childhood interactions with Dad were unpleasant, you may find yourself avoiding this type of interaction as an adult. You could also continue to repeat the negative events to get an opposite result for the child.

Reframed: What did Dad teach you about male connection? How does this information apply to your interactions with yourself and others in your adult world?

b) **Did your father say "I love you?" How did you feel?**

If you are a woman, the expression of affection by your dad teaches you how to receive affection from a man. If your dad said "I love you" and you felt comfortable with those words, as an adult it will be easy for you to hear the words "I love you" from a man. If your dad said "I love you" and you were not comfortable, you will feel uncomfortable when a man says the words "I love you."

If you are a man and your dad said "I love you" and you were comfortable with those words, it will be easy for you to say the words "I love you" to others. You will also have a sense of love for yourself. If you did not hear the words "I love you," it will be uncomfortable for you to say these words to others. You may also have a struggle within yourself regarding your own belief about self love. It is also possible you could do the opposite and frequently say the words "I love you." This behavior is a result of trying to make up for the lack of expression from your father.

Reframed: Your father taught you what the verbal expression of love from a man feels like for you. If you shared this expression with him and liked it, you realize the feeling it creates and you will want to share that experience with others. If as a child the words "I love you" were missing, you know the feeling that this void creates and you will be sensitive to others who also feel this lack in their lives.

c) **Did your dad hug you? How did you feel?**

If you are a man, this part of your interaction with your dad has to do with your ability to give affection. If you are a woman, this part of the question about your dad has to do with your ability to receive affection from a man.

If you are a man and you were hugged by your dad and you felt comfortable, as an adult it will be easy for you to show affection. If you were not hugged, you may find yourself uncomfortable giving affection to others.

If you are a woman and were hugged by your dad and it was comfortable, receiving affection from a man is comfortable for you. If your dad's hugs were uncomfortable or you were not hugged by your dad, then as an adult you will find yourself uncomfortable with physical expressions of affection from men.

d) **Did you feel loved by your father?**

If you felt love, you will be sensitive to the feeling of love and will not necessarily need words or touch to be a part of the experience.

If you are a woman and did not feel loved by your dad, you will have a difficult time feeling loved by a man.

If you are a man and did not feel loved by your father, you will have a difficult time feeling love for yourself. You may also find yourself having a struggle providing love to others.

Reframed: What does your personal experience in this area teach you. What can you learn about your interactions with others? For example, if you are a man and you did not feel loved by your father, then you know the deep feelings this has created within you. As a father, you can now give your children the love you felt was missing in your childhood. As a friend, you can give others the loving assurance you felt was missing in your interactions with you father.

e) Did you love your dad?

If you loved your father and you are a man, you will have feelings of love for both your father and yourself.

If you loved your father and you are a woman, you will have feelings of love for both your father and for the men in your world.

If you did not feel love for your father, you will struggle in this area with yourself and others. This struggle is the result of needing a deep connection of love and belonging from your father. When this does not occur, the child pulls back to protect himself and withholds love. Your struggle will end once you learn to reframe your experiences with your father and view him as your perfect teacher. Once this occurs, you can then look to the knowledge you gained from his presence in your life and apply it to all future relationships. For example, you did not feel love for your father because he was angry and distant. As an adult, you know to become the opposite of your father and strive to be peaceful and available to others. You can also be empathic with individuals who have been hurt by angry and/or distant people.

f) Did you like your dad?

If you are a woman, this answers the question, "Do I like men?" For men it determines how much you like yourself.

g) Did you feel comfortable around your father? Why or why not?

If you are a woman your answer to this question explains your comfort level around men. If you were comfortable with Dad, you will be comfortable around men. If you were not comfortable around your father, you will feel uncomfortable in the very situations in which you found yourself uncomfortable with Dad. Reframed: What did your father teach you regarding your personal placement with men? What placement works best for you? What placement does not work for you?

If you are a man, the answer to this question pertains to your comfort with yourself. If you were comfortable with Dad, you are comfortable with yourself. If you were uncomfortable with Dad, you will tend to have issues with your comfort about yourself. Reframed: What did Dad teach you about being comfortable with yourself? How can you use this information to help others become more comfortable with themselves? For example, you were comfortable with your father except in public. In public you never knew when your father was going to embarrass you by losing his temper or by becoming boisterous. As an adult, you now understand why you do not exhibit the type of behavior you observed in your father. You also avoid scenes and people who exhibit this type of behavior.

h) **Did your father have any addictions?**

If your father had addictions and you are a woman, you may tend to have relationships with men who have some form of addiction. You could also have learned from to avoid men with addictions. If you are a man and your father was addicted, you may tend to escape in the same way your father escaped. You may also be firmly committed to resisting any addiction.

Reframed: How can what you felt and observed with your father assist you in your adult choices? With the information the child obtained for you, how can you help others in the area of addiction? For example, your father was an alcoholic and was abusive to your mother when he drank. You felt scared and helpless during those times. As an adult, you take extreme care to nurture your relationships and not to be abusive. You also assist others who feel abused to make different choices in their lives.

Understanding specific addictions can be complex. I suggest you take time to become knowledgeable about any addictions that may have affected you as a child. With this knowledge, you will have greater adult options with regard to your behavioral choices. For the purpose of *LifeScripting*, observe the dynamics of any addictions your father may have had. Look specifically at what his behavior created for you in your belief system formation about men.

i) Was your dad physically attractive to you?

The information from this question has to do with your feelings about the physical attractiveness of men.

If Dad was good looking to you and you are a woman, you will want to be with good looking men. If Dad was not attractive to you, you will feel most comfortable with men who are not attractive.

If you are a man and Dad was good looking to you, your looks will be a major concern for you. If Dad was not good looking, then your looks will be less important to you.

Reframed: What did the child you were teach you about your need for physical attractiveness in a man?

The Total Effect Of Dad On Your Life

The overall effect of your father on your personal beliefs and behavior will unfold for you throughout your entire adult life. With the tools of *LifeScripting,* you will be able to reframe all past events, both positive and negative, that occurred with your father. As a result, you will view your father as a powerful teacher who positively impacted your adult life.

It is important to remember that your father could only give to you what he received from his parents and significant others. When you look at your father as the perfect teacher, your experiences with him will assist you in a positive reframe for all future behavioral choices.

If you are a man, look to your father for the answer to the question, "How is this man the perfect person to teach me all I need to know to become all I desire to be?" If you are a woman ask yourself, "How is this man the perfect person to teach me all I need to know in the area of male relationships?"

Remember, if a non-biological father figure was involved in your life, he too will add to your knowledge base about male behavior. However, your deepest beliefs about men are the direct result of your beliefs regarding your biological father.

67) **What kind of person did you perceive your mother to be prior to your being nine years of age? Give as much detail as possible.**

This question, like the question about your father, is very detailed and contains the core of your beliefs about women. For a woman it answers the question "Who am I?" For a man it answers the question "Who are women to me?"

Look closely at the description of your biological mother. How does this description match your beliefs about women?

If you are a man, how does your description of your mother match your current or past female relationships? If you are a woman, how does this description match your belief about yourself? If in your formative years you had a non-biological mother figure involved in your life, her influence provides additional information about women. However, your core beliefs come from your biological mother since she is half of you. As an adult, you will choose the same or opposite behavior of your mother based upon what you believed about your mom. Closely study your answer to this question before reading the following scenarios for assistance.

For Men

If you loved your mother and liked who she was, you will have a deep belief that women are wonderful. You will tend to find someone like your mother for a relationship. (Note: having the perfect mother can also create a dilemma for a man. What happens to create this dilemma is that the male child believes Mom is perfect and therefore Mom becomes the child's everything. As a result, having a relationship with someone as wonderful as Mom could create a feeling of betraying Mom. To prevent this betrayal, the man may engage in a relationship with someone who is opposite of Mom. The result of this type of relationship is usually turmoil.)

If you struggled with your mom and her interactions with you, you will generally find yourself in the same type of struggles in your adult female relationships. Remember, you will do this to prove to the child that if you find someone just like your mom and fix her, you were not the problem. To reframe this interaction with your mother, remember that your mom is the perfect teacher to teach you whom to avoid. Consequently, if someone like your mother enters your life, simply say, "Thank you for the reminder," and quickly move on. It is important to reframe your perceived past negatives with your mother. It is also important to recognize any positive interactions with your mother and acknowledge the gifts they provide in your adult life. Also, ask yourself how your mother's presence in your life has provided knowledge to help you assist others?

If your mom was absent in your life, you will feel women are absent in your adult life. Reframed: Mom could be the perfect teacher to assist you in understanding that your life purpose may not be to focus on women, but rather to concentrate on the gifts you have been given for yourself and others.

An exercise that may be helpful for you in developing an understanding of the role of female relationships in your life is to list on paper the positive and negative aspects of all your past female relationships. Describe the character of each person as well as the positives and negatives within the relationship. Compare this overview to your beliefs about your mother. Once you have completed your comparison to your mother, compare the relationships with each other. Look for the common threads in all relationships and try to trace them back to your interactions with your mother. What can you learn from this exercise to help you with your future choices?

For Women

If your mother was someone you admired and you were connected to her, you will feel a need to become equally as wonderful as your mother. You will also have a strong sense of self. However, if for some reason you should not live up to the standards you set regarding your mother, you will feel a deep sense of failure. Reframed: Having a mother that you admired will assist you in becoming all you are capable of becoming. Her direction will also assist you in sharing these qualities with others.

If you struggled with your mother's behavior, as an adult you will sometimes struggle with your sense of self. During the times you believe you are acting like your mother, you will not feel comfortable with yourself. You could also tend to have an internal contract with the child to never be like your mother. If that is the case, you will frequently do the opposite behavior of your mother. Reframed: Mom is the teacher who is perfect to instruct you in what "not" to do. Because of your interactions with your mother, you can now understand how people feel in their disconnect with themselves and others. One of your jobs could be to assist others in the process of connecting to themselves.

If your mother had standards you could not reach, yet you kept trying to meet her standards to gain her approval, as an adult you will struggle to be good enough. Oftentimes you will feel you are unable to succeed. Reframed: Your mother taught you to always work hard and to never settle for less than your best. This trait can be a gift to yourself and others, particularly if you let go of the need for approval from others.

If your mother was physically absent during your childhood, you will tend to struggle with the question, "Who am I?" Reframed: This lack of connection can create a deep search within yourself that may lead you to a spiritual connection that can be deeper than any connection you might have had with your mother. You can also help others by assisting them in their search for themselves.

a) **What kind of interactions did you have with your mother?**

If you are a man, the positive interactions you had with your mother will be the type of interactions that will create a closeness to women.

If you are a woman, the positive interactions you had with your mother will be the type of interactions that will give you the greatest pleasure as an adult.

If your childhood interactions with your mom were unpleasant, you may find yourself avoiding the same type of activity as an adult. You could also repeat the same situations with the hope of making them right for the child.

Reframed: What did your mom teach you about female connections? How does this information apply to your interactions with other women and yourself? For example, you are a man and as a child you felt your interactions with your mother to be superficial since she always appeared too busy for you. As an adult, you find yourself in situations with women who are too busy for any interaction with you. This occurs both at work and home. You can now get the needs of the child met by arranging for time and attention with those you love. You can also position yourself in business in such a way that the women you work with are present to your needs.

b) **Did your mother say "I love you?" How did you feel?**

If you are a man, the expression of affection by your mother teaches you how to receive affection from a woman. If your mom said, "I love you" and you felt comfortable with those words, it will be easy for you to hear the words "I love you" from a woman. If your mom said "I love you" and you were not comfortable, you will feel uncomfortable when a woman says "I love you."

If you are a woman and your mom said "I love you" and you were comfortable with those words, it will be easy for you to say the words "I love you" to others. You will also have a sense of love for yourself. If you did not hear the words "I love you" from your mom, it will be uncomfortable for you to say these words to others. You may even have a struggle within yourself in the area of self love. You could also do the opposite and constantly say the words "I love you" to make up for the lack of expression from your mother.

Reframed: Your mother taught you what the verbal expression of love feels like for you. If you shared this expression with her and liked it, you may want to share the same with others. If the words "I love you" were missing when you were a child, you know the feelings this lack of expression created. As an adult, you can now be sensitive to others who feel this missing dynamic in their lives.

c) **Did your mom hug you? How did you feel?**

If you are a woman, this portion of your interaction with your mom has to do with your ability to give affection. If you are a man, your answer to this question has to do with your ability to receive affection from a woman.

If you are a woman and you were hugged by your mom and felt comfortable, as an adult it will be easy for you to show affection. If you were not hugged, you may find yourself uncomfortable giving affection to others.

If you are a man and were hugged by your mom and it was comfortable, receiving affection from a woman is comfortable for you. If your mom's hugs were uncomfortable, as an adult you will find yourself uncomfortable when displaying affection. If you were not hugged by your mom, it may be difficult for you to receive affection from a woman.

d) Did you feel loved by your mother?

If you felt love from your mother, you will be sensitive to experiencing love without the need for words or touch.

If you are a woman, you will believe that others should understand and feel your love without the need for words. If as a child you did not feel loved by your mother, as an adult woman you will have difficulty feeling love for yourself.

If you are a man and you felt your mother loved you, you will feel the love of a woman with or without the need to hear the words "I love you." If you did not feel loved by your mother, you will have a difficult time truly feeling you are loved by a woman.

Reframed: What does your personal experience in this area teach you for your future interactions with others?

e) Did you love your mom?

If you are a woman and you loved your mother, you will have feelings of love for both your mother and yourself. If you believe you did not love your mother, you will tend to have a difficult time loving yourself.

If you are a man and you loved your mother, you will feel love for the women in your world. If you did not feel love for your mother, you may have difficulty believing in the possibility of deeply loving a woman.

Reframed: Your mother was your perfect teacher. What did she teach you about love of yourself and love of others?

f) Did you like your mom?

If you are a man, your response to this question about your mother answers the question, "Do I like women?"

If you are a woman, your answer determines your feelings about liking yourself.

g) Did you feel comfortable around your mother? Why or why not?

If you are a man, your answer to this question explains your comfort level around women. If you were comfortable with your mom, you will be comfortable around women. If you were not comfortable with your mother, you will feel uncomfortable in the very situations that created discomfort with your mom. Reframed: What did your mother teach you regarding how to best place yourself with women? What did she teach you in the area of what to experience or what to avoid during your interactions with women? For example, you were very comfortable around your mother and spent hours talking with her as a child. As an adult, it is important to have friendships with women with whom you feel comfortable. It is also important to have friendships with women to whom you can easily talk for long periods of time.

If you are a woman, the answer to this question pertains to your comfort level with yourself. If you were comfortable with your mother, you will tend to be comfortable with yourself. If you were uncomfortable with your mom, you will tend to have issues of discomfort with yourself. Reframed: What did your mom teach you about what you want to give to yourself and others? For example, you were uncomfortable around your mother because she never looked at you or talked directly to you. She always seemed to be preoccupied with other things. As an adult, you realize you want to be present for others, especially your children. As a result of your interaction with your mother, you consciously give others your full attention. You also pay close attention to your need for connection to others, making sure you place yourself where those needs are met.

h) Did your mother have any addictions?

If your mother had addictions and you are a man, you may tend to have relationships with women who exhibit some form of addiction. Because of your mother's addiction, you may also have learned the merits of choosing a woman without addictions.

If you are a woman and your mother was addicted, you could tend to escape the same way she escaped. You could also be firmly committed to resisting any addiction.

Look at your adult behavior for any long-term impact resulting from your mother's addictions.

Reframed: How can what you felt and observed with your mother assist you in your adult choices? How can you help others in the area of addiction with the information the child obtained for you?

i) Was your mother physically attractive to you?

This part of the information about your mother has to do with your feelings about the physical attractiveness of women.

If your mom was good looking to you and you are a man, you will want to be with good looking women. If your mom was not attractive to you, you will feel the most comfortable with women who are not attractive.

If you are a woman and your mom was good looking to you, your looks will be a major concern to you. If your mom was not good looking, then looks will be less important.

Reframed: What did the child you were help you understand about your need for physical attractiveness in a woman?

The Total Effect Of Your Mother On Your Life

The effect your mother had on your life will have great impact upon you throughout your entire adult life. By utilizing the *LifeScripting* process, you will be able to reframe the events you experienced with this powerful personal teacher. Your use of reframing will greatly add to your adult empowerment.

Any event that involves the question "What is a woman?" is about your childhood interactions with your mother. If you are a woman, your mom also affects your sense of "Who am I?" As a man, your mom represents "Who is a woman to me?" Your mom also teaches you, as a man, how to give and receive love from a woman.

It is important to remember that your mom's behavior was a reflection of what she was taught and what she experienced. Like you, she had the perfect parents. By looking at your mother as the perfect teacher, you can assist yourself in a positive reframe for your future understanding and behavioral choices.

If you are a woman, ask yourself the questions, "How was my mother the perfect person to teach me all I needed to know? How has she enabled me to become all I desire to become?" If you are a man, ask yourself, "How was my mother the perfect person to teach me all I needed to know about determining the right relationship for me?"

Remember, if a non-biological mother figure was involved in your life, she will add to your knowledge base about female behavior. However, your deepest beliefs about women are a result of your beliefs regarding your biological mother.

68) **Who of the siblings is most like your father? How? How are you like your father?**

This question helps you recognize the facets of you that are most like your father. It is helpful to review those traits in your father you liked, as well as to reframe the traits your father exhibited that created challenges for you. By recognizing any behavior that models your father, you will be able to better choose your future behavior.

As a child, when you observed your father's behavior, you were being taught behavior in two distinct ways: 1) If you were comfortable with his behavior, he taught you how to model his behavior. 2) If you were uncomfortable with his behavior, he taught you what traits to avoid.

69) **Who of the siblings is most like your mother? How? How are you like your mother?**

This question helps you recognize the parts of you that are most like your mother. It also helps you recognize those traits your mother exhibited you liked, and those you didn't like. By analyzing your answer to this question, you will be able to make more conscious behavioral choices. Remember, your mother is the perfect teacher because she has taught you how to be and how not to be. If you were comfortable with her behavior, repeat the behavior. If you were uncomfortable, do not repeat the behavior.

70) **What kind of relationship did you witness between your mother and your father when you were a child?**

When you observed the relationship, or lack of relationship, between your parents, you were absorbing information about possible ways to act within a relationship. As a result of what you observed, you will tend to do the same or opposite behavior in your adult relationships. When observing the behavior of your parents toward one another, you formed your beliefs regarding how to act within a relationship. Be aware that you were observing your parents' interactions, you were not participating in their relationship. This was much like watching a movie. When watching a movie, you process information then make decisions based upon what you see. The data you gathered from watching the movie of your parents can be easily analyzed since you were an observer to their relationship. Based upon your observations of what worked or did not work for your parents, you can easily pick and choose the parts of their relationship you want in your life. Be very aware that the deepest base for what you believe about your personal relationships is a result of your direct relationship to each parent. By watching their personal relationship, you received valuable information about how to act within a relationship.

The following diagram depicts this process.

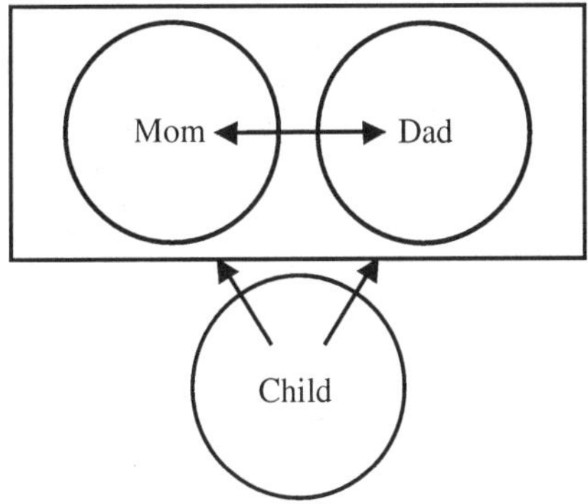

In your observations of your mom and dad, what parts of their life together do you want to have as a part of your life? What did you observe that you would prefer not to have occur in your relationships? How can you be grateful for what your parents taught you by what they did or did not do within their own relationship? Looking at their relationship as a learning experience also helps you better understand why you have exhibited certain behaviors in past and present relationships. Recognize how you may have repeated what you saw in your childhood. With this new knowledge, establish new and positive choices for your future behavior.

Secondary information about relationships is also obtained from observing the interactions of stepparents, adoptive parents, foster parents, grandparents, etc.

71) What kind of affection did you observe between your mother and father when you were a child?

This is the basis for your comfort regarding your display of affection within a relationship. Review how you have expressed yourself in past relationships and see how your behavior compares to your feelings and observations about your parents' display of affection within their relationship. You will find yourself expressing affection in the same manner as your parents, particularly if their behavior was pleasing to you. If their behavior was uncomfortable, you will tend to avoid similar expressions of affection in your relationships.

If your parents were not affectionate, as an adult you may find yourself having difficulty with displays of affection. If your parents were not affectionate and you wished they had been, you will desire to experience what you did not see.

What did your parents teach you regarding the display of affection? How can you apply this information in a positive way to your life? How does this information assist you in loving and understanding others?

72) Do you feel your mother loved your father? How did you come to this conclusion?

This question has to do with your feelings about women loving men.

If you are a woman and you believed your mother loved your father, you will feel a deep love for the man in your life.

If you are a woman and you believed your mother did not love your father, you could tend to struggle with the concept of love for your partner. You could also do the opposite behavior because you have a commitment with the child to deeply love your partner. This is a result of not liking what you observed as a child.

If you are a man and you believed your mother loved your father, you will feel that the women in your life love you no matter what the circumstances.

If you are a man and did not feel your mother loved your father, you will have a sense of not being loved by a woman.

Reframed: What did your mother teach you that applies to your adult relationships? How can you apply this to others as you interact with them?

73) Do you feel your father loved your mother? How did you come to this conclusion?

This question has to do with your feelings about men loving women.

If you are a man and you believed your father loved your mother, you will tend to feel deep internal love for the women in your life. If you are a man and believed your father did not love your mother, you may struggle with this very dynamic within your own relationships. Or you could strive for the opposite of what you observed with the hope of fixing the feelings of the child.

If you are a woman and you believed your father loved your mother, you will have a sense of being loved by a man no matter what the circumstances. If as a child you did not feel your father loved your mother and you are a woman, you may tend to feel that this dynamic is also occurring within your intimate relationships.

Reframed: What did your father teach you about the love of a partner that you can apply to your relationships? How does this influence your interactions with others? For example, you are a man and as a child you observed your mother's sorrow over feeling unloved by your father. You vowed that when you grew up you would treat your wife with kindness and love. As an adult, you are tender to and considerate of your spouse.

74) Who told you about sex? What was your experience about this information?

Your feelings and beliefs about sex are multi-faceted and clearly more complex than the scope of this book. Your deepest beliefs about sex can be discovered by applying the basics of *LifeScripting* to the questions in this section. Your feelings about your sexuality are a vital part of your feelings about yourself. It is important to realize that sexuality is a part of everyone's life and your decision as to where sex fits within your life is crucial. This applies even if your choice is to be non-sexual.

How and from whom you learned about sex establishes your comfort or discomfort in terms of discussing it. If you obtained direct information about sex with no awkwardness, you will be able to talk comfortably about sex. If you were given information and were uncomfortable with how the information was presented, you may tend to feel uncomfortable when talking about sex.

How you learned about sex also indicates how you generally discover the deeper information of life. For example, if you had to put the pieces of information about sex together yourself, you will generally find yourself putting the pieces of life together for yourself.

If you were told about sex by your mother and/or father in a thorough and comfortable manner, you will readily receive vital information without difficulty or extensive research. You will also tend to be comfortable discussing in-depth subjects.

Review this part of your life and reframe how it serves you, as well as how this information can best help you and others.

If as a child you learned about sex because someone was sexual with you, look to this experience for how it can best serve your future where decisions about your choices with others are concerned. How can this experience help you help others?

If you are a woman, it is also important to review your feelings about puberty and your comfort or discomfort about your bodily changes. How your father interacted with you at this time also plays a vital role in how you feel about your femininity and sexuality.

If you are a man, how did your mother and father interact with you during puberty?

75) **How old were you when you had your first sexual experience? Was it pleasant? Why or why not?**

This question has to do with your belief about the age at which you feel you should be able to approach life's events. If you were young when you had your first sexual experience and you chose the experience, you may find yourself wanting to do things earlier than your peers. If your first experience was later in life, you may find yourself cautious about events that have the potential to change your life.

If your first sexual experience was pleasant, you will try to repeat it. If your first sexual experience was not pleasant, you may also find yourself repeating the situation in an attempt to change the outcome. Once you understand the reasons why you are repeating undesirable behavior, simply realize what is causing what and avoid those situations. For example, you are a woman and your first sexual experience was forced. The experience left you feeling scared and degraded. As an adult, you have found yourself with men who force themselves upon you and degrade you. You have done this out of love for the child in an attempt to change the outcome. You can now realize what is causing what in your life and recognize the type of men who will act out this scenario. With this awareness, you can now avoid this type of man. Remember, the child learned for you. The lesson in this experience is to find men opposite of the man who forced himself upon you. You can also reach out to others by helping those who have been forced or degraded.

Since sexuality is an intricate part of your feelings about yourself, it is important to determine how you truly feel about yourself in this area of your life. To bury your sexual experiences and feelings could create lifelong blockages of your energy and greatly affect your future choices. To determine where sexuality best fits for you does not imply the necessity of sexual activity. It simply implies a need to understand yourself and your choices in this area.

76) Is sex okay for you now? Why or why not?

It is important to discover for yourself the dynamics of your sexuality in your present life. By recognizing any imbalances, you will greatly assist yourself in terms of available options for a totally balanced life. If sex is okay for you, enjoy your life in this area. If sex is an issue for you, spend the necessary time to look to your past and reframe your experiences for what they taught you in terms of how you can most effectively love and accept yourself and others.

(Note: There are many avenues for valid information to assist you with sexuality. Those avenues include books, therapy, seminars, etc. Be selective about where and how you gather information. The information gathering experiences should feel right to you. If the information does not fit for you, it does not have to be applied to your life. You are the only person who can determine what information and activity is correct for you.)

77) Who made the decisions in your home, your father or mother?

Your answer to this question will help you better understand your belief about who should make the decisions in your relationships.

If your father made the decisions, you will believe that men are to make the decisions. If you are a man, this will generally create a need to decide. If you are a woman, you will look to a man to decide.

If your mother made the decisions and you are a man, you will tend to look to the woman for decision making. If you are a woman, you will want to make the decisions.

If your mother and father shared the decision making process, you will feel most comfortable when you are sharing the decision making process with a partner.

If you find yourself in a partnership where both you and your mate believe they are to make the decisions, a possible solution to this dilemma would be to agree that each of you will make all personal decisions for yourself. It is also important to agree with your partner that you will come together and jointly make any decisions involving the partnership.

Reframed: How can the lessons provided by your parents in the area of decision making assist your life today? How can this information help in your interactions with others? If as a child you were taught to make the decisions, decision making will be a gift for you in your interactions with others. If as a child you were taught that others should make the decisions, it may work best for you to let others decide.

78) Did your mother and father ever argue openly? What did they argue about?

How your parents or parental figures interacted in this area taught you how to, or how not to, problem solve. (Questions 79, 80, and 81 will also add to this information.) Please do not become frustrated if you observed intense interactions in this area. At the end of this series of questions, I will present a simple problem solving technique enabling you to quickly and easily solve problems.

What your parents argued about will be the exact stressors that tend to be a part of your adult life and relationships. For example, if your parents argued about money, you will tend to have adult stress about money. If they argued about time spent with each other, look to this as an issue within your relationships. If your parents argued about infidelity, you will feel stress about your partner's faithfulness. If they argued about children, this will tend to be an adult issue for you. If your parents never disagreed, you will find yourself unable to deal with any issues of contention in your relationships. On a positive note, you may find you tend to have fewer problems than others. This occurs because your inclination will be to create the "problem free" environment you had as a child.

If you ever observed your parents disagreeing, you have a basis for problem solving. However, the manner in which they disagreed will become the method you will generally implement to solve your problems.

The next three questions will assist you in understanding the specifics of your problem solving skills. Before moving on to these questions, spend a moment reflecting upon the two areas of information provided in this question: 1) What basis do you have for your ability to problem solve? 2) Based on what your parents disagreed about, into what areas do your problems tend to fall?

79) How did these arguments progress from beginning to middle to end?

This question assists you in understanding your style in resolving issues from beginning to end. It will also help you understand, if pieces of data were missing, why you cannot complete a problem solving process.

Look to your answer for the details of your behavior. If you are a man, you will tend to respond to conflict in the same or opposite manner in which your dad responded. If you are a woman, you will tend to respond to conflict in the same or opposite manner your mom responded.

If as a child you perceived your parents' style of problem solving to be ineffective and you made a commitment not to become like them in this area, you will tend to respond to conflict in the manner the child determined was correct.

You may also find that your partner often responds in the same manner as one of your parents. What the child observed will assist you in determining what to do when interacting with a partner. For example, if one parent never worked toward resolution in an argument, you learned that to repeat that style will not solve your issues. If one of your parents' style was very effective in resolving conflict, to repeat that behavior will create effective problem solving for you.

Look again to your answers to determine your skills for effective problem solving from beginning to end. Is the entire area represented in your learning or are there gaps?

When your parents disagreed, if they talked the issues through and analyzed both sides while determining together the best solution, as an adult you will have the same basic behavior.

If your parents never fully resolved problems, you may have a difficult time deciding how best to bring closure to your conflicts.

The following examples will assist you in a better understanding of the intricacies of problem solving.

A) As a child, Sam saw his father totally overwhelm his mother when disagreements occurred. His father would yell until his mother left the room in tears. The issues were never resolved. They would just go away because his mom never talked about them again. As a result, Sam's dad would do whatever he desired in the area that was the problem. As an adult, when Sam finds himself in stress he yells at his partner until she leaves the situation in tears, then he does as he chooses about the issue. In business, he also finds himself controlling those around him with his voice and determination. If Sam did not like Dad's behavior, or if he realized the method was ineffective, he could do the opposite behavior to bring closure to his problems.

B) Julie saw her parents frequently yell and scream at each other over the least little issue. Neither parent would back down so there was constant tension in the household. As an adult, Julie finds herself in constant disagreement with the man in her life and feels helpless to resolve the tension. In business, she also finds herself in similar situations.

C) As a child, Grace saw tension mount between her mother and father. Her father would get angry and leave the house. As an adult, Grace feels that tension will create a situation where someone will leave her. Consequently, she avoids any confrontation with her partner and her needs within the relationship seldom get met.

D) Joe saw his mother totally dominate his father. When his mother would get angry his father would simply become quiet. As an adult, Joe handles tension and stress by withdrawing.

E) Norma observed that every time her mother got frustrated she ran from the house and didn't return for several hours. As an adult, when Norma is frustrated, she runs from the situation and does not return for several hours.

Reframed: Look at the interactions of your parents in the area of how their disagreements progressed from beginning to end. Observe this like you would watch a movie so you do not become emotionally involved. Ask yourself what you have learned as a result of observing your parents interactions with each other. How can you use this information for your future choices in serving yourself and others? For example: 1) If you are a woman and you saw Mom leave the situation for several hours, the child learned for you the importance of taking a break from issues before returning for final resolve. 2) If you are a man and you saw Mom leave the situation for a period of time, Mom taught you to give the woman in your life adequate space when there is a disagreement.

Remember, if you were comfortable with what you observed, you will want to repeat the behavior. If you were not comfortable with what you observed, use that information for what not to do in your adult life.

80) How did you feel about these arguments? What did you do when they occurred?

Your childhood feelings during your parents' disagreements will tend to be the feelings you will have when disagreements occur in your adult life. What you did during your parents' disagreements will be what you tend to do during conflict in your adult life.

For example, if you were afraid and went to your room, as an adult, when conflict occurs, you will feel afraid and want to retreat to your room or some similar place. If you felt overwhelmed and just stood immobile while watching your parents' arguments, you will tend to become immobile when conflict occurs.

Reframed: How can your present behavior assist you in understanding yourself and your future choices? How can this information help you in your interactions with others?

81) Whose side did you take and why?

Your answer to this question gives you information about whose side you will take during a disagreement.

If you are a man and you took your father's side, during disagreements you will find yourself believing you are right. If you took your mother's side, you will find yourself always seeing the woman's point of view. If you did not take a side, you will find yourself remaining neutral in the area of who is right or wrong.

If you are a woman and you took your mother's side during disagreements, you will believe you are right. If you took your father's side, you will find yourself seeing the man's point of view. If you were neutral, you will tend to remain neutral in disagreements.

Reframed: Look to your alliances during disagreements to understand your future behavior choices.

How To Problem Solve

Problem solving is a learned skill. If these steps are followed, problem solving can become quite simple. On a sheet of paper create five columns. In column one write the word PROBLEM. In column two write POSSIBLE ACTION. In column three write CONSEQUENCES. In column four write YES/NO. In column five write ACTION TO BE TAKEN.

Your paper will look something like this:

Problem	Possible Action	Consequences	Yes/No	Action To Be Taken

If in future you have an issue difficult to resolve, use this flow chart to crystallize your thinking and create an action plan.

In column one, labeled PROBLEM, write what you believe is the problem. Probe for the real problem rather than just the symptoms. If you have difficulty defining the problem (which many do since they did not see their parents argue and therefore are unable to problem solve as an adult), pretend you are talking to a good friend and he is describing the very issue you are confronting. After hearing his story, what would you tell your friend the problem is?

Next, in the column marked POSSIBLE ACTION, write as many options for action as you can imagine. If you have difficulty determining possible actions, again think of your friend. What would you tell your friend about his possible action steps. Brainstorm all options and do not leave any stones unturned. By writing all possible options, you will discover several valid steps toward a solution.

In the CONSEQUENCES column, write all the consequences that could occur for each specific action step. This part of the exercise will enable you to thoroughly analyze each possible action step. By doing this, you will eliminate later regrets that may occur from reacting too quickly.

In the YES/NO column, mark "yes" next to the action steps that, if taken, will result in acceptable consequences. Mark "no" next to the consequences that do not qualify. Action steps should not be taken where the response is no. If your response is yes, analyze the action more closely to determine if you want to initiate the action process.

The final column reads ACTION TO BE TAKEN. Look to the areas you marked "yes." From these responses, choose the action to best solve your problem and take the action.

Problem solving in this manner will assist you in both your private and business life. The method is simple yet the results are so very rewarding.

Do not forget to reframe your personal learning in terms of your ability to problem solve. What did your childhood experiences teach you, both in the area of "how to" and "how not to" problem solve? How can you assist others in these areas by understanding what they feel and need?

82) **Did your parents agree or disagree on the methods of raising children? If they disagreed, what did they disagree about?**

How you observed your parents with regard to their interaction about children formed your beliefs for what will occur in your relationship when and if you have children.

If your parents agreed on how to raise children, you will want agreement about children in your relationship. If your parents disagreed, you will tend to find yourself in the same types of disagreements about children.

If your mother made all the decisions about the children, you will believe the woman is the deciding factor regarding issues about children.

If your father was the deciding factor, you will want the man to make all important decisions regarding children.

If you disliked the method your parents used regarding the children, you may attempt to do the opposite behavior.

Reframed: From your childhood experiences, what behaviors did you perceive worked well with regard to rearing children? What behaviors did you learn do not work well? How can this information help you in the interactions you have with your children and spouse? How can this data help you better understand the behavior of others?

83) **What parent wanted the most for your life? What did your mother want for you and what did she do about what she wanted? What did your father want for you and what did he do about what he wanted? How did you feel?**

Your belief for who will support you in life comes from your answer to this question. Also, your belief regarding your need to live up to the expectations of others is inclusive in this question. Look closely at your answer and apply the dynamics of your childhood experiences as you analyze your adult feelings and behavior in this area.

The parent who supported you the most is the gender from which you will expect to receive adult support. If both parents supported you, you will experience support from both sexes.

If neither parent seemed to want anything specific for you, but rather just let your life happen, as an adult you may find yourself without clear direction. You may also do the opposite behavior and make major demands upon yourself. However, if this is the case, you may feel a deep sense of aloneness as well as a strong belief that no one will be there to encourage you. To reframe this experience, realize that you are an individual who has been trained to be self-sufficient and self-motivated. As a result, you will be able to assist others in becoming strong.

What each parent wanted for you is what you feel you must become in some form, to receive their approval. If you become something other than what they desired for you, you will experience tension. This tension is the result of your "perceived parental disappointment." It is wise to talk to your parents honestly to dispel any untruth about their desires for you.

If you are a man, what Dad wanted for your life will have an effect upon your view of "Who am I?" If you are a woman, what Dad wanted will influence your feelings of what you believe a man wants for you, and from you.

If you are a woman, what Mom wanted for you will effect your concept of self. If you are a man, what Mom wanted for you will influence your feelings of approval from women, as well as your feelings of being successful in the eyes of a woman.

For example, if you are a man and Dad wanted you to become the executive you have become and you like your position, you will be settled both inside and outside of yourself. However, if Dad wanted you to become the executive you have become but you do not like your position, you will feel a tremendous imbalance in your life. Unfortunately, unless you reframe your experience with your father, you will not be able to leave your position without feeling deeply that you've disappointed your father. If Dad's dream was for you to be an executive and you hated the thought, becoming instead something totally different, then regardless of your success, you will still tend to feel a sense of having disappointed Dad.

Reframed: What did your parents teach you about support from others in the world? What did they teach you about what you want for yourself? How can this information assist you in positioning yourself to accept joy in your life?

84) Did any other people live with your family? Describe him/her/them and your relationship(s).

If people other than your immediate family lived with you, they will add to your belief about extended family relationships.

Look to your answer for any information from significant others that has influenced your life. If someone lived with you and you enjoyed his/her presence, look in your present life to see who seems most like this person. If you were challenged by the presence of someone who lived with your family, look to your life at present to see if someone matches that person.

Reframed: What did these individuals teach you about human interaction? How can you apply this information to your life? If the interaction was negative, what did this interaction teach you about what "not" to do in your life?

Summary Of Parents

Questions 62-84 gave you an overview of your beliefs for, "What is a man?" "What is a woman?" "What is a relationship?" "What is my view of sex?" "How do I problem solve?" and "Who supports my life?" It would serve you well to pause at this point and invest some time integrating the information you have just uncovered. As you contemplate this information, add any additional data you recall. Reframe this new information for how it best serves your future interactions in relationships.

As your life unfolds, know that any memory about your biological parents or non-biological parental figures will fit into one of the categories of this section. Take each memory as it occurs and place it into the proper category. Over time, you will truly have an understanding of why you do what you do within relationships. With this understanding, you will be able to empower your future life choices.

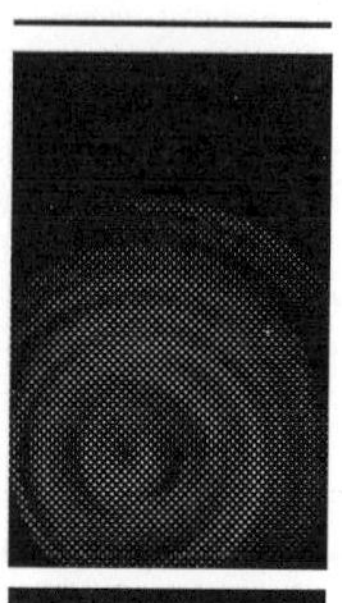

ADDITIONAL BELIEFS
Memories - God - Money - Dreams

Early Recollections-Your Past Is Your Present

85) Relax and allow your mind to recall three early memories prior to nine years of age. Do not judge the intensity of each memory. Allow the memories to appear on the screen of your mind one at a time. What age were you during each memory? What happened in detail? How did you feel at the time of the memory?

When you asked yourself to recall three early memories, your mind went through the card catalog of millions of past memories and picked three very specific memories. The selection of these memories was not a random event in your brain. Your brain chose three memories that exactly match your current life issues. Not only did your mind pick three matching memories, it also picked them in the exact order of importance. Your first memory is an event that matches the dynamics of your primary concern or thought at present. Your second memory matches your secondary thought or concern. Your third memory matches something that is happening in the present moment ranked third in order of concern for you. When your memories are analyzed, you will realize they contain the characters and dynamics in your life at present. There are no random memories. The memories that surfaced will assist you in understanding your present reality as well as your corresponding options.

It has been my consistent experience with *LifeScripting* clients that their past memories always have the exact ingredients of their now moment experiences. This occurs because your past beliefs run your present life. Therefore, you will choose situations that match your past experiences. You will also respond to situations in the present with the same feelings you had in the past. Connecting the memories of the past to the present becomes a meaningful way to understand what did or did not work for you in the past. With this information, you can make conscious choices regarding your future behavior. When you grasp the depth of your past memories and their relationship to your now moment challenges, you will come to an understanding that the past is the present and it governs all your choices. Your ability to experience free choice will come from your recognition of "what" caused "what" in the past, coupled with your ability to make conscious choices in light of that information.

The three memories you noted apply to your present day adult life. However, in two or three weeks, if you were to ask yourself to remember three past events, three different memories would surface. The new memories will again match your current now moment experiences.

Analyze your memories and determine what characters in your present experiences are similar to your past experiences. Carefully consider how the child felt and determine where in your present situation you are having the same basic feelings. Look to the end result of these childhood experiences for the possible end result in your present moment. With this understanding, you can predict what will happen in your present situation. If you dislike the predictable outcome, you can choose to alter the end results by changing your behavior.

To assist you in the process of interpreting your three memories, I will provide you with several examples:

The first example comes from the memory of Lucy who came to me because she was trying to make a decision in two areas. Her first decision was wether she should remain in her relationship. The second decision concerned her career. Lucy was at a point of burn-out in her job and needed to decide if the risk of leaving her field was advisable. Lucy's three memories were:

A) "I remember a family vacation to Virginia. We were going to see my father's family. We packed the station wagon and my grandmother went with us. I felt excited about going that far away. I also felt excited about getting to meet my father's family for the first time."

B) "No one could find my father. No one knew where he was. I went behind the garage and found him sitting back there making something. He was always good with his hands. He liked to make things. He was making a popcorn popper. I ran and told everyone I found him. He came in and we made popcorn. I felt it was fun. I enjoyed it. I still have the popcorn popper."

C) "I remember getting ready to go to the river. My father had washed the car. When getting ready to leave, my puppy had gotten under the car and my father ran over him. We had to bury my dog before we left. I was crying and was very upset. When we got to the river I realized I had forgotten my shoes. Everyone had to carry me because the rocks were hot."

Interpretation: It appears, at first reading, that these memories are random until you apply them to Lucy's present life. Remember, Lucy wants to make decisions in the areas of her relationship and job.

The first memory is a memory to remind Lucy of her deepest present desire. At a deep level, Lucy has a need to just take a vacation and have some fun meeting new people. She would prefer escape over confronting the decisions she is now facing. Her mind is telling her to remember that doing something new and exciting will assist in reducing her present stress.

Lucy's second memory has to do with defining her relationship and deciding how it fits in her life. In her memory, her dad was lost. In her present relationship, Lucy feels she cannot find the man she is with. In her memory, she searches for Dad and finds him doing what he loves, making something behind the garage. In Lucy's relationship, the man is doing what he loves which keeps him away from her. In her memory, Dad was making a popcorn popper for the family. He shared his creation with them by going into the house and making popcorn. In Lucy's relationship the man is professing to be working at what he loves with the hope that it will add to the dynamics of their relationship. This memory is reminding Lucy that if she is patient, supporting the need of the man to be away doing what he loves, the end result will add to the relationship, just as the popcorn popper added to the family fun.

Lucy's third memory has to do with Lucy's desire to change careers and her fear that something will go wrong if she does. She remembered getting ready to go to the river and that her dad ran over her dog. Presently, she is getting ready to make a career change. Her memory reminds her that when she does something out of the ordinary (going to the river) something awful happens (Dad running over her puppy). Her present feeling is that something awful will happen if she changes careers to do something different. She also feels she will not get the support of the men in her life. In fact, she feels they may even hurt her, just like her dad running over her puppy. Lucy's memory goes on to remind her that when she got to the river she did not have her shoes and had to be carried by others. Lucy's present fear is that she will make a career move and will not be prepared. Her memory reminds her that others will be there to support her since her family carried her over the rocks.

The second example of three early recollections comes from a male client named Frances. This client came to me because he was overwhelmed with the responsibilities in his life. He had three small children, a large financial overhead, and was in a commissioned sales position which depended on his daily efforts for survival. Fran's marriage was also stressed. Communications with his wife had broken down to the point where divorce was being contemplated. The option of divorce seemed overwhelming to Fran because of the children and his financial commitment.

Fran had four memories. They were:

A) "There were around six kids playing in my sand box. I didn't like them touching my stuff. Dad got angry at me. Scared me and spanked me. I was afraid."

B) "I had to fight or get beat up at home. I got teased about my name and Dad said if anyone laughs punch them in the nose. I felt pressure because I was supposed to punch them in the nose but I didn't. I didn't fight because I didn't see the value in it."

C) "One kid used to pick on me a lot, like everyday. I felt embarrassed. I couldn't tell my dad about it because he would get angry, thinking I was afraid or chicken or whatever."

D) "I remember being at a cottage. Early one morning I was sitting out on the dock fishing. It was peaceful. I felt great. I loved it because I was peaceful and alone."

The interpretation of these memories is clear when you look at Fran's life at the time he came for counseling.

His first memory of six kids in a sand box playing with his toys and getting into trouble with Dad because he didn't like it has to do with his home environment. Fran was feeling overwhelmed with the activity and responsibility of the children and his wife. He had no room or space to call his own (like the sand box). In his memory Fran was spanked and felt afraid and scared. In his present circumstance he is afraid to speak out about his personal needs because he will get "spanked by Dad" (represented by his wife who is saying "share your things and self," just like Dad had demanded of him in the sand box).

Fran's second memory had to do with him having to either fight or get beaten up at home. The fights were about his name. He saw no value in fighting and felt uncomfortable about fighting, yet he was supposed to punch people in the nose. This memory is directly related to Fran's feeling of pressure about his sales position and the effect of his job on his home life. Fran feels he has to fight for his position in the world or get beaten up at home from the pressure and demands of his wife. The fights of childhood were also about his name, which represents his identity. At present, Fran feels he must defend who and what he really is. As a child, he saw no value in fighting and refused to fight. As an adult, Fran also refuses to fight for survival in the world by "punching people in the nose" to get ahead.

Fran's third memory is about a boy who continually picked on him. He felt embarrassed and was afraid to tell anyone. This memory is directly related to his marital relationship. He feels "picked on" by his wife. He feels embarrassed because he thinks he should have a good relationship and doesn't. He also feels he can't tell anyone what is really happening in his marriage because people will be angry with him.

Fran's fourth memory occurred because his mind needed to provide him with hope in what seemed like a bleak situation. He remembered being at a cottage and sitting on the dock fishing. It was tranquil, and he felt great because he was at peace and alone. Through this memory, Fran is being reminded how to balance his life and return to the peace and quiet he deeply desires. This memory is what Fran would presently like to do in his life. This memory is telling him to take time for himself in a place of peace and tranquility.

Summary Of Memories

Your memories serve you with the information they provide regarding insights into your present moments. Do not judge your memories. Simply look to them for how they match your present experiences and what they tell you about your present choices. Also know that if all three memories are in the same category, they are informing you that only one primary event is happening for you, and it is demanding all of your attention. For example, you have three memories of fun experiences as a child, such as a trip to Disneyland, a great time at the park, and an evening with Mom and Dad watching television. Know that these memories are matching what life is like for you in the present moment. You may be planning a trip (Disneyland), you may be feeling like taking time out from your routine and going on an outing (park), and you may be needing rest and enjoyment by watching television (TV with Mom and Dad). These memories could also appear in sequence because you are stressed at present and your mind is saying, "slow down and take some time to enjoy life."

Applying the past to the present can be accomplished in two ways: 1) Ask yourself for past memories and see how they apply to your present. 2) Look at the present situations in your life and ask how they specifically apply to your past.

If you seem to have difficulty applying your present situations to your past memories, simply ask yourself how you would interpret your best friend's memories in relationship to his/her now moment life. If you are still somewhat confused, the following section on dreams includes an exercise that can also be applied to interpreting memories.

Ask yourself on a regular basis to recall past events. By doing this, you will open a whole new avenue to assist you in the discovery of your deepest desires and needs.

Dreams

Your dreams also add information on how your past and present come together.

86) **Did you have any reoccurring dreams as a child? What were they? How did you feel at the time of the dream?**

Dream analysis can be extensive and has become for some a field of its own. It is not the intent of this question to delve into your dreams at such a level. This question, in the context of *LifeScripting*, is simply designed to provide you with additional information about the child you were to assist in a deeper understanding of the adult you have become.

Dreams provide information about the child you were at the time of the dream. Dreams are best interpreted like you interpret a memory. How does the dream match what was happening for the child at the time of the dream? What does this information teach you about the child that can apply to your adult life?

For example:

Ken remembered a dream that began to reoccur after his parents' divorce. In the dream, he was with many people when suddenly they were gone. He would search for them and panic as he called out and no one answered. He would awaken in terror. This dream was a nighttime expression of his daytime fear. The dream stopped when his mother remarried and he felt secure with his stepfather.

Ken remembered this dream because it matches his present situation. Ken was feeling alone in his life and was terrified that he wouldn't find his place with others. The dream memory reminds him that in time things will work out and he will soon connect with the right people.

To interpret your dreams first, look to what was occurring for the child. Then look to your present life situations to determine the degree of the match.

It is helpful to keep a dream journal. We all dream four or five dreams per night. If you log the dreams you remember and look to your dreams the next day for information about your life, you will find a beautiful ever-expanding avenue to better know yourself. If you don't remember your dreams, know that you do have them. To help you remember your dreams, simply say to yourself before going to sleep, "If I have an important dream please let me wake up." With this command to your brain you will begin to awaken after important dreams. Have a pad of paper by your bed and jot down what you have just dreamed. This exercise does not disturb your sleep pattern and you will still feel as if you had a full night's sleep. In the morning, look to your dreams for information to assist in your daily decision making process.

Hopes And Dreams For Self

Questions 87-89 will give you information about your hopes and your dreams for yourself.

87) What was your favorite fairy tale or story as a child? What character did you relate to the most intensely? Why?

The character you most identified with as a child tells you about yourself. How are you like this character? Look at the details and similarities to this character and determine how these similarities are parts of who you are. Even if you choose a character who is common, determine what about the character is a specific part of you. Not everyone likes a character for the same reason. For example, someone could relate to Cinderella because she was happy during adversity. Someone else could relate to her because the prince saved her. Someone else may only see her oppression and feel she is similar to her in the area of oppression. What does your personal choice of characters say about you?

My favorite character was Tinkerbell from Peter Pan. I loved Tinkerbell because she had the fairy dust. She helped others believe in their dreams by giving them dust to accomplish them. She helped each person to truly discover his/her real self. I feel I do this with the *LifeScripting* process. I do not give people dreams. I simply ask them what their dreams are, and give them the tools (dust) to accomplish their dreams. I also help people to never forget who they really are.

If you had more than one favorite character, look to each character for what that character says to you about your hopes and dreams. I also suggest you find a picture or figurine of your favorite character and put it where you can see it daily. This will visually reminded you to always remember who and what you are.

88) Who were your heros? Why?

In Chapter 5, you learned that having a hero as a young adult is an important stage of growth and development. This is true because finding a hero opens your heart and therefore opens your brain to limitless possibilities. It is important to remember that heros are people who have accomplished something for themselves and others. A hero is not just a high paid athlete or celebrity.

Who you admire helps you understand the desires you want for yourself. Look to each hero for what you loved about him and for what he stirred in your soul. How can you become all that your connection to them suggests? The purpose of a hero is not for you to become the hero, but rather to fully become yourself by using him as a model and motivational aid. How can you use the memories of your heros to help you in your present life circumstances?

If you had no heros, in all likelihood, you are a person who motivates yourself from within. It is, therefore, important to look closely at your personal experiences for the needed direction in your adult life. It is equally important to remember that most who do not find a hero end up discouraged and confused. This occurs because when a hero is not found people tend to turn to the first two layers of their brain for satisfaction. In these layers, where physical and animal behavior dominate, true satisfaction can never be accomplished.

89) **If you could be any animal right now, what would that animal be and why?**

The animal you chose speaks to you of your personality traits. How are you like this animal? If you are far from the traits and characteristics you admire in this animal, how can you alter your behavior to incorporate the qualities of this animal?

Examples of some animal choices are:

A) "I want to be a house cat. House cats are independent and decide for themselves, yet they are cared for and loved by others." This individual wants and needs to be independent as well as cared for and loved by others.

B) "I want to be an eagle because they soar above everything and are free and peaceful. They are also loved and respected." This individual desires a life not totally connected to the mundane of the world. She wants a feeling of being above it all with a sense of freedom and peace. She also needs and must experience the love and respect of others.

I share the following example with you because I felt it was an unusual choice until I heard the explanation.

C) My client said, "I want to be a cow." I paused and asked "Why?" She said, "Because cows are so contented and all they have to do all day is eat and roam the land." This woman was totally stressed in her life and the cow reminded her of her deepest desire for contentment and a stress free life.

I again suggest that you find a picture or figurine of the animal you most relate to and keep it where you can see it. When you look at the animal, remember the parts of you that want to be like this animal. Find ways in your daily life to implement the characteristics that you admire in this animal.

Spiritual

This portion of the *LifeScripting* questionnaire is designed to address the spiritual part of you. The purpose is to assist you in understanding the beliefs you have formed about the concept of God. The questions are not intended to address religion, but rather to bring you to an understanding of your deep-seated personal belief about God.

At some time in life, each individual is invited to decide who and what God is to him/her. This phenomena can be seen by tracing recorded history and observing man's search for a higher power. This search is common to all races and all individuals. As a result of this search, everyone develops a concept of "who" and "what" God should be. Your concept of God provides the spiritual base upon which your life is lived. It also provides a basis with which to face death. Therefore, your belief about God is one of the pillars of your self-expression. With this understanding, it is vital to realize that your personal beliefs about God are based more on your experiences with your father, than on the dictates of society or the beliefs of a religion. Your answers to the next three questions will give you the information you need to understand your personal beliefs about God.

90) What was your concept of God as a child?

Look closely at your answer. How does this belief still apply in your life? If it no longer applies, what event or events changed your belief about God?

Look now to your answer to question 66. That answer reveals your view of your father prior to nine years of age. How does your description of the God of your childhood and the description of your father match? Remember, how you viewed your father before age six will program your beliefs about God. This occurs because we call both God and Dad "he" and "father." Consequently, if you had difficulty with your father, you will probably have a difficult time with the concept of God. One possible exception is that if, as a child, you were exposed to strong religious beliefs about God, then you have been able to establish a belief about God that is separate from your view of your father. Generally, however, the view of your father will prevail.

If a religious affiliation was an integral part of your childhood, look to this affiliation for any belief you may have formed. Ask yourself, " Did this teaching match what I believed about my father?" If it didn't, you may be confused about the character of God and who God really is for you. For example, your father was absent and yet the church said God loved you and would always be there for you. When stress enters your life, you may find yourself praying, while deep within you don't expect God to respond. Look to your past experiences to see what is true for you.

The awareness that God and Dad are connected in the belief system formation of a child will greatly assist you in understanding yourself as well as others. This is particularly true regarding the acceptance of, or the struggle with, God. If you have ever experienced a twelve step program, you may be aware that the second and third steps pose difficult struggles for many. Step two states, "Came to believe that a Power greater than ourselves could restore us to sanity." Step three states, "Made a decision to turn our will and our lives over to the care of God as we understand Him." Can you now imagine what happens to those who were hurt by their fathers as children? They truly want to complete the 12 steps, yet they have a deep contract with the child they were to never let anyone like Dad (God) hurt them again. They must honor this contract with the child. Yet they are being told that God (Dad) will restore them to sanity if they just turn themselves over to Him. This dilemma is further compounded when the people struggling with God observe how easily some individuals sitting next to them accomplish these steps. They are unaware, when they observe their friends ease with God, that these individuals did not have a struggle with their biological fathers. As a result of what they observe they feel even more deeply that something must be drastically wrong with them because they cannot as readily turn themselves over to God.

Once an understanding is reached regarding the depth of our programming as it pertains to God, new options will emerge. One such option is to discuss with individuals their relationships with their fathers. This should occur long before we ever ask questions or make requests regarding their relationships with God. This approach will enable everyone to feel equal in the process of finding God.

Some examples of God = Dad

If your dad was not present when you were a child, you will tend to believe that God is not present for you as an adult. If as a child you also believed, because of your dad's absence, that you were on your own, as an adult you will tend to believe you are on your own in life.

If Dad was there and supportive of you, your concept of God is that God is present for you.

If Dad physically abused you, you will feel that God could easily hurt you and/or punish you. In all likelihood, you will have a difficult time becoming close to God, unless you have experienced some form of spiritual intervention or personal awakening.

Reframed: How does your childhood concept of God assist you in the now? How can you have a deeper understanding for the needs of others as a result of your experience? How can you truly assist others in the future? For example, as a child your father was absent and you now struggle with an understanding of God. As an adult, find a way to discover God through classes or discussions with others who are knowledgeable. As you discover a God beyond your father, you can share your knowledge with others. In your interactions with others regarding God, it is important to understand their connections to their biological fathers. With this awareness, you can assist them in separating the concept of their fathers from the concept of God.

91) What is your concept of God now?

How does your answer to this question compare with your answer regarding your childhood beliefs about God? You will generally find many similarities between the God of your past and the God of your now. If your view has changed, what experiences created this change?

If as a child you struggled with your father, look to this answer for ways in which the God of your now can be different from your father. What did your dad teach you about love and belonging? What do you need to do that is opposite of your father's behavior? How can you give to yourself and others what you were not given?

92) Close your eyes and imagine yourself in a white room. There are white ceilings, white floors, and white walls. You are in the room alone and there are no windows and no doors. Write three words that describe how you feel in this room?

The three words you choose tend to match what you feel about the actual event of your death. Look to the words and see how they match your deepest feelings about death.

Like the concept of God, our concept of death is one we all must inevitably confront. Our beliefs about death merge with our beliefs about God since both are concepts that take us to our spiritual self.

If your three words were peaceful words and caused no stress for you, your beliefs about death are balanced.

If your words were stressful and intense, you may want to review your beliefs and possibly do some research to expand your understanding of death. There are several books and many articles about the actual death experience. These sources will greatly assist in expanding your perspective of death. This expansion will create a peace that will assist in both your daily life and your actual death.

Finding God

If you have a desire to find a God that fits into your life, there is a very simple exercise I have developed which has helped many of my clients. This exercise can also help you. The exercise is very effective because it tends to bring a sense of perspective about God into an individual's life.

First, it is important to understand that God is who and what God is, and your personal view of God does not change God. However, your personal view of God does drastically affect your life. If you believe God is a judging God, you will approach your life with this concept as a central focus. If you believe God is primarily a loving God, you will approach your life with this belief as the core of your reality. Your reality of God is based solely on what you believe about God. God does not change because you change your mind, but you truly change when you change your mind about God.

If you have struggles with your view of God, the following exercise will assist you in balancing your point of view.

Imagine you are sitting in a beautiful place. You are alone and just enjoying the wonder of the day. As you sit in this peaceful setting, a child approaches and sits beside you. The child looks into your eyes and says, "I heard the word God today and I don't know who God is. Tell me, who is God?" Before you answer the child, you need to understand that the explanation you give this child about God is the only information about God the child will ever hear. Also understand that the God you describe is the God he will live with, act upon, and trust for the rest of his life. What kind of God will you give this child? If possible write out your answer to the child so you can reference your description as the years pass.

I have found consistently that the God given to the child is a God of love, caring and presence. The adult always tells the child that God is there for him and loves him no matter what the circumstance. Let's again imagine that the child lives your description of a loving, caring God until he dies. What if you described God incorrectly? Have you hurt the child? No, because any individual experiencing the God of your description would live a well-balanced and loving life. He would face his death without regret because his life choices would have been centered on love.

Look again to the God you gave the child and ask yourself if this is the God you know and desire for yourself? If you do not already have this God in your life, how can you begin to experience this God? One method to accomplish this connection is to again imagine the child who asked you about God. Tell this beautiful child how to incorporate a loving God into his life. Now do this behavior for yourself.

Money

The next two questions pertain to your beliefs about money. They help you understand your beliefs about how to obtain money, what to do with money once you have it, and where money fits into the overall picture of your life.

In Western culture, money is a primary issue that must be dealt with for individual balance to be achieved. This is true whether you have money or do not have money. It is, therefore, helpful in obtaining personal balance to understand your beliefs about money.

93) **What were your thoughts about money as a child? How did you obtain money? What did you do with the money?**

Look closely at your answer and you will recognize your deep beliefs about money. Your answer will also help you understand how you believe money is obtained and how money is best used.

If as a child you worked for money, and as a result of your efforts always felt you had the money you needed, as an adult you will work for money and believe that what you need will be provided as a result of your efforts.

If you saved a portion of your money, as an adult you will easily save money.

If as a child you felt there was never enough money and made a vow to the child that you would work hard and obtain large sums of money, as an adult you will strive to fulfill that promise. But even if you do this, deep inside you may still find yourself fearing the loss of the money you have acquired.

Your answer about money is specific to your life. It is valuable to spend the necessary time to understand and reframe the child's learning for your adult empowerment and potential service to others.

94) **What do you believe about money now?**

Your answer to this question usually matches the answer to question 93. If your answer is different, what caused the change in your perceived belief about money? Ask yourself if your answer to this question is what you believe or if it is what you would like to believe.

Reframed: What do you know about money based on the child's experience? Look for how you create the same events about money that the child experienced. If your childhood beliefs about money were balanced, recognize how you require balance with money in your adult world for peace within yourself. If your money ideas and money interactions as a child were not balanced, determine how this creates the same or opposite behavior for you the adult. Based on your childhood learning, how can you best develop a winning perspective about money for your future? How can you assist others in this area?

What Are Your Hopes And Dreams?

There are two primary areas regarding your future hopes and dreams. One area pertains to your home life, the other to your dream for yourself. Your desires regarding your home life are addressed in question 95, and your deepest personal desires will be determined in question 96.

95) **If you put a neon sign above the door of your family of origin to let people know what to expect inside of the house, what would the sign say?**

The answer to this question reflects the type of home environment you desire as an adult.

If the neon sign over the door of your childhood home was positive, you will want to create the same type of environment in your adult home. For example, if the sign read "Everyone is welcome, this is a loving place," this would be the motto you desire for your adult home.

If your answer was less than positive, you will probably want to create the opposite environment in your adult home. However, at times you may find yourself in the same environment as the child because you are trying to desperately "correct" the original situation. An example of a negative sign would be "Danger, keep out, unpredictable behavior inside." Generally, people from this environment have a desire, at the deepest level, for a home that is safe and predictable.

Again, look to your personal sign for the information it provides about your desire for your ideal home environment.

96) **If you could design your life right now with no limits, what would your life look like for you? There is only one condition: you must be willing to live what you design.**

This final question will give you an overall perspective of your life. This question identifies the personal road you wish to travel. With the answer to this question you can determine the parts of your hopes and dreams already present in your life. You can also determine the parts of your hopes and dreams not yet in place. With this awareness, you will have a basis for all future goal setting.

I often find that when clients answer this question they are surprised at how many pieces of their present life actually match their desired life. It seems as if individuals often miss what is right in their lives because the focus is on what is wrong. It is extremely helpful to build your future on the parts of your dream already in place. Once you recognize what percentage of your dream is in place, you can take the necessary steps to accomplish the remaining portion.

It is of vital importance to realize the truth about your life. If you are on the "wrong road," your hopes and dreams cannot be accomplished. Remember, if you are on the road to Barstow and you really want to go to San Diego, if you keep driving without any changes, you will end up in Barstow. When you begin to make changes and turn your life into the life you want to live, stress will be reduced, positive energy flow will occur, and you will be on the road to total fulfillment.

An additional exercise to assist with your awareness regarding the match between childhood and adulthood is to cross reference your answer to question 96 with question 45. Question 45 asks about your ideals and dreams as a child. If you are on the right road in your life, you will find that the answer to question 96 will have many of the ingredients of the child's dreams and ideals as described in question 45. This is not an accident. The child knows what the adult is to become. Remember, the closer you are to what the child learned for you the less stress you will have in your daily life. I do not believe any child has ever been given a dream that the adult cannot live in some form. What was and is your dream? How can you best live it?

How To Goal Set Your Dreams

The following formula for goal setting will assist you in realizing your dreams. It requires three steps. On a piece of paper, draw three boxes that connect as the boxes do below.

In the first box, write one of your desires. This desire should be an ingredient in the dream life of both you the adult and you the child.

In box number two, write the words win/win connections. In or under this box, list all the win/win connections you will need to attain your goal. The list will include anyone who can help you arrive at your goal. The connections you list must include win/win interactions. Win/win connections are characterized by both parties mutually benefiting from the interaction.

In the third box, write the word action. In this box or below it, write the action steps needed to reach your goal. Without action, it is impossible to accomplish any goal. Also realize it is the action we take toward accomplishing a goal that can give us the most pleasure.

An example of goal setting is Julie, whose desire as a child was to become an actress. She feels she is now too old but is willing to attempt the process. Julie sets up her goal setting boxes and in the first box writes her dream: to become an actress. The second box contains the win/win relationships needed to reach this goal. They include: signing up at college for acting classes, contacting the local amateur theater, contacting the local acting guild, etc. The third box contains all the action steps she actually agrees to take.

If this process seems simple, it is. Life was meant to be a simple and loving process. To experience this reality all you need to do is take charge of your personal direction and strive toward your dreams. The following exercise will assist you in the accomplishment of your goals/dreams.

Imagine the child who asked you about God in question 92. If this child told you about his hopes and dreams for life, how would you encourage him to fulfill his dreams? Undoubtedly, part of your encouragement would be to tell the child how to proceed toward his dream. You would also spend time telling him how his dreams are unique and special. You would tell him how important it is for him to accomplish his dreams because no other person has been given his exact dream.

Apply the same encouragement you gave the child to your own dreams. Then take yourself by the hand and walk toward the dream you truly believe is your birth right!

Points To Ponder

The following nine concepts are valuable to consider before reading Section III.

1) There are far more than 96 questions involved in the total understanding of your life. In fact, the number of questions to unfold throughout your life will be limitless. The 96 questions simply provided you with a well-rounded basis for personal understanding. They also provided you with knowledge of where to place future information in terms of categories. The 96 questions assisted you in knowing how best to handle the initial information provided by your life experiences. Any future questions, about any subject, can be addressed by applying the techniques and principles you have acquired through experiencing each of the *LifeScripting* questions. Now that you can answer any question that may arise in your life, you will be able to experience a knowing about life that is constantly unfolding and growing. This process is much like being in love and having that love grow deeper with each passing day. As the knowledge of the person you love unfolds layer upon layer, you begin to experience a deeper and more wonderful

relationship. This is not only true in relationships with others, but also in relationship with yourself.

2) *LifeScripting* is not an excuse for behavior, it is an explanation. An excuse says, "I can continue my behavior." An explanation allows for an understanding of your behavior which can help you accomplish positive future behavioral change. Thus, it is crucial to know why you do what you do!

3) Life is a day by day, minute by minute process. Do not rush your life. Your life will unfold for you with perfect timing. For some, life is fast-paced, for others it is slow. When life is moving at a pace that dissatisfies you, patience is required. There are many times when we immediately want what we feel is important to us. If we don't get what we want, we generally feel a part of us has been cheated. Yet when we look back with hindsight at the picture of our life we can usually see that if we had gotten what we wanted at the time we wanted it, our life would have been drastically different. When looking with hindsight, which is always 20/20, we are most often grateful.

4) Life happens. Experience life as it happens and feel it to the fullest. Remember, there is a time to look at the past, a time to ponder the future, and a time to be fully in the now. If the feelings of the present are appropriate, do not confuse them with a trigger. Only review your past when it is necessary to enhance your present.

5) When you experience a past trigger, your now moment has become a gift to help you understand more about yourself and your choices. Do not miss the opportunity to love yourself by learning more about yourself at this time.

6) Be your best friend. If you ever have difficulty with the process of *LifeScripting*, do not give up. Simply

ask yourself, "If my best friend were telling me my story, what would I say were her issues? What would I tell her to do?" Do what you would advise your friend to do.

7) Keep your heart open and love yourself no matter how life appears at any given moment. Remember, all events are neutral. It is you who attaches meaning and significance to an event by what you think. If what you think is not creating an open heart, choose a different thought.

8) Be involved in your own life. Get as involved with your life as you would want to get involved in the life of someone you deeply loved.

9) Take action regarding who you are and what you desire to become. If you are taking right action, joy should be immediate and lasting.

SECTION III

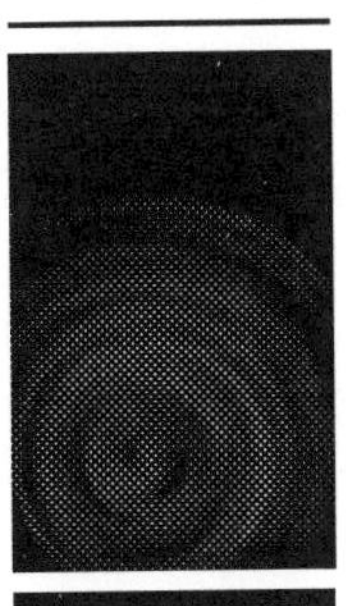

Your Internal Connection With Yourself

In Section I and Section II you were given the information necessary for you to connect with the experiences you had as a child. With these insights, you can now obtain any desired information concerning why you do what you do. You can also discover what new behavioral choices you have as you face your future. This blueprint for empowerment, if applied, will create joy for the rest of your life.

Section III offers additional possibilities for greater personal connection. It is important to note that Section III is not for everyone. Some may find it uncomfortable to approach their lives in the in-depth manner suggested on the following pages. If that becomes the case for you, then it is perfectly acceptable not to do the exercises. Nevertheless, it is important to read this section for an understanding of the processes.

In this section you will be given methods that, if used, will daily connect you in conscious love to the child you were and are. A daily connection to the child is helpful when making adult choices of life. This connection does not imply that you are to become two people inside. It simply means that to love yourself at the deepest level is to love both the child you were, and the adult you have become. They are the same person! The deeper your internal connection to yourself, the more you will feel love for yourself, for the child, and for others. This is much like falling in love and nurturing that love because you desire it to last forever. The deeper you love, the more you want to know about the person you love. The more you love, the more you feel love within yourself. Loving the child you were is the key to a total experience within yourself.

If you feel awkward approaching yourself in this deeply personal way, keep in mind that no one needs to know the intense experience you are about to have.

The following steps are usually easier for women than for men. However, they do work equally well for both. If you are a man and start to feel uncomfortable with the suggestions within these pages, know that the events you are being asked to experience were the things you longed to have occur for the child you were. To put this exercise into perspective, simply go back in your mind and remember the feelings of being small and wanting to curl up with someone who would lovingly hold you and talk to you. Now think of having that same experience with a child in the present moment. Can you imagine how fulfilling it would be for both you and the child? You are equal to this child, and the experience of connection is as close as your willingness to risk feeling somewhat awkward for a moment. I encourage you to take the chance and see what happens.

To assist in your comfort, I will share several of the countless experiences from individuals who have taken these steps to achieve an in-depth connection with the child.

1) Don is an MD from Canada. Don spent years on a personal search, not only for himself, but for the meaning of life. Part of his search involved trips to India where he explored Eastern philosophy. After completing *LifeScripting,* and the processes to connect with the child, Don was tearfully overwhelmed by his experience. He told me, "While studying Eastern philosophy I was told about the possibility of discovering and connecting to the divine child. Until my experience with *LifeScripting,* that connection was an illusive theory. I now believe the process of *LifeScripting* is the path with connect to the divine child, the place of our total divinity."

2) An inmate reported, "After connecting with the child, I felt filled with light, and had a sense of carrying a beautiful baby with me at all times. Everything finally began to have meaning."

3) A friend used the "Birth Of Me" meditation tape and had such an overwhelming sense of oneness inside she decided to share the process with her mother and sister. She chose the day of her grandmother's funeral for this experience. All three women laid on a bed and listened to the audio tape. The result was such a loving experience all three of the women are now enjoying a more complete and loving experience with life. I met the mother shortly after the process, and she cried when she talked of the depth of experience.

4) After connecting to the child that she was, Mary began to regularly ask the child what was necessary for joy in her life. Answers always followed.

5) Andy, who was adopted, now feels a total bonding, not only to himself but to his biological mother, who he has never met. This occurred as a result of seeing through the child's eyes and experiencing life with this new dimension.

Ways To Connect To The Child

The following approaches are just some of the ways to deeply connect to the love of the child that you were and are. This connection will create a more empowered you. Remember, you and the child are one and the same.

1) How do you fall in love with a child? Your answer to this question is the beginning of how to fall in love with yourself, and the child that you were and are.

To fall in love with a child, you do not have to do anything. You simply need to be fully present for the child. This process involves eye contact and a connection at a feeling level. A simple way to accomplish this is to look into a mirror. While looking into the mirror, look at your eyes as you would look into the eyes of a child. Send love through your eyes to this child. After a few minutes of eye contact, say to the child in the mirror "I love you." Make a commitment to this child that you will treat yourself in the exact manner you would treat this child. Also commit that you will only say to yourself what you would say to this child. Make this commitment with the realization that you and this child are one. As a final step, recognize we are all in this life together. Therefore, make an additional contract that you will not say, or do, to another what you would not say, or do, to this child.

The results of this exercise are profound and life changing. They can be experienced as often as you choose.

2) Hug yourself as you would hug a child. Pause to feel the feelings of this hug. If you hug yourself and truly feel the feelings of the hug, as though you were being hugged by someone else, a feeling of connection begins to occur. Try touching your own hand as if you were touching

the hand of another. If you pay close attention, you will experience an intense sense of oneness. Not only do you feel the sensation of touching yourself, but you also feel the sensation of being touched. Commit to touching and hugging yourself as often as you would like to be touched or hugged by someone you love.

3) Get pictures of yourself as a child and look at them often. If you do not have pictures, then find a child that you can relate to, and regularly see that child in your mind. What does this child need on a daily basis? How can you meet these needs for yourself?

4) Take time every once in awhile to review your life and its direction. Do this by imagining a child sitting next to you. Talk to the child about who you are, and ask what he/she feels and thinks. In short, if the child could talk, what would he/she say about your life? What would the child need you to do differently?

5) If you were the sole provider for a child, what would you need to do for that child on a daily basis? Are you already doing these things for yourself? How do you provide for the basic needs of a child? What about food, shelter, clothing, sleep or social, mental, spiritual, intellectual, and physical needs? Make a list of your needs and determine how you are fulfilling each.

6) What did the child you were value and love most? What do you as an adult value and love most? What do you do about what you love? What can you do about what the child valued and loved?

7) Be fully alive in your adult life. The greatest gift you can give any child is a happy, healthy, fulfilled adult to care for them.

8) Keep a journal of your now moment triggers. Your journal is not a daily journal, it is simply a record of your triggers. In the journal, write about any event that triggers you and what you did about it. You will then want to determine when you first felt the way you felt when you triggered. Then log what the child learned for you. Also list the possible adult choices that are now options due to childhood information. This journal will help you recognize what is occurring in your life on a daily basis. With a journal of triggers, you will be able to visually track the events that create over/under-reactions. As a result you will better understand why you do what you do, and be able to develop desired behavior.

An integral part of the total *LifeScripting* process that I present to clients and inmates involves the use of a personalized journal. To better assist you in setting up a personal journal, I have designed an audio package. The back of this book contains details about this package.

Additional ways to love yourself are as countless as your imagination allows. Ask yourself, "How could I demonstrate love to someone else if I were free to unconditionally love?" Ponder, "How would I want someone to love me?" Experience the behavior you just described by doing it with/for yourself.

The Birth Of Me Meditation

To further connect to the child within, consider experiencing the meditation on the following pages. This experience will connect you to the baby that you were at the time of your birth. It will create a feeling of embracing your life at a level that is visually depicted by the picture on the next page.

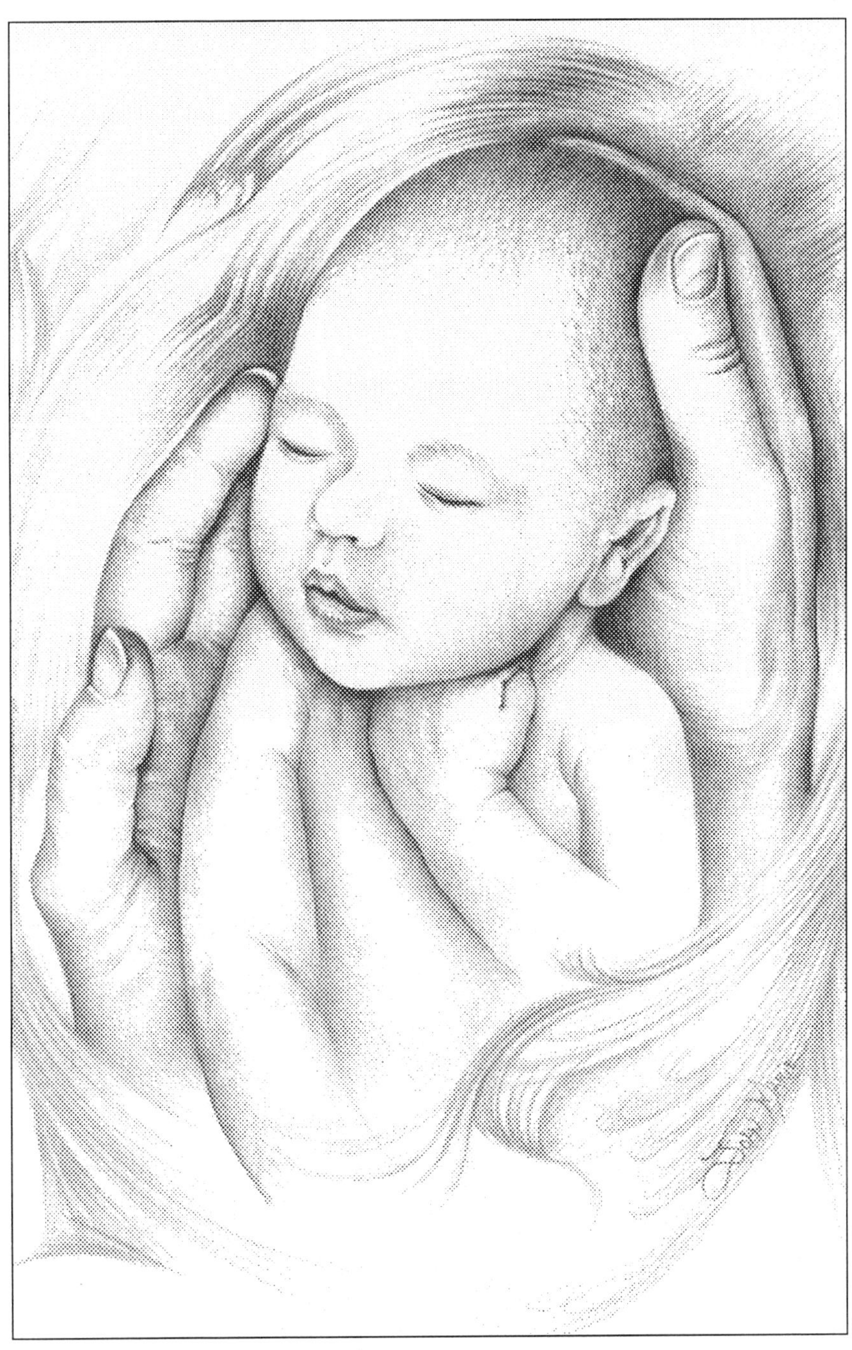

"The Embrace"

The meditation you are about to experience should be read several times before attempting to visualize the process with closed eyes. Reading the meditation several times will lock the steps into your mind and will enable you, when you close your eyes, to accomplish what you desire to experience. Music can be played quietly in the background as you close your eyes and visualize the dynamics of the meditation. Remember, the end result will be a connection to yourself similar to the one you see in the picture of the baby wrapped in loving hands.

Before beginning this meditation, please be aware that each individual experience is unique and should not be judged in any way. Know also that this process can be experienced more than one time, so do not expect everything to happen for you all at once, even though it can!

It is helpful to understand before attempting any internal meditative exercise that everyone experiences the world through all five senses. However, each individual generally has a dominant preference for one of the senses. Knowing this, do not judge your personal internal experience when you close your eyes. If, when you close your eyes, you actually see pictures in your mind, then that is your experience. If you have a sense of what is occurring without pictures, then that is the correct experience for you. If your preference is auditory, then incorporate sound into your experience.

The overall goal of this meditation is for you to embrace yourself by creating your perfect birth. As a result, you will have a greater acceptance of yourself and your life. I know this experience will assist you, as it has countless others, in bonding to yourself for the remainder of your life. This meditation was created because of a need I felt for my clients to go deep within themselves to bond to the babies they once were. Consequently, I began guiding them with a mediation to the places of their births. This process is now on cassette tape with music. Information about this cassette is in the back of this book. A general overview of this tape follows.

The Birth Of Me

This meditation in no way has been designed to negate your actual birth. The birth you had was perfect for you and for what you are to become. This meditation is simply inviting you to experience a connection to yourself at the deepest possible level.

Find a place to be involved in this process where you will not be disturbed. Assume a comfortable position, either sitting or lying down. In this position, ask your body to be fully cooperative and relaxed. Check for any tension in your body and simply breath it out by saying the word "relax" as you exhale. Notice any tension you may have in your face. Relax your forehead and make sure your eyelids are not tightly closed. As you breath in, think life, and as you breath out, think relax.

In your mind, find a space in which you would like to be born. Imagine now that your mother is with you and, without judgement, realize she is the perfect mother to give birth to you. In this scene, your mother will be delivering to you the baby you were at birth. Your mother is simply an instrument in this scene, and is not in pain or labor. As she gives you birth, feel honor and love for her for being the one to give you life.

Imagine now that you are in a position to receive the baby that is being born from your mother's body. That baby is you. Watch the baby slowly come from your mother's body and receive the baby into your hands. Take the baby to your body and observe it from head to toe, realizing that this baby is you. Look into the baby's eyes and let it know with your eye contact that you are the adult it has become. Let the baby know with your eyes that it is safe and loved. Welcome the baby into your life. Let the baby look at you and recognize that you are the beautiful person it has become. Hold the baby next to your heart. Let the baby feel your heartbeat as you feel the heartbeat of the baby. Feel how they beat as one. Look into the eyes of the baby and, with your eyes and words, make a commitment to the baby that you will never exhibit behavior that would harm it in any way. Tell the baby that you honor its life and, therefore, you will honor your life because it is the same life. Spend time telling the baby what you hope and dream for its future and what you want for its life. Let the baby know that you will follow these dreams because they are the dreams that inspire the purpose and direction for your life.

When it feels right, take the baby to your mother and, without letting go of the baby, say thank you to your mother for giving you the life of this child. Let her know that you see her as the perfect instrument for your birth and the perfect teacher for your life.

Imagine now that your father is in the room; go to him with the baby and, without letting go of the baby, say thank you to your father for being the instrument to your life. Thank him also for being the perfect teacher to help you become all that you were intended to become.

Again, spend time looking at the baby that you were and feel the unconditional love you have for this child. Make a commitment to the baby that you will always remember its presence in your life. Assure the child that you will hold it sacred in your heart and in your life. Tell the baby that you will return often to your mind and remember the connection of this moment.

When it feels absolutely comfortable, imagine that you are taking the baby into your body and placing the baby in a safe place such as your heart. When the baby feels comfortable inside you, assure the baby it is safe and you will return often.

At the right moment for you, take a deep breath in as you say the words awake and refreshed. Take another breath as you open your eyes.

This exercise can be done as often as you wish. The connection that results is one that will empower and direct your life. Once you feel the honor of embracing the beautiful baby you were, you will hold your life sacred.

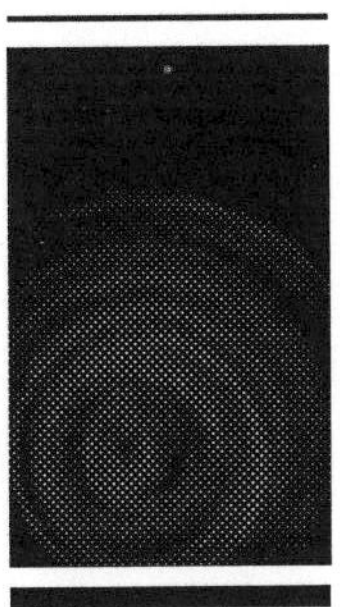

A Final Note

It is difficult to express in mere words my deep desire for your life to become fully alive. Alive, with not only the vision of who you are, but with the reality of accomplishing all that you were created to become. I know at the very core of my being that it is possible for all of us to realize the true depth of the love we have for ourselves. I also know that with this realization comes the desire to share that love with others. When this sharing occurs, our planet will become a more loving place.

Writing this book has been one of the most challenging experiences of my life. Many times, the only thing that kept me motivated was knowing that your life, as a reader, could be positively affected with the information contained within these pages. Foremost in my mind, and in my heart, was the knowledge that *LifeScripting* has truly assisted countless lives, and through this book I could share that reality with you. I know, as you now know, that *LifeScripting*, when applied, will create a lifelong foundation for loving yourself and others.

It has been an honor to have been allowed to enter your life and share with you this workable method of love. May your future be filled with deep internal love, joy, and peace!

Virginia

About The Author

Virginia Dunstone, M.S., is living proof that a loving, tender, self-affirming approach to therapy, and life, works best to attain personal joy and fulfillment. As a therapist, she has assisted thousands of individuals through private counseling, public seminars and prison workshops. Her innovative approaches have enabled individuals to find their true purposes and reach their full potentials.

Virginia has five wonderful children and four grandchildren. She graduated from the University of Nevada, Las Vegas, with a bachelor's degree in Psychology, and a master's degree in Counseling. Both degrees were conferred with high honors. All of her college credits were earned while raising five children and working fulltime. Her life is living proof that goals, when accompanied with the proper attitude and effort, can result in meaningful accomplishments.

In addition to her private practice in Scottsdale, AZ, Virginia speaks for corporations, associations, conventions and U. S. Senators' conferences. She has also designed and implemented several life changing programs for inmates. She not only facilitates a 52-hour *LifeScripting* program, but has also developed a series of seminars that assist in the alleviation of stress, addictions, and phobias. The results for the women who are about to re-enter society are phenomenal.

LIFE ENHANCEMENT SERIES

12 Tapes To Empower Your Life

This audio series is designed to complement the LifeScripting materials presented in this book. For most individuals, these tapes are like owning a psychological toolbox and are the equivalent of 12½ hours of private counseling. This series will greatly assist you in your future discovery of self.

WHAT PEOPLE SAY BEYOND WORDS. Connection with others includes more than words. How to know what others are saying even when they aren't speaking.

INSTANT CONNECTION. How to establish and maintain rapport in relationships and business interactions.

WHY DO I REPEAT PATTERNS? Learn why you repeat behavior, and what to do to empower your life.

SELF IMAGE. What is it? How do you get it? How do you enhance or change it? The role of self talk.

EMOTIONS. What are they? Why do we have them? What do we do with them? How to understand anger, depression, and grief?

RELATIONSHIPS. Unravel the complications of relationships. Learn what can go wrong and what to do.

WHO AM I - WHERE AM I HEADED? The role of thoughts in your life. How to create your own life. How to find your purpose.

TAKING CONTROL OF YOUR LIFE. Stress is a major factor in life. What it is, what it does, and how to eliminate it forever.

BEHIND YOUR EYES. What happens during sleep and relaxation. How to benefit from both processes.

YOUR PERFECT SELF. A relaxation tape that will help you discover the perfect person you have always wanted to become.

WHEN LOVE IS DIFFICULT. A relaxation/meditation tape designed to help you be at peace with individuals that have been difficult for you.

THE BIRTH OF ME. A relaxation/meditation tape that will connect you to the deepest part of yourself. This tape is life changing.

Complete Set: $89.00

THE BIRTH OF ME TAPE

At the conclusion of Section III you were introduced to an overview of a meditation that is life changing. The complete meditation which is called THE BIRTH OF ME is available on cassette tape. This meditation is one that individuals have reported is the piece of *LifeScripting* that connects them to themselves forever. This tape is a composite of words, music and sound effects and is truly a moving experience.

Meditation Tape $9.95

JOURNAL KIT

Your personal journal is an integral part of the LifeScripting process. This journal is not a daily diary where you simply monitor thoughts and activities. It is designed to assist you in better understanding the patterns and issues in your life. Its function is to provide you with a systematic approach to charting your over/under-reactions, triggers. It is also designed to assist you in maintaining an overview, of your life and your choices. With this overview, you will consciously recognize what is occurring and where to set or adjust your behavior and goals. *LifeScripting* journals have been used extensively by my clients and women in prison. All report that their journals truly make the difference in feeling connected to, and in charge of, their lives.

The JOURNAL KIT contains a one-hour tape with instructions and ideas on how to set up and maintain your journal. It also contains the journal master files which you can photocopy.

Complete Kit $15.95

"THE EMBRACE"

Virginia would be honored to send you a signed lithograph of the heart-warming picture on page 337 of this book. This touching embrace is the ideal gift for every new parent, and the perfect gift to your own inner child.

8" x 10"	**$12.95**
11" x 14"	**$19.95**
16" x 20"	**$24.95**

CREATING YOUR OWN WORLD

An Entertaining And Educational Way To Help Children three to eleven Reach Their Full Potentials.

This audio series was created by American Family Resources. These powerful vignettes teach children valuable life principles. Music, sound effects, and the use of five unique characters greatly add to the value of the program which is fast paced, entertaining, and educational. Included is a 90 page picture book and an audio tape just for parents. On this tape, Virginia shares vital parenting skills.

1. **Create Your Own World**...life is choice and each of us can learn to make the right choice and create a better world.
2. **Give Up Your Excuses**...excuses are out and responsibility is in for the cast of characters and the kids.
3. **Learn From Your Mistakes**...it is easy to learn valuable lessons from mistakes and turn them into positive experiences.
4. **Make Friends With Yoursel**f...being your own best friend is an option available to everyone who has the desire.
5. **Begin Your Mental Diet Today**...learning to replace negative feelings with positive ones can become reality for each child.
6. **Direct the Movies of Your Mind**...now young people can learn how to sit in the director's chair and create their own worlds!
7. **Dissolve Your Problems**...problem solving can be attained by all, but first it requires the creation of a new movie.
8. **Transform the World**...positively affecting others is the key to transmitting success attitudes to people everywhere.
9. **Believing in Yourself**...accomplishment is the by-product of putting positive effort and energy into each endeavor.
10. **Get it Done and Still Have Fun**...work can be an enjoyable task when approached with the proper attitude and perspective.

Album $69.95

VIRGINIA DUNSTONE & ASSOCIATES
P.O.BOX 4261, SCOTTSDALE, AZ. 85261
1-800-443-2644 or (602) 991-2660
Fax: (602) 661-4091

YES! Please rush me:

________BIRTH OF ME MEDITATION tape/s ($9.95 per tape)

________set/s of MY PERSONAL JOURNAL kit ($15.95 per kit)

________set/s of the LIFE ENHANCEMENT album ($89.95 each)

________set/s of CREATING YOUR OWN WORLD album ($69.95 each)

signed lithograph, "THE EMBRACE"
________ (8" x 10" $12.95)
________(11" x 14" $19.95)
________(16" x 20" $24.95)

________SUB TOTAL

________Sales Tax (AZ residents add 6.7% sales tax)

________Postage & Handling (Add $3 for every $45 in merchandise)

________TOTAL INVESTMENT

Charge My: VISA MasterCard Check Enclosed

Card No.________________________________ Exp. Date____________

Name____

Address____

City____________________ State____________ Zip__________

Telephone ( ) ____________________

Home ( ) ____________________

PLEASE SEND ME:

________Volume discount pricing for the book.

________Information regarding Virginia Dunstone Seminars.

________Place me on the mailing list.

VIRGINIA DUNSTONE & ASSOCIATES
P.O.BOX 4261, SCOTTSDALE, AZ. 85261
1-800-443-2644 or (602) 991-2660
Fax: (602) 661-4091

YES! Please rush me:

________ BIRTH OF ME MEDITATION tape/s ($9.95 per tape)

________ set/s of MY PERSONAL JOURNAL kit ($15.95 per kit)

________ set/s of the LIFE ENHANCEMENT album ($89.95 each)

________ set/s of CREATING YOUR OWN WORLD album ($69.95 each)

signed lithograph, "THE EMBRACE"
________ (8" x 10" $12.95)
________ (11" x 14" $19.95)
________ (16" x 20" $24.95)

________ SUB TOTAL

________ Sales Tax (AZ residents add 6.7% sales tax)

________ Postage & Handling (Add $3 for every $45 in merchandise)

________ TOTAL INVESTMENT

Charge My: VISA MasterCard Check Enclosed

Card No.________________________ Exp. Date____________

Name____

Address______________________________________

City________________ State____________ Zip__________

Telephone ( ) ____________________

Home ( ) ____________________

PLEASE SEND ME:

________ Volume discount pricing for the book.

________ Information regarding Virginia Dunstone Seminars.

________ Place me on the mailing list.